# THE SINGLE PARENT
# TRAVEL HANDBOOK

by Brenda Elwell

An informative and humorous guide to planning
and executing an exciting, fun-filled, educational
vacation, indispensable for all single adults
traveling with kids.

GlobalBrenda Publishing, LLC
Secaucus, NJ
www.GlobalBrenda.com

Elwell, Brenda
    The Single Parent Travel Handbook/Brenda Elwell.—1st ed.
    Includes appendices and index
    ISBN 0-9723627-0-3
    Library of Congress Control Number: 2002112 104

Published by GlobalBrenda Publishing, LLC 755 9th St. 2nd fl., Secaucus, NJ 07094-3321 201-866-9991. First edition. www.GlobalBrenda.com www.SingleParentTravel.net

Edited by Dina Horwedel Dina@RedRockRain.com www.RedRockRain.com
Cover design and concept by Rambo Design Group www.RamboDesignGroup.com
Cover photo by Thaddeus Harden www.ThaddeusHarden.com
Styling, props and wardrobe done by Vanessa Baran 212-473-3763
Hair and makeup by Yuseff Smythe
Typesetting by Sagrario Gallego Simón sagrariogallego@ctv.es
Printing by C&C Offset printing in Hong Kong
Production coordinated by Monique Elwell

# What People Are Saying About Brenda's Work

*"I enjoy your newsletters and Web site and will continue to read them and pass on the info to other single parents that I meet."..."Thank you for your time and for having such an informative web-site."— C.C.*

*"No, thank YOU, and your DAUGHTER! Thanks for the tips, sharing your memory (about Shakespeare), and your positive attitude. Enjoyed all your newsletters archived so far. I'm sure you are an inspiration to many! And thank you for the photo tip. Have a great summer!" — P.S.*

*"I just subscribed to "Single Parent Travel" a month ago and I'm very, very pleased with it. Finally, some information for those of us who refuse to let single parenthood mean nothing but trips to Disney World (which I absolutely hate!). Keep up the good work!............ Many thanks for a great newsletter." — G.B.*

*"Your listserve service is just wonderful and I am sure it has helped more people than you can imagine. There is so little done to help those of us in single parent positions and with the amount of us out there — we need to be addressed." — S.A.*

*"I am a single female and love to travel with my nieces all the time. This book is a keeper. Brenda's reasoning is brilliant and the book will fascinate any single parent travel aficionado." — S.R.*

*"...And special thanks for performing this service. It's greatly needed and appreciated." — L.B.*

*"Well can I just say I have just finished reading your biography and list of destinations from your web page and you are my new icon Brenda!! If all single mums had a fingernails worth of the courage that you've had then a lot more kids would have seen and learned about the world. Having extra language skills must be a real bonus and I am only sorry to say that being British and having everyone speak English to you its only too easy to be lazy and not learn other languages. Still, the best piece of travelling advice ever given to me has been to learn how to say thank you - it being the most important word of all. ..."*

*"I just wanted to say thank you for the inspiration it certainly seems a lot less scary doing it on my own if I know others have done it before!!..."*

*"I wanted to say you should include if you haven't done already about the fact that if you are travelling alone with kids you need to have written permission from the other parent — I would never have known that in a million years if I hadn't just read it in one of the articles of your web page, but maybe you could include it in a news letter for other mums? Cheers" — M.O.*

*"You've given me hope that it's not too late to travel with my 11 and 13 (soon to be 12 and 14) year old daughters!"*

*"I found your writing to be engaging and delightful. It took me right there with images dancing in my brain. Thank you for that." — J.D.*

*"Thank you SO much for the advice. I've copied this into a permanent folder we use for planning. I really appreciate the time it took you to do this!" — S.P.*

*"As a recent widow (my husband passed away 10 days before Christmas, 2001), I have been trying to find a site that would help me in my pursuit of ways my 6 year old son and I could travel without being ruled by the "double occupancy" gods. Thank you so much for starting this site. I believe that your advice is going to be invaluable to me. Keep up the good work." — D.T.*

*"I'm a member of this yahoo group, and also a member of Parents Without Partners. thanks for the excellent article on the PWP Web site!" — Cheryl.*

*We are pleased to announce the creation of*

## SINGLE PARENT TOURS

Commencing summer of 2003 my single parent travel company will offer a series of weekend packages and one-week tours to exciting destinations. I will host these tours and design them for single parent and other non-traditional families. Look for further announcements on the Web site, **www.SingleParentTours.com**, and in my monthly newsletters. Look for the discount coupon for the inaugural season of Single Parent Tours at the end of this book. We hope to see you on a tour soon...

*Would you like to be informed when the tours are available to book? Then send an e-mail to Brenda@SingleParentTravel.net, or send your name, phone number, fax (if you have one) and address to:*

**Single Parent Tours**
755 9th St. 2nd fl.
Secaucus NJ 07094-3321

Fax it to 413-208-6105

www.SingleParentTours.com

# ABOUT THE AUTHOR

A veteran of over thirty years' experience in the travel industry, Brenda Elwell has held management positions for global companies such as Carlson Wagonlit Travel, Uniglobe, Diners Fugazy, and CHA (Cultural Heritage Alliance), a renowned global student tour company. Her most recent position was Director of Product Development for Amisto.com, a global Internet adventure travel company. A worldwide adventurer since the age of nineteen, Ms Elwell has lived abroad and traveled to over sixty countries and forty-five states, half of them as a single parent with two kids in tow.

Ms. Elwell is the founder of GlobalBrenda Publishing, LLC, which publishes www.SingleParentTravel.net, an informative Single Parent Travel newsletter and "The Single Parent Travel Handbook"; and founder of Single Parent Tours, the first and only nationwide tour operator focused on serving the needs of single parents and non-traditional families. Her work has been highlighted in the New York Times' Practical Traveler Column, Rudy Maxa's Savvy Traveler radio show, Frommers.com, Time Magazine, the Washington Post as well as numerous other national publications, nationally syndicated radio shows and Web sites.

In addition to her lifetime addiction to travel, Ms Elwell is an avid hiker, photographer, swimmer, movie and museum buff, and connoisseur of exotic cuisines. Her most unusual dish to date has been lemon ants — eaten live off the tree in the Ecuadorian Amazon.

## How to Contact the Author

Brenda Elwell is available for speaking engagements, book signings, interviews and any other event that offers an opportunity to educate the travel industry of the enormous (and long neglected) marketing potential of single parent and non-traditional families. Please contact her through her publicist, Monique Elwell, via phone 917-623-1896 or via e-mail at Monique@Single ParentTravel.net. Monique and Brenda can also be reached via postal mail at the following address.

GlobalBrenda Publishing, LLC
755 9th St. 2nd fl.
Secaucus NJ 07094-3321

*Sign up for the* ONLY *listing of*

## SINGLE PARENT SPECIALS

GlobalBrenda publishes the **only** listing of specials that cater to single parent families worldwide. It is available **free** once per month via our electronic newsletter. Travel suppliers must meet at least one of four criteria:

- Single supplement that is eliminated or reduced.
- Kids discounts based on ONE ADULT traveling, not two.
- Activities that cater to BOTH the adult and the children, or an even mix of both adult's and children's activities.
- Provide environments where single parent families can meet other single parent families.

The newsletter and the accompanying Web site,

### www.SingleParentTravel.net,

are chock full of useful information, entertaining articles, not to mention tips, suggestions and recommendations from all our single parent readers!

To sign up for the newsletter, go to **www.SingleParent Travel.net** and follow the sign up instructions.

*Dedicated to my two wonderful and adventurous children,
Monique and Gregory, who have been my inspiration
for this book and with whom I have shared so many
"trips of a lifetime."*

## ACKNOWLEDGEMENTS

An enormous debt of gratitude goes to my daughter, Monique Elwell, who, in addition to being the Webmaster for my Web site, www.SingleParent Travel.net, has also been the unpaid research assistant, publicist and major cheerleader for my book. As the primary force in coordinating the business arrangements necessary to bring this book to print, she has devoted countless hours to the project without complaint. Parents all over the world will know what I mean when I say, "Payback is sweet." Thank you, Monique.

I also would like to thank my dear friends, Diane and John Harris, who provided me with a home and a place to work on my book after I sold my home of twenty-three years. Their gracious hospitality, along with their much-needed cable lines, enabled me to bring my Web site and this book to fruition. Your former "Resident Writer" is forever grateful.

Special thanks go to all the wonderful Single Parent Dads who took the time to write their inspirational stories for this book. May all my readers have as much joy in reading them as I did.

**Attention Single Parent Organizations, travel agents and other travel suppliers**—Quantity discounts are available to help you raise funds and attract clients. Brenda Elwell, the author, is also available for speaking engagements. Special books, booklets or book excerpts can also be created to fit your specific needs.

For more information contact: Monique Elwell at Monique@SingleParent Travel.net or 917-623-1896.

Further information is available at www.SingleParentTravel.net.

# Table of Contents

INTRODUCTION .................................................................................... XV

I. PREPARATION (ANTICIPATION) ...................................................... 1

DECISIONS, DECISIONS .................................................................. 1
RESEARCH .......................................................................................... 2
CREATING AN ITINERARY ............................................................ 7
    *Why create and type up an itinerary?* ...................................... 7
PLANNING AHEAD TO MEET THE LOCALS ............................. 25
PACKING .............................................................................................. 29
    *First Aid Kit* ................................................................................ 29
    *Packing List* ................................................................................ 30
    *Travel Books, Maps, Documents, Confirmations, Insurance*
    *and Emergency Information* ...................................................... 34
    *Appropriate Luggage* ................................................................ 35
    *Packing Snacks* .......................................................................... 36
DOCUMENTS AND VACCINATIONS .......................................... 37
    *Valid Passports* .......................................................................... 37
    *Obtaining a U.S. Passport for a Minor Under Age 14* ......... 37
    *Permission to Take the Children Out of the Country* ........... 39
    *Tourist Cards* .............................................................................. 40
    *Visas* .............................................................................................. 40
    *Government Warnings About Travel* ....................................... 41
    *Vaccinations* ................................................................................ 42
    *Where do I get these vaccinations?* .......................................... 43
    *Travel Insurance* ........................................................................ 44
MONEY MATTERS & RESPONSIBILITIES .................................. 45
    *Estimating Expenses* .................................................................. 45
    *How to Save on Hotel Expenses* ............................................... 46
    *How to Save on Meal Expenses* ............................................... 47
    *Other Ways to Save* .................................................................... 47
    *What Type of "Wampum" to Carry* ......................................... 48
    *Family Member Responsibilities Before and During the Trip* ............ 49
    *Let's Start with Some Ideas for Younger Children, Ages 3-9* .............. 49
    *Ideas for Children Ages 10 and Older* ................................... 52
    *The Uniqueness of Single Parent Travel* ............................... 52
    *Things Single Parents Must Remember* ................................. 53
TAKING THE PLUNGE — Assuaging Fears — Your Own, Your Kids' ..... 54

EXECUTION OF RESERVATIONS .............................................. 55
   *When to Book* ................................................................. 55
   *Last-Minute Specials* ..................................................... 57
   *Booking on the Internet* ................................................. 59
   *Travel Agents — To Use or Not to Use?* ........................ 60
   *Reserving Your Air Tickets* ............................................ 61
   *Reserving Hotels* ........................................................... 63
   *Pre-Booking Activities and Excursions* .......................... 64
   *A Final Word on Frequent Flyer Programs* .................... 64


**II. THE TRIP ITSELF — (REALIZATION)** ............................. **67**

MODES OF TRAVEL ................................................................. 67
   *Airplane Travel* .............................................................. 67
   *Car Travel* ..................................................................... 71
   *Fly/Drive* ....................................................................... 74
   *Train Travel* ................................................................... 75
   *Bus Travel* ..................................................................... 79
   *Miscellaneous Modes of Travel* ..................................... 82
DEALING WITH ISSUES .......................................................... 83
   *Tending to "Business" on the Trip* ................................. 83
   *Managing Conflict* ......................................................... 84
   *Major Life Decisions* ..................................................... 89
   *Emergencies and Health Matters* ................................... 89
   *Carrying Your Money and Valuables* .............................. 94
   *Keeping You and Your Children Safe* ............................. 94
BREAKING THE ICE ................................................................ 97
   *Learn Local Customs in Advance* ................................... 98
   *Learn Some Words of the Local Language* ...................... 98
   *Do What the Locals Do* ................................................ 100
   *Come Bearing Gifts* ...................................................... 104
   *A Few More Field-Tested Suggestions for Making Friends* ............... 107
   *Final Goal* .................................................................... 108


**III. STORING AND RELIVING THE MEMORIES —**
    **(RECOLLECTION AND PAY-OFF)** ................................ **111**

RECOLLECTION ..................................................................... 111
   *Photo Albums* ............................................................... 111
   *Slides and Videos* ......................................................... 113
   *Diaries* .......................................................................... 113
   *Scrapbooks* ................................................................... 115
PAYOFF .................................................................................. 115

IV.  SINGLE PARENT DADS TELL THEIR STORIES ........................... 119

THE ORIGINAL STAIRMASTER: A TALE OF MUNDO MAYA
  by LEWIS FLINKMAN ............................................................... 120
CAMPING AND CANOEING THE ADIRONDACKS
  by MARDEN ELWELL ............................................................... 123
PACIFIC NORTHWEST TRIP 2000
  by DON BAHAM ...................................................................... 128
TRIP TO UNIVERSAL STUDIOS AND WALT DISNEY
WORLD FLORIDA
  by VICTOR KATZ ..................................................................... 131
A TRADITIONAL BRITISH SEASIDE ADVENTURE
  by COLIN BENNETT .................................................................. 134
THE POISON CONTROL AFFAIR
  by PETER KOZA ....................................................................... 136
GROWING DOWN A RIVER
  by GREGG P. BOERSMA ............................................................ 140


V.  ALTERNATE VACATION IDEAS ........................................... 149

KID EXCHANGE ....................................................................... 149
BLENDING FAMILIES ................................................................ 150
THE ADULT TAKES A BREAK — THE DELICIOUSNESS OF
TRAVELING ALONE ................................................................. 151


VI.  RECOMMENDED DESTINATIONS & ACTIVITIES ...................... 153

GROUP #1 — DRIVE OR FLY/DRIVE VACATIONS ........................... 155
*Niagara Falls* ....................................................................... 155
*Mid-Atlantic Historical Tour* ................................................ 159
*Arizona* .............................................................................. 167
*National Parks of Southern Utah* .......................................... 178
*The Oregon and Northern California Coast* ............................. 195
GROUP #2 — GOING TO THE NEXT STEP ................................... 208
*Riviera Maya* ...................................................................... 208
*Costa Rica* .......................................................................... 213
*Hawaii* ............................................................................... 227
*Alaska* ............................................................................... 235
GROUP #3 — TRIPS OF A LIFETIME ......................................... 248
*Egypt* ................................................................................ 248
*The Galápagos Islands* ........................................................ 260
GROUP #4 — SPECIAL MENTION DESTINATIONS ......................... 268
*Europe* ............................................................................... 268
*Our Nationals Parks* ............................................................ 270

**VII.  WHERE DO WE GO FROM HERE?** ................................................. **275**

**APPENDICES** ................................................................................ **281**

SINGLE PARENT SURVEY INFORMATION ......................................... 281
TRAVEL AGENTS WHO SPECIALIZE IN SINGLE PARENT TRAVEL... 287

**INDEX** ........................................................................................... **295**

# Introduction

After nearly 20 years of traveling independently around the globe and the U.S. as a single parent, I finally asked my now-grown kids, "What was your favorite trip?" Without hesitation they simultaneously replied, "All of them, Mom. They were all great." That answer was not a result of good luck, a big budget, or easy-to-care-for kids. It was a result of accrued knowledge, meticulous planning and research, and some creative travel ideas.

Single Parent Travel as a niche group has been woefully neglected by the travel industry. There have been a few feeble attempts by resort hotels, tour operators, and travel agencies to lure single parents and their kids with special "single parent pricing," but all make the common mistake of assuming that the needs and desires of single adults traveling with kids are the same as double-parent families. Resort hotels, for example, have wonderful programs that place the kids in day camp so parents are free to play tennis or golf during the day. Romantic evening programs are "couples-friendly" by design. All of this is great if you are part of a couple. The single parent, on the other hand, prefers to spend time during the day doing fun activities with his or her child. During the evening, the single parent, neither a "swinging single" nor part of a couple, feels like the "odd man out" during candlelight dinners and hot tub events. Not knowing where to go or how to plan an independent family vacation, single parents often take the easy route and just book a resort hotel.

Eager to have other single parents share the special joy of an exciting and successful travel adventure with their children, be it local or far away, I wrote the *Single Parent Travel Handbook*. This book is not meant to be a destination guide, although it does contain insightful destination information. Rather, it is meant to serve as an inspirational planning tool that will demonstrate simple ways to prepare and execute an exciting, fun-filled, and educational trip that *both* you and your kid(s) will enjoy without blowing your single parent budget.

Sometimes people say, "Oh, it's easy for you. You are in the travel business." Twenty or 30 years ago, that statement rang true. Now, with the wonders of the Internet, everyone who has access to a computer, either at home or at the library, has access to all sorts of travel information. With the proliferation of airline frequent flyer programs and other loyalty programs; business travelers sometimes have greater access to discounts and free travel than I do.

Contrary to popular belief, people in the travel business do not travel for "free." As a single parent I often paid regular airfares for my kids since companion discounts only applied to spouses. I had to find creative ways to save money while traveling and learn to hunt down bargains before we left. I also learned to budget for our annual family vacation. Our Sunday family outings usually consisted of free or inexpensive activities such as summer blueberry-picking outings and winter museum visits. We rarely went out to dinner, and when we did, it was usually budget Chinese. But come summer, we were off on an exciting two-week vacation to a faraway place. If not rich in greenbacks, we were certainly rich in experiences.

Both of my children are now grown. Like their mom, each of them could be dropped in the middle of a city or town anywhere in the world, and, within hours, they would feel at home, having found their way around town, checked out the local attractions, eaten tasty local cuisine at an inexpensive restaurant, and made new friends along the way.

Besides the fun and enjoyment of traveling together and having memorable adventures as a single parent family, they have developed exceptional life skills and a deep appreciation of history, foreign cultures, the importance of a clean environment, education, and the privilege of living in a free country. Like an education, travel memories are something you can never take away from a person. I hope you will benefit from our experiences and venture forth to share a similar legacy with your children.

*Although the book is primarily for the working single parent, who wants to spend a one, two or three-week vacation with his or her kids, it is also an indispensable guide for any single adult traveling with children – a grandparent, aunt, uncle, big brother or sister, older cousin, or even a married adult who finds it necessary to travel alone with children from time to time.*

From our traveling family to yours - Happy Adventures!

*"Travel is fatal to prejudice, bigotry, and narrow-midedness."*

—MARK TWAIN

# I

## Preparation (Anticipation)

### DECISIONS, DECISIONS

*Where's the best place to go?*

*How long should we spend there?*

*What should we do when we get there?*

These questions, commonly asked by all travelers, are especially poignant when asked by a single parent. A single parent, by definition, is a working parent, and unless you happen to be Ivana Trump, your vacation budget is limited. Also, as a single parent, you have unique travel and vacation objectives, which include:

1. Wanting to spend quality time with your kids, but not just doing kid activities.

2. Wanting everyone to have a good time, maybe even an adventure, without spending all of your vacation time attending to travel details.

3. Wanting to get the biggest bang for your limited buck.

How do you begin to plan your trip? Start with three easy steps:

1. Determine how much money you can comfortably afford to spend.

2. Decide how much time your vacation should last — one week, two weeks, or even a long weekend.

3. Start researching destinations that interest you (You must have some ideas!).

Let's look at an example.

You are a single parent with one child, age 10. You have one week of vacation, a budget limit of US $2,500, and you live in the Northeastern U.S. You have done the Walt Disney World route with your child and want to do something different for your next vacation. You have thought about flying out West and renting a car or perhaps visiting California or Arizona , but you are not sure you can afford it. You also don't know where to go or what to do once you get there. Another idea is to drive to Montreal and Quebec, but you are not sure if your child will enjoy visiting just big cities. What do you do next?

It is now time for research. Get your child involved in the process to make the vacation a family effort.

## RESEARCH

The first reaction I often hear is, "Oh my God, I don't have time for this!" You are correct. Single Parents never *have* time; they must *make* time. You will need to budget time to research the Internet or make toll free phone calls.

### PHASE I

**Plan on taking one to two hours to complete these four steps of your Phase I research.** *Start this research as soon as you have decided to take a trip.* **It may take weeks to get information from tourist boards. Also keep in mind that some trips require booking hotels many months in advance, such as U.S. national parks in summer.**

1.  First check the Internet for sample airfares to your proposed destinations. Some sample Web sites are: www.travelocity.com, www.orbitz.com, and www.expedia.com. You can also check on the airline Web sites directly, such as www.continental.com or www.aa.com (American Airlines) using a search engine such as google.com. Do an Internet search if you do not know the Web site address for a particular airline. If you do not have access to the Internet, locate the toll free airline numbers listed in the Yellow Pages® of your local phone book. Remember, you are not booking at this time, but are just checking to see if the airfare costs fit into your budget and allow you to consider flying to a faraway destination.

2.  Next, contact the local tourist boards and have them send you any and all information about the places you want to visit (it's all free). Your child, if he or she is old enough to read, can assume this task. If your children

are younger, they can enjoy the pictures while you do the research. An excellent Web site for this project is www.towd.com, which offers information on regional, state and worldwide tourist boards. Another site is www.OfficialTravelInfo.com. You should allow anywhere from 10 days to several months to receive tourist board literature, so *this should be a priority project.*

3. Check out the links on my Web site, www.SingleParentTravel.net under the "Single Parent Travel Specials" and "Outside Resources" sections. SingleParentTravel.net and the accompanying newsletter is the *only* comprehensive source for specials designed for single parents. One of my newsletter subscribers recommends posting a notice on "The Thorn Tree" on www.LonelyPlanet.com. He was taking his young son to China and connected with an English teacher from China, on the Thorn Tree, who planned to visit the same areas. They decided to travel together.

4. Finally, gather information wherever you can. Talk to people you know — friends, co-workers, and neighbors. Tell them you are planning a trip to Arizona or Canada with your child and ask for suggestions. Keep in mind that your friends and associates may not have the same budget and interests that you do and therefore their recommendations may not be appropriate for you. Ask specifically why they recommend a place or hotel and if it is appropriate for *single parent* families. Check out newspaper articles in the travel section, review travel videos, or peruse travel magazines. Other than *National Geographic Traveler, Frommer's Budget Travel Magazine,* and specific interest magazines, most travel magazines tend to feature articles that are glossy pieces of fluff, but your research may produce something worthwhile. You can also call a travel agent for destination ideas, but, understandably, he or she may be intent upon selling you a trip rather than providing free information.

## PHASE II

**Once you have decided on your destination, you are now ready for Phase II of your research.** *This will take about three to four hours, not including reading time for the guidebooks:*

1. Go to your local bookstore or to the Web and buy one or more good travel guidebooks, specific to your chosen destination. Although I often purchase books on the Web, when searching for travel guidebooks, I prefer to browse through several in a bookstore, checking for weight as well as content. If you are a member of AAA, they also provide

guidebooks for free, but are not as extensive, so you will want to supplement them with a good guidebook. Your public library is also a good place to browse for guidebooks before you shop (you will still want to buy a guidebook, since libraries do not always have the most recent editions and you cannot always take the library's books with you on your trip). Sometimes you may have to go to more than one bookstore to find what you want. Three good choices that contain information useful for single parent travel are the Moon Handbook, Lonely Planet and Arthur Frommer Series, detailed below:

➢ The Moon Handbook series is my overall favorite because it provides detailed discussions of activities, places to stay (from budget to deluxe), flora and fauna (fun, educational info for the kids) as well as a bit of history. Unfortunately the Moon Handbook series doesn't cover as broad of a range of destinations as Lonely Planet or Frommer.

➢ Lonely Planet covers destinations all over the globe and is a great budget guide. However, the series focuses only on budget hotels or very Spartan hotels, often not in the center of town, and not always appropriate for single parents with small children. These guidebooks are great for adventurous "off the beaten path" travel if you are a bit more adventurous.

➢ The Arthur Frommer series offers good overall guidebooks, but they usually do not have extensive flora and fauna sections. The Frommer City guidebooks are excellent and provide a most appropriate lightweight companion for a weekend getaway.

I also recommend the Michelin green guides for visits to overseas cities. The green guides offer superb walking tours, and their excellent rating system helps you to determine what to see and what to skip.

After this book is published, we will start a destination series designed specifically for single parents. If you would like to be notified when they are available, please send me an e-mail at Brenda@SingleParentTravel.net. Be sure to tell me what destinations interest you.

2. Skim through the guidebooks, searching for ideas on activities and exciting places to visit. Jot down the page numbers on the inside front cover with notations. This will assist you in final itinerary planning as well as providing a quick reference when you are on the road. At a later date you can go back and read the sections on history, hotels, and restaurants.

3. Recruit your kids. Assign them the tasks of searching the Web, checking books in their school library, even asking their teachers for help. Teachers absolutely love it when a student comes to them and asks for book recommendations to read for a trip. Often a teacher will then ask the child to give an oral report upon return from their vacation. Extra credit!

4. Obtain maps — state, regional, city, or country, if you are going abroad. They may be ordered free from the tourist boards or you can obtain them from your local AAA or other motoring club. If you are not a member, it is a good idea to join. AAA tour books also contain some good maps of local attractions, making it easy to find your way around town. You can also plan your trip with TripTiks online, and if you are driving, you get roadside services if you need them, and hotel discounts. (For our Canadian readers, there is CAA, the Canadian Automobile Association).

5. As you begin building your final itinerary, have a family meeting to determine how long you need to overnight in each place, the travel time between each place, and the activities you want to do. Don't worry about hotels. That will come later, unless during your research you uncover a special place to stay and want to build your itinerary around it

*It is very important at this stage to get buy-in from your kids.* If you want to do an exciting mid- summer desert hike, the kids have to agree to get up early that day. Let them be part of the itinerary creation process. Listen to their feedback. When my son was 12 and we were planning a big driving tour out West, he suggested rerouting our trip to include Monument Valley. After nipping some time off another destination, and tossing in some extra driving time, we were able to fit it in. We were glad we did; Monument Valley turned out to be one of the highlights of our trip.

## PHASE III

**Once you decide what you want to do and how long you want to spend at each place at your destination, you are ready for Phase III — the final planning stage.** *This stage will take anywhere from a couple of hours to a couple of days, depending upon whether you choose to take a tour or travel independently.* **Now you need to make some decisions.**

**Should you take a tour?**

There are two types of "tours" in the travel industry:

One is the *fully escorted tour,* where nearly every moment of your day is pre-planned and you have a guide with you from morning to night. I don't recommend spending your entire vacation on this type of tour, especially if you are a single parent with young children. There is little room for spontaneity, and the spontaneous things you do on your trips are often what children remember the most.

My son was 5 and my daughter was 12 when I first took them to Europe as a single parent. It was an unusually hot summer day in Switzerland, so we decided to take a cable car ride high up into the mountains, visit an ice cave at the snow line, and then ride the cable car back down the mountain. Once up in the mountains, my son, seeing all the hikers, asked if we could walk down. Sure, I agreed, thinking he would quickly tire and we would pick up the cable car at one of the lower stations, and then ride down. Five hours later we had hiked all the way to our starting point, having stopped along the way to say hello to several dozen cows, roll in the meadow grass, and smell the wild flowers. Not once did he ask to be carried. When I tucked him into bed that night, he asked, "Mommy, can we walk down another mountain tomorrow? That was so much fun!"

Although independent travel allows you the flexibility to have a spur-of-the-moment excursion such as the one described above, there are times when a short escorted tour may be the best option, especially in foreign countries. Before my kids and I set off for an independent trip to Scandinavia, we pre-booked a three-day tour departing from Helsinki, Finland for Leningrad in the Soviet Union (now called St. Petersburg, Russia). With the exception of a brief four hours of free time to roam the city on our own, the three days were jam-packed with sightseeing, but we did see the major sights of this beautiful, interesting city. At that time, under Soviet policy, independent travelers were not admitted into a museum until a group showed up, which could mean a wait of several hours. The three-day escorted tour was definitely the way to go.

The other type of tour is called a *package tour.* You prepay your airfare, hotel, and transfers, but once you arrive at your destination, most of your days are free to spend as you choose. Optional excursions are available at additional cost. Package tours are especially popular for resort destinations, such as the Caribbean, Hawaii or Mexican coastal resorts. The best "deals" are usually offered for one-week vacations where you stay at only one hotel. This type of vacation is not always the most welcoming environment for a single parent adult who often feels like the "odd man out," drifting some-where between the swinging singles and the double parent families.

## Should you travel independently?

If you can find a tour that takes you where you want to go, does what you want to do, at a price you want to spend, then consider going that route. If not, think about planning an independent trip with your kids. You can mix and match sightseeing and leisure days as you please, taking into the account your special interests and those of your children. You can also mix and match hotels within your budget, combining such diverse accommodations as a resort hotel, inexpensive B&B, and perhaps even a jungle lodge. It will take a little work and time on your part, but you and your kids will be free to plan an exciting, interesting, tailor-made family vacation, one that gives you both structure and flexibility.

Let's get started planning your trip!

## CREATING AN ITINERARY

### WHY CREATE AND TYPE UP AN ITINERARY?

Single parents that travel with their kids have different needs than double-parent families. Single parents must be twice as organized, twice as patient, and twice as creative to have a successful and fun trip with their kids. A good itinerary helps you to stay organized and remain patient while also allowing for built-in flexibility.

In all of the years I traveled as a single parent with my kids, from kinder-garten through college, we never once argued about what we were going to do that day (we argued about a lot of other things on our trips, but never that). The kids simply got up each morning and asked, "What's on the itin-erary for today?" Although our itineraries were always flexible, and often could be changed on a moment's notice, the kids took for granted that what was on the itinerary was what we were doing that day. End of dis-cussion.

1. *Itineraries create a framework for your trip and help you get and stay organized before and during your trip.* All confirmation numbers, hotel directions, and special instructions can be written into your itin-erary.

2. *Itineraries eliminate family argument, allowing you to be more patient.* The hour or two you spend typing an itinerary with rainy day alternatives will save you hours of time and frustration during your vacation.

3. *Itineraries save you time.* By geographically planning out and writing down our daily activities we spent more time having fun. For example, by pre-planning and writing down our ride sequence at theme parks, we never waited in long lines, even at Walt Disney World in high season. *Birnbaum's Guide to Walt Disney World* is an excellent guidebook for the most efficient ride sequence at Disney.

4. *Custom-made itineraries allow you to be creative.* You can include side trips to schools, local sporting events, and get more deeply involved with the local culture.

5. *Itineraries make a nice memento.* You can keep them with your photo albums or videos. (Years later you may have trouble remembering all the names of places that you visited). You can leave itineraries with family members and envious co-workers who will be eager to hear about your adventures when you return.

Before discussing what to include on a successful itinerary, let's take a look at the following sample single parent vacation itinerary I created for a two-week summer vacation in Alaska. We decided on Alaska that year because Continental Airlines was offering a One Pass "two-fer" special to Alaska. I had accumulated enough frequent flyer points to cover the airfare for two people and the third fare was "free," making it an easy destination decision.

**IN SEARCH OF TIMBER WOLVES**
**ALASKA, THE ARTIC CIRCLE AND MORE**
**THE 1993 ELWELL ADVENTURE**

**JUNE 30, WEDNESDAY**

Limo pick up at 6:30 a.m. We begin our journey (which will take us halfway to Japan) at 8:30 a.m. on CO #1289, due to arrive in Denver at 10:36 a.m., departing Denver at 2:20.p.m. on CO #1272, due to arrive in Seattle at 4:08 p.m. In Seattle Monique and Greg's Aunt Betty Lou, Uncle Tom, and various cousins whom they have never met will greet us. After several hours of "getting to know you" we board CO #1191 at 9:15 p.m., due to arrive in Anchorage at 11:49 p.m. There we pick up our Hertz mid size car CF #833713F0CF2 and head wearily to our hotel (If space is available, try to fly Seattle/Anchorage on CO #726 leaving Seattle 6 p.m., arriving Anchorage 8:36 p.m. What about the luggage?).

## JULY 1, THURSDAY

Today is a shopping and strolling day. First off to the Sears Mall for wolfie T-shirts and then to Alaskan Native Arts and Crafts Association (no retail mark-up) at the Post Office Mall. Possibly check out the Alaskan Food and Gift Cache, 419 D Street, for seafood gift packs. Time permitting we can visit the Alaska Experience Theater and the adjoining Earthquake Exhibit. "Must See" south of Anchorage is Beluga Point at Turnagain Arm. Check out tidal timetables. Eight-foot waves bring in the second highest tidal surge in North America (30 feet). Don't step in the quicksand, Greg!

## JULY 2, FRIDAY

Leave early a.m. for the Kenai Peninsula. En route we will visit the Portage Glacier, where the visitor center houses an ice cave, a real iceberg, and the elusive ice worm. We'll hike the Moraine Loop and the Byron Glacier Trail. From there we'll drive through Soldotna and then to the town to Kenai, the second oldest settlement in Alaska, founded by Russian fur traders. In the late afternoon or early evening (daylight doesn't end until midnight) we head south to Homer, the Acapulco of Alaska.

## JULY 3, SATURDAY

At leisure to enjoy Homer, the fabulous scenery, interesting galleries and shops. Stop for a beer at the Salty Dawg Saloon, near the end of Homer Spit, dating from 1897. Cruise along Skyline Drive to view the gorgeous homes. We could try our hand at the fabulous fishing... Monique, are you game?

## JULY 4, SUNDAY

North to Seward to view the 4th of July footrace up the mountain, and then overnight at Anchorage. Since it doesn't get dark until midnight, I wonder when the fireworks start? Hmmmmm...

## JULY 5, MONDAY

We head north five hours to Denali National Park, site of North America's highest peak and home to oodles of wildlife. It is here that we chase the bears and timber wolves, or is it the other way around? We overnight in Healy, north of the park entrance, in a dome-shaped Bed & Breakfast, aptly called the Dome B&B. Reconfirm our shuttle reservations for July 7.

## JULY 6, TUESDAY

At leisure to check out the park activities and hotels. The Denali Park Hotel has free half-day guided hikes starting at 8 a.m.

## JULY 7, WEDNESDAY

We take our pre-reserved 8 a.m. shuttle bus (cars not allowed beyond the hotel area) to the area where we disembark for hiking into timber wolf country. Bring water, food, sunscreen, and toilet paper, gang. There are no facilities in this part of Denali.

Nada. Required reading for this part of our trip is page 293 of the Alaska-Yukon Handbook, the section titled "Unexpected Bear Encounters."

## JULY 8, THURSDAY

Head north to Fairbanks, Alaska's second largest city located in the heart of Alaska's interior. We stop en route at Nenana, famous for its yearly Ice Classic, "Alaska's Biggest Guessing Game." Now in its 75th year, the prize for guessing when the ice on Tanana River will break up in the spring runs about $100,000. Onward to the town of Ester, where we check in at the rustic and historical Cripple Creek Hotel, and then to the city of Fairbanks, where there are more Chevy Camaros per capita than anywhere else in the world. (Eat your heart out, Monique).

Must-see attractions in Fairbanks are ALASKALAND (Alaska's answer to Disney World, Alaskan frontier-style) and the Dog Musher's Museum. Tonight we spend the evening in the Howling Dog Saloon, the most northern Rock and Roll bar in the world. Call to reserve the Alaskaland salmon bake for tomorrow.

## JULY 9, FRIDAY

This morning we must be at the Fairbanks Museum by 10 a.m. for a two-hour student-guided tour. This fabulous and beautiful museum in the heart of the University of Alaska campus has mind-boggling wildlife and gold exhibits, exceptional permafrost displays, and superb Russian artifacts. Lunch is a salmon bake at Alaskaland. We'll do the Alaskaland theme park Saturday afternoon.

After lunch we drive five hours north on a gravel road, paralleling the Alaska Pipeline, to the little town of Coldfoot, 50 miles north of the Arctic Circle. Temperatures in Coldfoot have been recorded as low as -82 degrees Fahrenheit in the winter (hence the town name) and as high as 90 degrees in the summer. Coldfoot, billed as the northernmost truck stop in the world, is halfway between Fairbanks and Prudhoe Bay, on the North Slope. We are almost at the top of the world, gang. Bundle up tonight, as temperatures will drop. Mom will have a shot and a beer and off to bed. Before leaving Fairbanks, we must rent or borrow a sleeping bag for Greg; window gravel protectors and a tail pipe guard for the car.

## JULY 10, SATURDAY

We head north for a while, watching for elk, caribou, and flying gravel, and then turn south for Fairbanks. Upon arrival in Fairbanks, we do the Alaskaland theme park and finish up the must-see attractions in Fairbanks. Tonight we are confirmed for the 10 p.m. show at the Malamute Saloon at the Cripple Creek Hotel. The show includes dancing, singing, and a reading of Robert Service poems.

## JULY 11, SUNDAY

Check out the Unitarian church services in Fairbanks before heading south on the famed Alaska Highway to the North Pole, where we will send postcards to all of the little kids in the family. We stop at the town of Delta and stroll through history at the Big Delta State Historical Park. Then onto Tok, where we overnight at a B&B for horses and people. The horse rate is US$10 and includes morning oats. The B&B owner used to raise Arabian horses in California. Lots of sled dogs are raised here. Eat your heart out, Monique.

## JULY 12, MONDAY

Today we leisurely drive four or five hours south through fabulous mountain scenery to the beautiful port of Valdez, site of the infamous 1989 oil spill. Afternoon at leisure. Reconfirm tomorrow's tour.

## JULY 13, TUESDAY

We depart 7 a.m. by boat (bring food and lots of lots of warm clothes) for a four-hour tour with Stan Stephans Charters through Prince William Sound to the famous Columbia Glacier. Columbia Glacier is 42 miles long and more than three miles wide at its face, which rises up to 300 feet above the water and plunges an incredible 2000 feet below. Here we look and listen up close to the awesome sights and sounds of icebergs calving off the face of the glacier. Afternoon at leisure for last minute shopping and photo opportunities in Valdez.

## JULY 14, WEDNESDAY

We sleep late and take a leisurely five-hour mountain ride back to Anchorage, stopping along the way at the town of Palmer. In Palmer we take the Glenn Highway north of town to mile 50, turn left on Archie Road (first left past Fishook Road), then continue another mile to mile 51.8 where a secret surprise (open 9 a.m.–8 p.m.) awaits Monique and Greg. This is something we will all enjoy and will be a fitting end to our Alaska Adventure. Make sure to have film left. We head back to Anchorage Airport (late dinner in Anchorage or en route?) and drop off our rental car at 11 p.m.

## JULY 15, THURSDAY

We leave Anchorage 12:50 a.m. on CO #759, due to arrive in Seattle at 5:15 a.m. Then we change to CO #184 leaving Seattle at 6 a.m., arriving in Denver at 9:35 a.m. We change to CO #321 leaving Denver at 10:26 a.m. and arriving in Newark in 4:10 p.m. We transfer to CO #3575, which leaves Newark 5:23 p.m. and arrives Philadelphia 6:13 p.m. This last one is a commuter, Monique. Take your Dramamine. Totally whacked out, we arrive home safely and hope our luggage makes it when we do. Sorry for the triple connection, kids, but the price is right.

Next year, Ecuador, señor and señorita. Until then, Hi-Ho, Hi-Ho, it's back to work we go.

My son was 15 that summer and my daughter, freshly graduated from college, had just turned 22. We opted against taking an Inside Passage cruise to Alaska; they were expensive and we wanted more freedom to hike and explore. We chose to rent a car in Anchorage and drive down the Kenai Peninsula, and then up and around the interior of Alaska, sort of like a figure eight, with Anchorage in the middle. We wanted to include three nights in Denali National Park (we love to hike and we love national parks), and we wanted to overnight one night north of the Arctic Circle so we could experience 24-hour daylight (besides, it seemed like a really cool thing to do).

I booked our flights as soon as Continental announced the frequent flyer special, about eight or nine months before our trip. About a month later I booked our rental car and hotels (Alaska has a short tourism season and summer sells out early). Wherever possible we decided to stay in B&Bs, rather than hotels, mainly because the rates were within our budget (at that time well under US$100 a night for three, including a full breakfast). The B&Bs turned out to be a great choice. The owners, several of them older single women, regaled us with pioneer stories of the "old" Alaska *before* the Pipeline. The accommodations were at minimum comfortable, and some were quite luxurious, including a microwave, VCR, and other amenities. Video rental is very cheap and popular in Alaskan towns.

With every independent itinerary there is always the unexpected: some of it good, some not so good, and some of it downright spectacular. You just have to go with the flow.

About three days into our trip, we were picnicking at the tip of scenic Homer's Spit, a narrow sandy finger of land extending out to sea from the Kenai Peninsula. As I bit into my sandwich I felt one of my molars shatter into pieces. Although there was no pain (the tooth had unexpectedly died), I was frantic to reach my dentist, an unlikely prospect until Monday since it was now Saturday evening back home. All of the dentists on Homer's Spit were fishing for the weekend. For the next two days my delicious, freshly caught salmon and halibut dinners were sprinkled with bits of enamel. Not a good start to our trip.

Later that day, once I got over the shock of my tooth's sudden death, we began inquiring about a local adventure excursion, something we try to include in every family vacation. We decided on a midnight kayak trip that evening. The cost of the kayak trip was well above my allotted budget but it sounded so exciting that the kids and I decided to make it our one and only special excursion. At 4 p.m. we were met by our "water taxi," manned by a family of five with a small, fast boat. Both parents were schoolteachers and had moved to Alaska with their young children from upstate New York several years prior. (No one, it seems, ever moves to Alaska from a southern state). About 40 minutes later our taxi deposited us on the small dock of a remote hunting lodge where we met our kayak guide, a former Manhattan maitre d', who was as knowledgeable on New York City restaurants as he was on Kenai Peninsula tides. After 20 minutes of instructions, we strapped ourselves into life jackets and our two-man cocoon-like kayaks. I was terrified. Although I have no fear of water, I was afraid of flipping the kayak in the chilly bay and not being able to climb back in the wiggly thing before hypothermia set in. For that reason I rode with the guide. I figured I might need rescue more than the kids, and wanted him close at hand.

After 10 minutes of steady paddling without turning my head, I finally began to relax and stopped to take a few snapshots. Otters were splashing about; the snowcapped mountain peaks formed a magnificent backdrop for the inland waterways in front of us, and always watching over us, the vast murky Alaskan sky. My newly purchased Alaskan fishing gloves felt good on my hands. Recommended by locals to keep our hands warm and free from blisters, they were one of the few bargains in Alaska at US$2 a pair. As we continued to paddle, our guide pointed out the tidal high-water mark on the islands we passed. Some disappeared completely under high tide, making it impossible to find your way back without knowing the area well. Time began to stand still. Suddenly it was after 11 p.m. and we were back at the dock. It was still daylight; that soft, gentle early twilight seen only in northern climes.

Shortly thereafter our family "water taxi" picked us up. This time only the father was on board. As we headed toward Homer's Spit he asked if we would like to join his family for salmon that his son just caught. Ravenous after several hours of aerobic exercise, we quickly agreed. Their compact summer home, accessible only by water, was perched on the water's edge, surrounded on three sides by heavy forest, with a view of the mountains to die for. As we devoured fresh grilled salmon and homemade cornbread, my son suddenly jumped up, grabbed my shoulders, and shrieked "Mom, it's after midnight. It's *still* light out. Here we are feasting on fresh caught salmon in the home of someone we just met, and if you look out the front sliding door, there are four, count 'em, *four* bald eagles, eating the salmon leftovers! This *must* be Alaska!!!"

Our day had gone from not so good to very good to downright spectacular. As I said before, sometimes you just have to go with the flow.

## What should you include in your itinerary?

### 1.  Your daily activities

Write into your itinerary any activities you might like to do each day, be it a museum visit, a special hike you read about, or a festival you hope to attend. Include the names of the museums, trails, etc. If you are in transit that day, indicate the number of hours you expect to be traveling. Don't forget to include hours of operation in case you would like to change your plans at the last minute and as a double check that the activity you are planning to do is available at that time.

By organizing and putting this information into the itinerary:

➢ You are not likely to forget things.

➢ You are better equipped to make changes on the spot. The kids and I often juggled our schedule to include some special activity we weren't aware of beforehand. Having an organized itinerary in front of us made our decision much easier.

➢ Years from now, when your friends ask you about what to see and do in a particular area, you may have forgotten the name of a trail or how long it took to drive from Flagstaff, Arizona to Monument Valley. Referring back to your itinerary will give you all of the answers.

Remember, the purpose of the itinerary is to maximize your time so everybody gets to do a favorite activity and everyone has a fun-filled exciting vacation with ample time for making new friends, chasing pigeons, or a dip in the pool. This book was not created for people planning to spend one to three months overseas at a vacation villa. Single parents usually do not have that financial luxury. As such, they want to make the most of their one, two or three week family vacation.

### 2.  Use a one-third formula

My children's pediatrician, a global adventurer who has taken his family all over the world, once told me, "When you take your kids on vacation, plan one-third of your time doing things that you like, one-third of your time doing things that the kids like, and one-third of your time doing things that you all like." This formula has worked very well for our family and for other traveling families that have asked for my advice. Obviously you cannot divide each day into three equal parts, but overall the itinerary should have a balance of activities that appeal to each family member.

When my children were little, we planned our European itineraries so that we could visit a museum in the morning and swim in a local mountain lake in the afternoon. Sometimes in the evening we would visit a local amusement park. Unlike the large, impersonal and expensive theme parks in the U.S., these amusement parks have no entrance fee and are social gathering places for extended families. It was a great way to mingle with the locals and engage in new experiences. These parks sometimes included a full band with free music; and tented restaurants serving inexpensive, local tasty cuisine. The kids were told in advance that they were limited to two or three rides and one snack so I didn't blow my budget. As the kids grew older, we modified our activities to include more strenuous and sophisticated excursions, such as kayaking or evening theater performances, but we always kept the one-third formula in place.

On some days, particularly when you are in transit, the itinerary will be fairly "set." On other days, when you are stationed in one place for a day or more, generally list all activities that interest you and try to do as many as time, interest and energy allow. People sometimes read my itineraries and say, "Oh, they are so busy. You have no time to relax." I liken writing an itinerary to eating from a buffet. You don't necessarily eat everything you see; sometimes you rest between courses; and you may only take a tiny bite as a sample, but you like to view all possibilities before making your final choices. The same applies to itineraries. List everything you think you *might* want to do and you can make your final decisions when you arrive.

Our Alaska itinerary showed a very busy schedule on July 1, our first day in Anchorage. Our "must-see" attraction, the tides at Turnagain Arm, turned out to be a "no-see" attraction for us. The local Anchorage tourist board advised us the high tides occurred in the morning and after nearly 20 hours of sitting in planes and airports the day before, none of us were in the mood to hop in the car, even for a short drive. We were content to stretch our legs and walk, enjoying the city's attractions.

## 3. Include rainy day alternatives

Except for those days in transit, you should list some fallback rainy day activities. Museums, shops, and strolling around town are the obvious choices, but also consider activities that are a combination of indoors and outdoors, such as forts or tented activities such as arts and crafts shows or local festivals.

Unless you are going to a rain-free climate, such as a desert, wet weather gear should be part of your packing list so you shouldn't be entirely deterred by rain. Ranger-guided hikes at national parks are often held in rain. We attended one in Denali National Park in Alaska. In spite of the chilly wet weather, more than a dozen people showed up for the walking tour, and we enjoyed a fascinating two hours learning about the habits of moose, bear, and elk; and how to identify their footprints and droppings. As we came upon fresh moose prints, the ranger guide explained that moose are extremely territorial. Unlike in a bear encounter, where one should back off slowly, we learned that when a moose charges, one must run away immediately because the moose is intent upon driving a trespasser out of his territory. When my son asked, "How do you know which way to run?" the ranger replied, "Don't worry. If you are wrong, the moose will soon correct you." My son decided it was worth getting a little cold and muddy to bring that bit of information home to his friends.

During a spring trip to Arizona, we decided to take a short late-afternoon hike up Sedona's Bell Rock. Clouds were gathering and we knew we risked getting caught in a shower, but we threw on our rain jackets and decided to turn back if we felt drops. Unaccustomed to Arizona's sudden showers — there were no droplets — a curtain of water immediately engulfed us as we neared the top of the rock. The rock platform under our feet became a slippery series of fast-moving rivulets. Rather than risk a fall on the sloping rocks, I chose to travel partway down on my bum. Alternately giggling and shrieking, the three of us, soaked to the skin, finally made our way safely to our rental car. Before we climbed inside my son yelled, "Look at Bell Rock!" We turned, and in the space of two or three minutes, we watched the glorious red rock turn from bright orange to deep red to burnished brown and then deep purple, and finally jet black. It was a sight worth getting wet for.

### 4. Hotel List

Attached to the itinerary, I always carry a list of hotels with confirmation numbers, addresses, directions, deposits sent or guaranteed, and any other pertinent information. I also include confirmation information for rental cars and pre-booked excursions.

On the next page is a sample hotel list for our Alaska vacation. In this particular case I did not include hotel directions in the hotel list, since each B&B sent me a map and directions with my deposit receipt. On other vacations I have found it handy to keep all vital information in one place, on one sheet, stapled to my itinerary. In addition, in a separate envelope, usually tucked in my backpack, I carry all original written hotel confirmations (sent to me by the hotels), including printouts of e-mail confirmations and deposit receipts. If I confirmed the reservation by phone, I carry the original

## HOTEL LIST — ALASKA — JUNE/JULY 1993*

HERTZ CF# 833713FOCF2/ $146.99 per week, unlimited mileage, includes 30% T/A discount off US$209.99/booked 10/28, reconfirmed 5/12/93, mid-size car

JUNE 30-JULY 2
Anchor Arms Motel
433 Eagle St.
Anchorage, AK 99501
deposit sent US$87.32 11/13/92

JULY 2-4
Seekins B & B
P. O. Box 1264
Homer, AK 99603
907-235-8996
CF# 1069/ deposit sent US$58.50

JULY 4-5
Anchor Arms (see above)

JULY 5-8
Dome Home B&B
P. O. Box 262
Healy, AK 99743
(near Denali National Park)
Guaranteed to VISA by Terry Miller 12/5
$80 plus 4% tax, no T/A discount
8 a.m. shuttle confirmed for July 7

JULY 8-9
Cripple Creek Resort
P. O. Box 109
Ester, AK 99725
907-479-2500
Confirmation #78BE/guaranteed to VISA
10 p.m. Malamute Saloon Show, confirmed for 7/10

JULY 9-10
Arctic Acres Inn
Coldfoot, AK
907-678-5201
confirmed by phone 10/28 w/Lorraine
US$125 rate, no deposit guarantee required
(If cabin available, rate is US$65, must bring sleeping bag)

JULY 10-11
Eleanor's Northern Lights B&B
Dept VP, 360 State St.
Fairbanks, AK 99701
907-452-2598
US$75 less 10% T/A discount, guaranteed to VISA 12/9

JULY 11-12
The Stage Stop B&B for horses & people
P.O. Box 69
Tok, AK 99780
907-883-5338
US$51.80 rate, deposit sent US$30

JULY 12-14
Best of All B&B
P.O. Box 1578
Valdez, AK 99686
907-835-4524
$75 for three less 10% T/A discount
deposit sent $30

JULY 13
confirmed for 7 a.m. Stan Stephans
Charter to Columbia Glacier
Deposit sent US$27.67

---

* Author's note: This hotel list does not in any way act as a recommendation for any particular property. Although we were very satisfied with almost every place we stayed, there is no guarantee that prices, services and amenities are unchanged since 1993. For further information, readers may contact the author directly via email: Brenda@SingleParentTravel.net.

scratch sheets or transpose the information onto my hotel list. Scratch sheets should indicate what reservation telephone number you called in addition to the confirmation number you receive. If you called the hotel direct, note the name of the person you spoke to and the time and date of your call.

Does this seem like a lot of unnecessary details? Not at all. Computers go down, people make mistakes, and hotels overbook, especially during high season. More than once sold-out hotels have "lost" my reservation or claimed that I was confirmed for an incorrect rate. Armed with my notes, I have stood my ground at the front desk patiently, politely, and firmly. Without exception, I have always received a room or a rental car at the previously confirmed rate.

When the time comes to pack for your return home, you can discard your reservation notes, except information pertaining to changes or cancellations you made en route. This information should be retained for at least three months to be certain you are not incorrectly billed as a no-show. When canceling or changing a reservation, always note the cancellation number and/or the name of the agent and the time and date of your call.

Lastly, when traveling to a hotel that is in a major city or near a main highway or airport, call or e-mail ahead to get specific directions and include the directions in your hotel list. There is nothing more frustrating than arriving at a city after a long or delayed flight and having to shuffle through papers or a map to find your hotel's location. Make it the responsibility of one of your older kids to read the hotel directions to you and help you navigate so that you can concentrate on your driving.

## 5. Pictures and Drawings

When traveling with little children, you need to find creative ways to get and keep them interested in the trip. This is especially important if the trip involves a lot of sightseeing and physical travel. One way to do that is through pictures and drawings.

When my son turned 5, I took him and his 12-year-old sister on their first trip to Europe. Some of my acquaintances and co-workers chided me, saying, "Oh, your son is too young to travel to Europe. He won't appreciate it or remember anything." Appreciate what? Europe is not only museums and churches. It is cable cars, mountain lakes, and interesting people. Undaunted, I planned an independent rail itinerary that included a number of countries and all types of activities.

Attached to the itinerary, on a sheet of paper I drew pictures of all the types of transportation vehicles we would use. My son was fascinated with moving vehicles. Next to each drawing was a series of small boxes so my son could check off a box each time we used that vehicle. Besides trains, planes and double-decker buses, I had pictures of cog railways, cable cars, ferry boats, lake cruisers, even a picture of hiking feet!

Certain that my advance preparation had covered everything of interest to my son, I packed up our itinerary and drawings in my fanny pack. On the second day of our trip, while in England, I noticed Greg was fascinated with European toilets. Back in the 70's most European rest rooms and hotel bathrooms still used the old pull cord or some other European system of flush. Once we reached France, Greg was in his glory. Every place we stopped had a different flush system. He insisted I make a new page of drawings so he could check off every kind of flush toilet that we found. Inevitably we encountered the "footprints" style of French toilet, prompting Greg to fire away with all types of scatological questions. By the time we left France, Greg had discovered more than 21 different ways to flush a toilet and we had recorded them all. When we returned home, my son easily remembered all the places we visited by the type of toilet we found there. Not only were my simple drawings a success, but also my son had taken my idea to a new and even more creative dimension.

You needn't be a skillful artist to draw pictures for your children. Just use a little imagination. Your child will be entranced by any effort on your part. If all else fails, you can rent books from the library and photocopy some of the drawings that pertain to your next vacation. You can also download photos from the Internet or cut out magazine photos. On a later trip to Arizona, we came armed with drawings of some of the major cacti such as saguaros, jumping chollas, and barrel cacti. My son, then 7, was thrilled that he could identify so many of the common types of cacti during our desert hikes. [1]

## 6.  Personalization of Your Itinerary

Personalize your itinerary by including activities that are of unique interest to you and your kids. Reference this in your itinerary. Don't be afraid of sounding corny or silly. The kids will love it.

---

[1]  I intend to create a workbook for a series of destinations like the one I describe here. If you would like to be informed of the print date, please e-mail me at Brenda@SingleParentTravel.net.

If your son or daughter is interested in becoming a doctor or nurse, arrange for a visit to a local clinic. If your child is interested in sports, get advance tickets for a ball game or make an itinerary note to arrange for tickets when you get there. My son was interested in vehicles, so we targeted transportation museums in our vacations.

You may have noted there were numerous references to timber wolves in our Alaska itinerary. At that time my daughter's outdoor pet was a beautiful wolf-hybrid named Kashmir. Kashmir had served as her soccer team's mascot, aptly called the "Wolf Pack," and later played a cameo role in her high school play "Dracula." After Kashmir came into our lives, the three of us became fascinated with wolves and learned everything we could about these intelligent, loving creatures. (No, they don't eat children!) The "secret surprise" at the end of our Alaska trip was a visit to a wolf-hybrid breeding farm, which delighted us all, but most of all, my daughter.

A few, final comments on itineraries...

➢ If you have not done this already, show your itinerary to your kids to get final "buy-in" as to what you will see and do and how long you will stay in each place. Plan on one last family "powwow" before you begin typing up the itinerary and making reservations.

➢ Keep a master copy of the itinerary in your backpack or fanny pack, or whatever will be with you throughout the trip. Keep additional copies in your luggage. Send copies to relatives in case of emergency. Keep a couple of clean copies at home, which you later can add to your photo album.

➢ Lastly, when all is said and done, you may still have some doubts as to whether you planned the best possible trip for you and your kids. Friends, family and co-workers, and even your travel agent, may say things like "You should spend more time (or less time) at this place," or "This is too fast (or too slow) a pace for children this age," or "You really should see (this) instead of (that)." My favorite is always "Aren't you afraid of...?" When in doubt, *go with your gut instincts!* There were many times when we decided to do things our way, often against the advice of well-meaning friends and family. After all, it was *our* itinerary.

In May 2001 I published an article on this very topic on the Web site of Parents Without Partners. It is an interesting story and bears repeating here:

## TRUSTING YOUR TRAVEL INSTINCTS
BRENDA ELWELL, CTC

After traveling the world for 40 years, including twenty of them as a single parent, I have come to trust my gut instincts about travel and where I think my kids and I will find a special experience for our annual family vacation. After some book and Web research, and listening to a few travelers' opinions, I present my ideas to my kids in a family "powwow" and, with their input, we hammer out a final itinerary together.

One such example was a 1997 10-day summer trip to the Belizean mainland and Tikal, Guatemala. We had read that if we crossed the border by land from Belize to Guatemala we would surely be beaten, eaten, robbed and raped. We also noted that tour groups spent only a day or two at Tikal National Park, flying in and out of nearby Flores Airport. I had really good feelings about Tikal; my kids and I love national parks, we are interested in history, and the animal life and Mayan temple climbs seemed to be superb. So, contrary to public opinion, we decided to cut a day off our Belizean itinerary and add a third night to Tikal National Park. We also decided to travel overland to Guatemala.

Since we would be crossing a foreign border mid-trip, we opted against renting a car and instead hired a local driver and car for our side excursion to Guatemala. We inquired with the locals about the safety of an overland crossing, and, not surprisingly, found that U.S. press accounts were grossly exaggerated. As a precaution, the driver stashed our cash in four different hiding places in the car. My daughter, who majored in International Business, made certain that each batch of cash was counted and witnessed before it went in. We were told to keep US$20 on our person ready to hand over if we were stopped and robbed. The three-hour drive was completely uneventful.

Tikal National Park was everything we hoped it would be. This was the New York City of the Mayan World: towering temples that seemed to stretch on forever, all nestled in a magnificent jungle setting. It was thrilling to spot the famous ones featured in such movie epics as "Star Wars" and the James Bond series. Each morning we headed out for a pre-dawn hike to the top of one of the temples, accompanied overhead by chattering, colorful papagayos (macaws) and, at our feet, such critters as the curious and friendly coatimundi. By late morning we returned to our hotel for lunch and a swim in the pool, while watching the monkeys swing from tree to tree. By late afternoon we were refreshed and back at the ruins.

No matter what the advertisements lead you to believe, there are only three hotels located within Tikal National Park: The Jaguar Inn, the Jungle Lodge, and the Tikal Inn. All are similar in price, style and amenities, with each offering a meal package, a pool, and bungalow accommodations ranging from modest to Spartan. You are surrounded by lush jungle with a museum, handicraft shops, and the Mayan ruins only a short walking distance away. For those seeking nightlife or more deluxe accommodations, the town of Flores is only 40 minutes by car.

The Tikal generator goes off (and lights go out) at 10 p.m. After all, this is the jungle. If you are planning an early morning hike, chances are you may not need to set the alarm clock. More than once we were wakened by the 5 a.m. clamor of howler monkeys. The kids and I recognized the sound from a previous trip to the Amazon. If we hadn't, I think we would have been too terrified to leave the room until noon. It is hard to believe such little monkeys can create such loud, piercing sounds.

Rusty, but still conversant in Spanish, I quickly made friends with our wait staff at the Jaguar Inn and, on the second day, my son was invited to play in their regional soccer tournament the following day. It was the final set of matches between the hospitality staff (waiters and hotel managers) and the security staff (park rangers and security guards). My daughter was disappointed that she was not asked, so, with her prompting, I diplomatically explained to our waiter that she was also an experienced soccer player. Without hesitation, the waiter invited her to play as well.

Satisfied with my linguistic and people skills, I turned to face my two grown children, both of whom had a look of concern on their faces. It had suddenly dawned on them that our gracious hosts might not have uniforms and shoes to fit them. My son was six feet tall (182 cm), with my daughter not far behind, and, like many Americans, they have big feet. The Guatemalans, especially those of Mayan descent are a petite people, with tiny feet to match.

Late the next morning we followed our hosts down a narrow trail to a huge clearing in the jungle which served as the soccer field. Surrounding the field were dozens of spectators (human and otherwise), a full marimba band, and a smiling Miss Tikal, the local beauty queen. My kids were given their uniforms and soccer shoes, all of which miraculously fit. We soon discovered that women do not play sports in Guatemala, but my daughter was easily accepted as "one of the boys" because the Guatemalans had watched American women play soccer on TV. Monique was the only female playing in the tournament that day.

My kids were placed on opposite teams, and after a half hour warm-up, play began. In Guatemala the ball is much lighter than in the States. There are a lot more headshots, far less dribbling, and very little physical contact. As the whistle sounded my son and daughter came charging for the ball, and immediately locked into head-to-head, or should I say, foot-to-foot combat. There was a loud crack as their bodies met, followed by a sudden hush in the crowd as Monique seized the ball. Even the marimba band stopped playing for a moment. A loud cheer followed once the Guatemalans recovered from the shock of witnessing a woman play sports as aggressively as a man.

I was busy running around the sidelines tending to my dual tasks of water bearer and sports photographer. After 20 minutes of furious play in the noonday jungle sun, my two kids, now red-faced and dripping with sweat, shrieked across the field at me "How do you say 'Get me outta here' in Spanish?" They were quickly relieved from play. Lying prostrate on the grass with a newfound respect for their hosts' stamina under the burning sun, they decided to call it quits for the day.

That night was the monthly regional dance in Tikal National Park. The outdoor museum exhibits were moved aside to make room for a dance floor under the canopy. The national social dance of Guatemala is called La Punta. You stand close to, but apart from, your partner and endlessly undulate your hips. It wasn't hard to learn, which was good, because that was all they played. When we arrived, Monique's entire soccer team lined up to dance with her, while Greg's teammates lined up their single sisters for him. Meanwhile I was pursued by the older men in the crowd, most of who reached only to my chest. Not exactly conducive to cheek-to-cheek dancing. Thank God for La Punta.

At 11 p.m. my daughter and I decided to retire for the night. My son, happily guzzling beer with his soccer buddies, indicated he would stay until the dance ended at midnight. As I flopped into bed, I had some concerns about Greg getting back safely to our bungalow. Had he remembered his flashlight? Would he get lost in the pitch-black jungle and get bitten by a snake? I voiced my growing concerns to my daughter, who by then was fast asleep. Deciding to let go of my motherly worries, I did the same.

Shortly before 1 a.m. I awoke to loud footsteps, a flashing light beam, and a slurred familiar voice saying "Grahshus (Gracias) Señor" several times over. On the way home from the dance, Greg had fallen behind his comrades and wandered off the path. Without his flashlight he had gotten lost. Fortunately the nighttime security guard, with whom I had chatted in Spanish two days earlier, came upon Greg stumbling about in the darkness. Assuming he was my son (he is tall and blond like his mom), he deposited him safely on my doorstep.

The next morning we said adios to our Guatemalan friends, leaving with sweet memories, great photos, and happy that once again, we had trusted our travel instincts.


## PLANNING AHEAD TO MEET THE LOCALS

In Part II of this book — The Trip Itself — we will discuss ways to meet locals and enjoy an interesting cultural experience, once you have arrived at your destination. However, well before you leave, there are many things you can do to prepare and lay the foundation for this vacation experience, be it within the U.S. or anywhere else in the world.

1. *Ask everyone you know if they have a contact at your vacation destination.*

   Ask your friends, acquaintances, co-workers, neighbors, doctor, dentist, kids' teachers, even your kids' parents' friends. This advice applies whether you are traveling domestically or overseas. Have your kids ask everyone they know, too.

2. *Use your business contacts.*

   Thanks to the Internet and a global economy, it should not be too difficult to track down contacts from your company or your company's suppliers that reside at your vacation destination. If you are in the educational field, you can contact local schools or universities at your destination. Even though you may be traveling during your school vacation, school may be in session at your destination.

3. *Call on your church/mosque/synagogue, Rotary Club, gardening club, whatever you belong to, and get information on domestic or overseas chapters and contact personnel.*

   Parents Without Partners is one such international organization. College alumni listings are another great source.

4. *Considering joining an organization just for the contact benefits.*

   One such organization is Women Welcome Women, an international organization designed to promote cultural understanding and friendship. There is a membership fee. Members are free to e-mail or write one another and offer information or hospitality as they see fit. I recently joined and have an e-mail pal from the UK who is planning to come to my

area to visit her daughter. The Web address is www.womenwelcome
women.org.uk.

5. *Contact tourist boards for information on cultural exchanges.*

    In some major cities overseas you can pre-book afternoon tea with a
    local family.

6. *If you or your child has a special interest, capitalize on that and contact
    the appropriate organizations in advance.*

    Perhaps your son recently prepared a paper on the Battle of Gettysburg
    or your daughter was asked to do a presentation about the history of
    women in journalism. Why not contact the local historian or editor of the
    newspaper at your destination? Often these contacts can be uncovered
    through an Internet search or by checking with that area's newspaper.

OK, now that you have all these contacts, what do you do with them? What
do you say?

First of all, don't be shy. Send a message, either through e-mail, fax or snail
mail that is brief, friendly, and to the point. For example, perhaps for your
next summer family vacation you are planning to take your two kids out
West for a fly/drive trip starting in Denver. Your co-worker, Katie Crandall,
knows a former neighbor who moved to Denver a year ago. She gives you
her name (Angie Olivetti) and address. Drop Angie a note like the following
example:

```
Dear Angie,

Your former neighbor, Katie Crandall, is my
colleague at Optical Instruments. Katie sug-
gested I drop you a note. My kids and I are
planning a summer vacation out West and will
be in Denver the weekend of June 20. We'll
have a day in Denver for some sightseeing
before we head off to Rocky Mountain National
Park for hiking. I thought perhaps you might
have some suggestions about what to do that
free day in Denver. We have read that the
Natural History Museum is very good. We are
also eager to visit any sites that are famous
for Wild West history. Do you have any moder-
ately priced restaurant suggestions? Perhaps
```

```
you might be available to join us for dinner,
my treat? Katie also gave me your home number.
I'll give you a call the evening of March 5ᵗʰ
or you can call me at 727-767-1011.

Katie says hello and promises to visit you
soon.
```

The purpose of writing or e-mailing ahead is to give the person you are contacting a chance to think about what he or she would like to recommend and if they want to join you. Perhaps Angie may want to call or e-mail her friend Katie and ask about you before she decides to offer her services as Denver tour guide or join you for dinner. Follow-up with a phone call as promised.

When contacting a person overseas, unless you are certain that he or she speaks fluent English, it is best to e-mail or fax. If you don't have a response within a week or so, try e-mailing or faxing again. In third world countries it is not uncommon for e-mails to get "lost" during heavy rains or for faxes to disappear when phone lines are down.

If you are fortunate enough to be invited to visit someone's home in a foreign country, be sure to bring a small gift. Flowers or candy are usually appropriate if the invitation comes unexpectedly. If you are not sure of local customs, ask hotel front desk personnel what would be an appropriate hostess gift. If you know or suspect beforehand that you might be invited to someone's home, bring along some gifts from the States. They need not be expensive — a pretty scarf for the ladies, small toys if you will be meeting children. Regional gifts are always appreciated, such as maple syrup from Vermont, a bottle of wine from California, or salt-water taffy from the Jersey boardwalk. In Part II of this book I'll devote a chapter to the art of gift-giving.

In addition to entertaining guests from around the world in our home, my family has had the pleasure many times of visiting someone's home overseas. All of these experiences have been both educational and delightful. One overseas single parent experience, in particular, stands out.

In 1994 my kids and I headed off to Ecuador for a long-awaited two-week summer vacation to the Galapagos, Quito, and Ecuadorian Amazon. At that time I was working for a global travel management company and a colleague gave me the business card of the General Manager of Operations of our company for Ecuador, whom she had met at our company's convention. I sent her a fax mentioning the date we would arrive in Quito and inviting her and her husband to have dinner with us. She accepted the invitation.

They were a handsome and charming couple, both fluent in English, so conversation flowed readily throughout dinner. Their opening question was "How are things going with OJ?" My kids and I groaned. We thought we had escaped the OJ Simpson circus by traveling to Ecuador. Our hosts had HBO and knew about the police chase down the L.A. freeway. We were astonished to learn how much our hosts knew about American culture. Our Ecuadorian hosts were astonished to learn that many Americans actually sat and watched that entire freeway chase on TV. (I was too embarrassed to admit I was one of them).

Our gracious hosts insisted on picking up the dinner tab and promised to call the evening we returned from our Amazon excursion, which they did. Four days later they brought us to their home for evening coffee and to meet their children. My daughter wasn't feeling well and went upstairs to lie down. (At the time we were concerned she had picked up a "bug" in the Amazon, even though we took all necessary medical precautions. We found out later that her electrolytes had become unbalanced during our Amazon visit. She had consumed plenty of water, but not enough salt).

Throughout the evening our hosts received calls from their three teenage children. "Can you pick me up?" "Can I go to my other friend's house before I come home?" Can I stay at my friend's house tonight?" It was just like a scene from American suburbia. Dad jumped in the car to fetch a child, only to discover when he returned home that another child called needing a ride. Eventually one of the children was brought home, a stunningly beautiful 17-year-old girl. As she entered the living room, she walked over to her mother, kissed her on both cheeks, and then greeted me as the oldest guest with a kiss on both cheeks. Lastly she did the same to my 16-year-old son and then sat beside him on the sofa, chattering away in English. Immediately my son visibly stiffened. I was surprised at his reaction. Normally a poised and gregarious teenager, he long ago had overcome his painful childhood shyness. Had it suddenly returned? Shortly thereafter the father brought home his 19-year-old daughter, who was just as beautiful and charming as her younger sister. She greeted everyone in the same fash-ion and then sat on the other side of my son. By this time Greg had turned to stone. He was answering, but not initiating questions, and not moving a muscle of his body other than his mouth. With one child sick and the other behaving strangely, I did my best to carry the conversational ball for our family.

After our hosts drove us back to our hotel I asked, "Greg, what was going on back there? Guys spend big bucks at bars hoping some pretty girl will sit next to them and, here you are, 16-years-old, surrounded and kissed by two world-class Latin beauties, and you looked so unhappy to be sitting next to them!" He promptly replied, "Mom, my sneakers smelled so bad from the Amazon, that when the girls sat down next to me I was afraid to move. I thought if I did, they might smell them too, and I would be so embarrassed."

## PACKING

Although packing is something you usually do the night before your trip, it is important to discuss it as part of the preparation section so that you can think about what to purchase in advance. Some essentials:

### FIRST AID KIT

Keep it simple. The contents should vary according to climate, destination, and children's ages. These ten items are staples:

1. *Pepto Bismol®* — Whether traveling in the U.S. or abroad, someone may get tummy troubles.

2. *Eardrops* — Apply them to your children's ears before and after any swim in any body of water, natural or otherwise. This helps to ward off infections. There are several over-the-counter brands available. Ask your pharmacist.

3. *Adhesive tape, gauze pads, alcohol swabs, Band-Aids* — I carried a large supply of these items when my kids were little and constantly chasing pigeons or tripping over stones. Now I just bring Band-Aids.

4. *Any medication you or your children normally take* — such as asthma or allergy medicine.

5. *Insect repellant and anti-itch creams or lotions* — if you will be in mosquito-infested areas

6. *Tweezers* — to remove splinters, bugs, whatever. Remember to sterilize the tweezers first with alcohol or a match flame.

7. *Soothing creams* — for chapped hands and faces if going to a cold climate plus lip balm with sunscreen.

8. *Sunscreen and sunburn cooling sprays* — if you plan to be outdoors in the sun. Children should never be allowed to get sunburned, so apply

sunscreen liberally and keep their bodies covered with hats and shirts when possible.

9.  *Aspirin* — If you are going to carry one-size-fits-all, label the bottle with the dosage for your kids.

10. *Airsickness bags* — Take some from a plane if you don't have them already. They also double as great diaper bags.

Think ahead to possible exceptional needs. On our first single parent trip to Europe, we had planned one overnight train trip. At that time my kids were little and very prone to sudden, painful ear infections. Anti-bacterial ear-drops were not readily available over the counter like they are today. I knew we would be frequently swimming in mountain lakes, so I asked my pediatrician if he would prescribe a small amount of antibiotics in case the kids were struck down with an ear infection on the long train ride. I just needed enough for about 24 hours, until we were able to contact a doctor. They didn't get sick, but we were prepared.

### PACKING LIST

Once your kids are old enough to read, hand them a packing list and let them assemble the items on the bed and check them off. If they are missing an item, such as batteries, have them circle it on the list, alerting you that it needs to be purchased. Praise them for their thoroughness and then show them how to pack everything into a duffel or suitcase. By the time they are pre-teens (10, 11 or 12), they should be able to pack everything on their own, with the help of a detailed packing list.

1.  Little kids like packing lists because it makes them feel grown-up.

2.  Teenagers like packing lists because it eliminates the need for communication, especially of an instructional nature, from a parent

3.  Grown-up kids like packing lists because it keeps them organized. My college-age son suffered from brain meltdown after final exams. Without a packing list to prepare for our summer family vacation, he, without a doubt, would have forgotten important items.

Following are two sample packing lists. (More packing lists may be found on my Web site, SingleParentTravel.net). The first one was created for a three-week driving trip through the American West. On that trip we borrowed a friend for my 12-year-old son, hence the "Rules of the Road," which the boys had to sign off on. This list dates back to 1990. Since then we eliminated canteens in favor of water bottles. As carry-on luggage restrictions tightened up, we were required to check duffel bags, and later traveled with duffels on wheels.

The second packing list, updated in 1999, was designed for travel to Latin America. (*For all of you geographically challenged Americans, Latin America refers to all countries in Central and South America, not just Mexico*). As you see, the packing process became more refined as my children got older. You will note I do not mention a hair dryer or electrical converter. I found converters do not work as well in Latin America and other third world countries as they do in Europe. Even though I posses a global set of converters, more than once I have blown my hair dryer in overseas outlets. When I need to primp for a nice dinner or a show, I borrow a hair dryer from the hotel front desk. Most hotels that are three stars and up will provide one. Other than those occasions, my daughter and I style our locks "à la wash and wear" while traveling in faraway places. Make sure your teen-age daughter is made aware of this fact.

One final note: when traveling to places that might be infested with mosquitoes or ticks, such as jungle, forest, or lakeside hikes, make certain you and your children are wearing hats and clothing that covers your wrists and your ankles. The Capri pants that reach to mid-calf may be stylish for the ladies but are not suitable for this environment.

**Packing List for U.S. West—Three Week trip**

- 2 or 3 pair jeans, 1 pair cotton or khaki slacks
- 4 pair shorts
- 6 or 7 T-shirts (We'll buy a couple more along the way)
- One nice shirt
- 7 sets of socks and underwear (should include 2 sturdy pairs of socks for serious hiking days)
- 1 or 2 sweaters or sweatshirts, lightweight jacket (optional)
- Rain jacket or poncho (essential)
- 2 pair of sneakers
- 1 baseball cap to protect from sun
- Sunscreen
- 2 bathing suits

- Pajamas or night clothes
- Binoculars (optional)
- Pocket knife (can not be carried onto plane)
- 2 water bottles
- 2 small backpacks
- Camera and lots of film and camera batteries
- Stamps for postcards
- Games and toys
- Walkie talkies
- Toothbrush and personal hygiene items
- Clock radio and lightweight flashlight
- Extra batteries for anything that needs batteries
- Sunglasses
- First Aid kit
- Shampoo and conditioner
- Pack everything in a large duffel suitable for carry-on
- Additional articles such as toys, games etc. for flight may be carried in a flight bag

**Rules of the Road**

1) Seat belts worn at all times in the car.

2) Remain absolutely quiet when Mom drives over the Continental Divide.

3) Everybody carries and is responsible for his or her own luggage.

4) Everybody takes a turn helping Mom with the laundry.

5) We stick together at all times, especially on trails and in the woods. Anyone that departs from the group must notify Mom where they are going and when they will return. The boys must always use the buddy system. When returning to our cabin after a nighttime national park activity, we stick together without any exceptions, i.e. no running ahead to hide behind trees and scare us.

6) Do not feed or approach any dangerous wildlife, especially the bears.

7) Respect and obey all ranger rules regarding wildlife and trails or risk being fined and thrown out of the park.

8) Absolutely no littering.

## Packing List for Latin America—One Week or longer

- One week's supply of socks and underwear (laundry service is often slow in Latin America)
- 3-4 short sleeved shirts or cotton tops such as T-shirts
- 2 tank tops
- 1 long sleeve durable lightweight, light colored cotton shirt which acts as a sun protector for daytime jungle hikes as well as a mosquito protector for evening walks in jungle areas
- 2-3 pair of lightweight loose fitting slacks
- 1 pair of jeans (2 pair if traveling to the Andes Mountains)
- 1 or 2 pair shorts
- Bathing suit
- Raingear
- Suitable foot gear for hiking and walking around cobblestone streets
- Hat (for sun protection) & sunglasses
- 1 sweater or sweatshirt (rainy evenings can get chilly even in the tropics)
- 2-3 bandanas, 3 hair bands
- Sleepwear
- Personal toiletries such as toothbrush, toothpaste, shampoo, conditioner, shaving gear, moisturizing lotion, etc.
- Flashlight, batteries, pocket packs of tissues (for use in public toilets), small travel-size sewing kit, all purpose
- Pocket knife, sink stopper for soaking laundry (not always present in moderate-priced hotels)
- Small roll of electrical tape (comes in handy for a myriad of things, including binding up gifts to take home)
- Large plastic trash bag (handy for lots of things including covering your luggage in the rain), 6 gallon-size and 6 quart-size zip-lock plastic bags (handy for packing things that may leak while traveling or carrying food snacks)
- First Aid Kit

## First Aid Kit

Keep it simple. The contents should vary according to climate, destination, and ages of children.

**Pepto-Bismol or equivalent** — Whether traveling in the US or abroad, someone may get tummy troubles.

**Acidophilus, Culturelle or equivalent** — Good tummy bacteria to prevent the need for Pepto-Bismol.

**Ear Drops** — Apply them to your children's ears before and after any swim in any body of water, natural or otherwise. This helps to ward off infections.

**Adhesive tape, gauze pads, alcohol swabs, Band-Aids** — I carried a large supply of these items when my kids were little and constantly chasing pigeons or tripping over stones. Now I just bring Band-Aids. My daughter who gets frequent blisters uses a fairly new product called Compeed. It is currently packaged by Band-Aid. Not only does it prevent blisters, but it allows you to continue walking if you have one. We have also heard that Moleskin is good. For some, foot powder does the trick.

**Any medication you or your children normally take** — such as vitamins, asthma or allergy medicine.

**Insect repellent and anti-itch creams or lotions** — if you will be in mosquito infested areas

**Tweezers** — to remove splinters, bugs, whatever. Remember to sterilize the tweezers first with alcohol or a match flame.

**Soothing creams** — for chapped hands and faces if going to a cold climate

**Sunscreen and sunburn cooling sprays** — if you plan to be outdoors in the sun. Children should never be allowed to get sunburned so apply sunscreen liberally and keep their little bodies covered with hats and shirts when possible.

**Aspirin** — If you are going to carry one-size-fits-all, label the bottle with the dosage for your kids.

**Eye Drops** for dry eyes on plane or dry locations.

**Lip Balm** Also for plane or sunny locations.

**Motion Sickness medication** — Ginger tablets, Dramamine, patches or wrist bands. Bring whatever works.

**Fever, Cold, Allergy Medication**

## TRAVEL BOOKS, MAPS, DOCUMENTS, CONFIRMATIONS, INSURANCE AND EMERGENCY INFORMATION

As noted on the Latin American packing list, all of these items need to be packed in such a way that you carry them with you at all times, either in a fanny pack or lightweight backpack.

If you are a female single parent or grandmother, now is the time to ditch that inappropriate purse and buy yourself a suitable fanny pack for travel. Not only will it free up your arms to take better care of young children, but also it will substantially reduce the likelihood of theft. Think about it: You are the only adult. You are carrying *all* valuables and documents on the trip. What would happen to your trip if your purse were snatched?

Through the years the kids and I developed a system that worked well for us. I wore a fanny pack and carried a camera on a strap and we took turns carrying a lightweight backpack that contained snacks, water, extra sunscreen, tour book and maps. When we traveled to major amusement parks or Walt Disney World, we stashed the backpack in our hotel room and I wore lightweight slacks or shorts with pockets deep enough to fit a water bottle and sunscreen. As the kids grew older and I invested in more expensive camera equipment, we wound up traveling with two backpacks, which we alternated. Ways to carry money will be discussed in Part II.

## APPROPRIATE LUGGAGE

Keep in mind that as an independent traveling Single Parent Family, you and your kids should be able to walk at least two blocks with your luggage. Keep that in mind when you pack your bags or buy a new suitcase.

When traveling by train in Europe, the train station may only be a block or two from your hotel. Why hail a cab? When arriving at an airport in Latin America, it may save you many dollars (or pesos) to walk a couple of blocks out of the airport area and hail a cab near the main road. Many airports in Latin America are quite small, even in the capital cities.

Today there are many types and sizes of luggage that come on wheels, making it very easy for each member of the family to be self-sufficient. A small child can easily pull along a suitcase designed to hold his or her clothing. Bigger kids may prefer a duffel. For some of our more remote trips, such as the Amazon or the Andes, we found double duffels on wheels to be most appropriate. They can be carried or pulled and can easily be squished to fit into tight compartments or onto transfer canoes.

For a variety of luggage, check out a Web site called www.ToughTraveler.com or call 800-GET-TOUGH. The company offers a wide variety of high-quality luggage, backpacks, fanny packs, and camera bags for adults and kids. I haven't tried their merchandise yet, but welcome comments from readers. Other luggage companies that offer kids gear are:

➢ www.Landsend.com or call 800-963-4816

➢ www.LLBean.com or call 800-441-5713

➢ www.ContainerStore.com or call 800-786-7315

➢ www.FamilyOnBoard.com or call 800-793-2075

## PACKING SNACKS

Plan to take healthy snacks on your trip. Besides saving you money and aggravation, your kids' tummies will feel better and you will be prepared for unforeseen delays.

The night before a trip I prepare the following:

1. A half-dozen easy-to-make sandwiches. My daughter recommends PB&Js because they last days without refrigeration and still taste pretty good after being squished.

2. One or two bagels with cream cheese cut up into small pieces.

3. Bottles of water and juice.

4. Fresh fruits such as apples, oranges, and grapes.

5. Cut-up carrots or other favorite raw veggies.

6. Brownies or cookies (I make these a week before and freeze them so they are fresh for the trip).

7. Sometimes I bring some packaged treats, such as cheese and crackers or locally made Tastycakes.

Your snacks should fit into a book bag or small backpack. If there is a flight delay, or the kids are too excited to eat breakfast, they can comfortably munch on healthful food and won't badger you for money to buy overpriced junk sold at airports. If they don't like what is served on the plane, they have their own food. Fruit and desserts usually last another day and make a nice healthful snack in the hotel room (Keep in mind you cannot bring fresh fruit and vegetables into a foreign country, but the kids will appreciate the familiar desserts from home while they last).

Remember to leave yourself a big note on the door so you don't leave food in the refrigerator. Prior to one of our long distance foreign trips, the commercial transfer vehicle showed up at our doorstep a half hour ahead of schedule. We skipped breakfast and hurried to finish dressing. As we approached the airport, I realized I had left our snacks in the refrigerator. My son, then a teenager, missed having his food bag close at hand and it cost me an extra US$20 in airport snacks before we even took off on our flight. After that lesson I left a note for myself, and yes, I also switched transport companies.

## DOCUMENTS AND VACCINATIONS

For U.S. Citizens, traveling within the U.S. requires no special documents. Of course you should take any documents or memberships cards that may entitle you to travel discounts. Some examples are AAA cards, AARP cards, and student ID cards. For single grandparents out there, did you know that at age 62 you can buy a Golden National Park Pass for only US$10? The Golden Pass is good for a lifetime and includes anybody traveling with you in your car. It's a pretty good deal considering a yearly National Park Pass runs US$50.

The following is a summary guide for documents for overseas travel for U.S. citizens. Rules change, so please check the appropriate government agency before making your plans.

### VALID PASSPORTS

Overseas travel requires a separate passport for each member of your family, even the children. U.S. Passports are valid for 10 years. If your child is under the age of 16, he or she will receive a passport valid for five years. The following U.S. government Web site provides instructions on how to apply for a passport and print out passport forms. You may need to download Adobe Acrobat Reader from the Adobe Web site onto your computer. Instructions are given on the site at http://travel.state.gov/download_applications.html.

Read the instructions, gather up the necessary documents and photos, and submit your application(s) to your local passport agency, county clerk's office, or post office. Allow six to eight weeks for first-time passport processing. Bargain hint: Don't get passport photos taken near a passport office; you will pay top dollar. Shop around and don't be afraid to bargain for a better "family" rate. AAA has reasonable photo rates for its members. We also found good rates at photo shops in the mall.

### OBTAINING A U.S. PASSPORT FOR A MINOR UNDER AGE 14

On July 2, 2001 a new law went into effect outlining the special requirements for children under the age of 14. Detailed requirements for obtaining a passport are on the U.S. Department of State Passport Service's Web site at http://travel.state.gov/specialreq.html. In this book, I address only those

requirements that deal with parental permission. To satisfy the new requirements for parental permission, either:

1. Both parents must appear together and sign, or;

2. One parents appears, signs, and submits the second parent's written statement of consent (including the child's name and date of birth) authorizing passport issuance for the child, or;

3. One parents appears, signs, and submits primary evidence of sole authority to apply (such as one of the following):

   ➢ Child's certified U.S. or foreign birth certificate (with translation, if
     necessary) listing only applying parent, or;

   ➢ Consular Report of Birth Abroad (Form FS-240) or Certification of
     Birth Abroad (Form DS-1350) listing only applying parent, or;

   ➢ Court order granting sole custody to the applying parent (unless
     child's travel is restricted by that order), or;

   ➢ Adoption decree (if applying parents is sole adopting parent), or;

   ➢ Court order specifically permitting applying parent's or guardian's
     travel with the child; or

   ➢ Judicial declaration of incompetence of non-applying parent; or a
     death certificate of non-applying parent.

If none of the above documentation is available, the applying parent/guard-
ian should submit a signed statement to the passport agency (including
the child's name and date of birth) explaining why the non-applying par-
ent/guardian's consent cannot be obtained.

If someone other than the parent of the child is applying for a passport
on behalf of a minor under the age of 14, then they must do the following: Submit a notarized written statement or affidavit from both parents
or guardians authorizing a third-party to apply for a passport. When the
statement or affidavit is from only one parent/guardian, the third-party
must present evidence of sole custody of the authorizing parent/
guardian.

Our research also uncovered the fact that parents who are in arrears of child
support payments in excess of US$5,000 are ineligible to receive a U.S.
Passport.

## PERMISSION TO TAKE THE CHILDREN OUT OF THE COUNTRY

*This is extremely important information for any single adult taking a child out of the country.*

Technically, U.S. citizens do not need permission to leave the U.S.; they need permission to *enter* another country with a minor child and without his or her other parent. So, what kind of documentation do you need to bring? The answer is it depends not only on the destination, but also often on the whim of airline, cruise and customs officials. That point has been driven home time and time again when readers who fully researched the topic *still* had trouble (I list all readers' comments in the documentation section of SingleParentTravel.net).

Don't take my word for it, though. DO YOUR OWN RESEARCH. This is critical because requirements change (If you find information that conflicts with mine, please drop me an e-mail at GlobalBrenda@SingleParentTravel.net for future updates on SingleParentTravel.net and future editions of the book).

So how do you research this topic on your own? Follow these three steps:

1. Read the Consular Sheets at http://travel.state.gov/travel_warnings.html. The sheets provide contact info for embassies and consulates, and are kept fairly up-to-date by the U.S. government.

2. Contact the embassy or consulate at your destination. The destination country has the final say, but remember, what you hear from a bureaucrat over the phone may not equate to what you hear from immigration officials upon entering the country. Make certain to document phone calls by jotting down the name of the person you spoke to, the date, and the number you called. This may help you in a difficult situation.

    For a list of phone numbers and Web sites, try this Web site www.consulate.travel.com.hk/.

3. Contact your airline, cruise line or tour operator and ask what they require for your particular situation. Airlines, cruise lines and tour operators are subject to enormous fines from the destination country. As such, they may be overly cautious and require more documentation than the destination country. Also, the documentation requirements for a destination may differ based on the time spent in that country and the way that you enter the country (airport, seaport, land).

I recommend that you err on the side of over-documentation. This is particularly relevant if your name differs from your child or if you look significantly different from your child. Regardless of the situation, you should bring the child's passport, his or her birth certificate, and a notarized letter of permission from the non-accompanying parent. If you are unable to obtain the letter, provide a substitute: documentation proving you have custody of the child, a death certificate of the other parent, or any other documentation relating to your situation. A sample letter of permission is available on my Web site at www.singleparenttravel.net/ Articles/Documentation/Notarized%20Letter.htm courtesy of Family Travel Forum.

I list the documentation requirements for entry into various countries in the documentation section of my Web site, SingleParentTravel.net.

While I am on this subject, if you are a non-parental or non-custodial adult traveling with a child traveling within or outside of the U.S., you should also carry with you a letter giving you permission to authorize any emergency medical treatment the child may need during your trip. Bring a copy of the applicable insurance card as well. I will mention this again under emergencies in Part II.

## TOURIST CARDS

Many Latin American countries require you to complete a tourist card before entering the country. Most are free, some require a small fee. Usually this is done at the gateway airport at the time you check in for your flight.

## VISAS

A passport gives you permission to *leave* your residential country and a visa gives you permission to *enter* a particular country. Although visa requirements are gradually being waived on the Eastern European scene as Communism fades into history, some countries in other areas of the world, such as the Middle East, Africa or the Orient, do require visas for entry.

There are two ways to go about getting a visa. You can contact a Visa Service which will handle everything for you for a fee, in addition to the fees charged by each government; or you can do it yourself, saving anywhere from $50 to hundreds of dollars. Do an Internet search for your destination country's government Web site. You can print out their visa application form or send them an e-mail asking them to mail the application to you. The next step is to send them the completed form along with the fee and any required photos. Carefully read the application instructions to determine if the photos need to be signed. Always send your documents via some type of express mail with a return receipt. It is also a good idea to send along a pre-addressed express mail airbill so the documents are returned to you express mail. Allow three weeks for the process, although most visas take less time. I recommend making a follow-up phone call to the consulate after a week or 10 days to make certain the application is being processed. After one of these phone calls I discovered our Syrian Visa applications were sitting on the desk of someone who was out of the office sick.

## GOVERNMENT WARNINGS ABOUT TRAVEL

Even though a foreign government may issue you a visa to enter their home-land, there may be times when certain areas become unsafe for travel, for reasons such as political unrest, floods, etc. It is *your* responsibility, as a parent and a traveler to be aware of these situations and to get the proper facts.

The media tends to exaggerate these occurrences and their effects, so it is best to check with destination country government Web sites (and the U.S. State Department Web site) to determine whether or not to go ahead with your travel plans. Just because there is an isolated outbreak of violence in Belfast, Ireland, doesn't mean that all of Ireland is unsafe. Travelers, in particular American travelers, frequently and mistakenly assume that if there is trouble in one country, then it must be dangerous to travel in all of its neighboring countries as well. This is like saying if there is political unrest in Quebec, Canada then it must be unsafe to travel in the U.S.

To get the facts, not the hype, and develop an informed opinion, go to government Web sites.

Start with your country, then try a few other English-speaking government Web sites. You will find the U.S. tends to be the most cautious in its assessments. If you do not have access to a computer, you can call information for the number for the U.S. State Department. There is usually a recorded message once you punch in all of the options to get to your particular destination country, but this is a laborious and expensive way to get information. It is better to ask a friend with a computer to help you find the information or go to your local library and do the research on a computer there. Some good Web sites are:

| | |
|---|---|
| U.S. State Department's Bureau of Consular Affairs | www.travel.state.gov |
| Britain | www.fco.gov.uk/travel |
| Canada | www.voyage.dfait-maeci.gc.ca |
| Australia | www.dfat.gov.au/consular/advice/ |

## VACCINATIONS

This will date me, but I remember the days when a smallpox and typhoid shot were required to travel to Europe. Back then typhoid shots were a series of painful injections, not the pop-in-your-mouth treatment we have today. Nowadays, unless you are going into the jungle or to a remote third-world country, there are few vaccination requirements, but there are some recommendations.

### Typhoid Fever

If you plan to travel with your children to places where it is not safe to drink the tap water, then I recommend considering booster shots for typhoid fever.

### Tetanus

Not a bad idea if you will be hiking, camping or doing any adventure stuff with your feet. Get a tetanus shot if you are venturing anywhere where horses were kept in the area within the past 100 years (i.e. ranch vacations, the American West, etc.), according to some doctors.

### Hepatitis A and Hepatitis B

I recommend these shots if you are going into countries where sanitation conditions may be less than ideal. Other than Western Europe, Canada and the U.S., that covers the world. The initial treatment includes a series of shots and then, a year later you can get one injection that gives you lifelong immunity. Keep in mind that lifelong immunity varies with each person. Some people lose their immunity after 10-20 years.

People assume that hepatitis A and B only apply to people that are sexually active. That is not the case. You could be traveling in a remote village in Mexico or Central America, get into an accident, need medical treatment, and be treated with a needle that was not properly sterilized and contract hepatitis. There have even been recent outbreaks of hepatitis in the U.S.

Although there are vaccinations for hepatitis C, I have been told by medical authorities that the vaccination is currently not very effective and they do not recommend it.

## Malaria Pills

If you are traveling to a jungle area you absolutely should take malaria pills. There are several different types and what type you get depends on your destination. Make sure your pharmacist and physician know what is current and appropriate.

### WHERE DO I GET THESE VACCINATIONS?

Check with your physician as to cost, where to get the vaccinations, and when to take the medications. If he or she does not seem knowledgeable on the subject, go to the U.S. government Web sites for vaccination recommendations and requirements, or check with your local health department, local city museums or universities. For example, the University Museum at the University of Pennsylvania sends many archeologists to remote locations. The medical department at the University Hospital in Philadelphia is very knowledgeable on this topic.

For an up-to-date list of required and recommended vaccinations and preventive medications, the Web site address for Center for Disease Control (CDC) is www.cdc.gov/travel.

Find out what is included on your medical insurance. When my kids and I needed medication for the Guatemalan jungle, we were on different insurance plans. I purchased and picked up my prescription at the pharmacy, took it to my doctor, paid his fee and a small prescription fee, about US$50 total. My son was then working evenings at UPS, so his plan worked by going to the doctor and getting everything done there for a US$10 co-pay. Unfortunately my daughter's insurance didn't cover anything.

*Lastly, once you have your shots, have your doctor mark what you received and the dates on an International Yellow Health Card. Always carry that card with your passport. If you are ever in an area that has an outbreak of a disease or are involved in an accident requiring a shot, your vaccination record will be with you.*

## TRAVEL INSURANCE

If you are traveling with a group, you can usually purchase medical insurance at a reasonable cost. If you are traveling independently, you should check with your local health insurance company to see if you have coverage for your destination country in the event of major accident or illness. If you do not have coverage, you may wish to consider purchasing travel medical insurance. It is a personal decision and can be expensive. Often in countries that have a Socialist form of medicine you may be able to avail yourself of its medical services with little or no charge. Medication and doctor's visits are usually cheap in a third- world country. For further information on travel insurance, check with your travel agent or do an Internet search using the key words "Travel Insurance."

## MONEY MATTERS & RESPONSIBILITIES

### ESTIMATING EXPENSES

Are you in a quandary trying to figure out how much an independent trip will cost? Are you wondering whether you can afford to travel for seven days, 10 days, more, or not at all? You can lay out a proposed budget with a few simple steps. Let's take the following example:

Laura is a single parent mother with a 10-year-old son named Jason. The two of them have decided on a July fly/drive vacation from their home state in New Jersey to Arizona. It is their first trip out West, so they want to see as much as possible. They have tentatively planned to spend a couple of days each in the Phoenix area, Sedona and the Grand Canyon. They would also like to see either Monument Valley or drive east to visit Winslow Crater, the Painted Desert, and the Petrified Forest, but Laura doesn't know if she can afford to extend the trip to 10 days. Her budget limit for all travel expenses is US$2500.

The following sample sheet shows how Laura can compute her estimated travel expenses. The purpose of this calculation is to show you how to estimate. It is not meant to recommend what you should spend; each family's travel preferences and budgets are different.

## Laura's Arizona Trip — Estimated Expenses

| | | | |
|---|---|---|---:|
| Airfare | $400 × 2 = | $ | 800.00 |
| Hotel | 2 nights × $100 = | | 200.00 |
| | 5 nights × $60 = | | 300.00 |
| Car Rental | 8 days = | | 230.00 |
| Meals | $30 × 2 people × 8 days = | | 480.00 |
| Misc. — gas admissions,etc. | | | 140.00 |
| **Subtotal** | for 7 day trip | $ | 2,150.00 |
| | 2 days hotel | $ | 120.00 |
| | 2 days meals | | 120.00 |
| | 2 days car rental | | 33.00 |
| | misc — 2 days | | 40.00 |
| **Subtotal** | | $ | 323.00 |
| **Total** | for 10 day trip | $ | 2,463.00 |

Let's see how Laura arrived at the estimated total for each item:

## Airfare

Laura searched a couple of Web sites (or called airlines) to get some fare ideas from her home state to Phoenix. She found airfares running between US$380 and US$413, so she estimated US$400. (We'll talk more about searching for lowest airfare and hotel prices in the Execution of Reservations section).

## Hotel

A quick search on the Internet combined with conversations with friends who had recently traveled to Arizona helped Laura arrive at an estimated figure. Motels run between US$40 and US$80 a night in Arizona. Some places, like Phoenix, are in low season in the summer, while others, like the Grand Canyon, are in high season. Laura's employer does business with a major hotel resort chain, so she is hoping to get a discounted rate at one of their resort properties in the Phoenix area since it is their low season. If so, she will go "deluxe" the first couple of nights and then stay on the hotel budget path for the rest of the trip.

## Rental Car

Once again, Laura searched the Internet (or called a few rental car companies) to get estimated costs for a compact car rental for one week including all taxes and surcharges. Weekly rates ran about US$200 to US$230 with taxes. Additional rental days are pro-rated off the weekly rate. Given the amount of driving Laura will be doing, she may choose to use a coupon she has for a free one car-class upgrade.

## Meals

US$30 a day per person for meals and snacks can easily be brought down to a lower figure, but this figure is appropriate for Laura. Except for the Phoenix resort hotel stay, Laura plans to pick up cereal and milk and store it in the hotel room's mini fridge. This will save her time and money so she and her son can get off to an early start. She also plans to buy fresh fruit, sandwiches, and snacks at local grocery stores so she and her son can enjoy a picnic lunch at a scenic spot. Laura plans to treat herself and her son to a nice dinner in a gracious restaurant a couple of times during the trip, perhaps in Sedona and at one of the famous national park lodges in the Grand Canyon.

The remaining items — gas, admissions, miscellaneous — are general estimates. Laura's friend will drive her to the airport so she has no parking or transfer fees. Her son has saved US$50 from his allowance and his grandmother is chipping in a little more, so he will buy his own souvenirs. Laura decides to do most of her Christmas shopping while out West, but she did not include this estimated amount in her trip costs. After tallying up her estimated costs, Laura was pleased to discover that she is able to stretch her trip to 10 days, rather than eight, and still stay within her budget limit. Now the problem is to decide where to spend those two extra days. Decisions, decisions...

### HOW TO SAVE ON HOTEL EXPENSES

1. Chain hotels often have specials, especially moderately priced ones such as Holiday Inn, Best Western, etc. Ask about them.

2. Ask about AAA rates, AARP, and student discounts when getting quotes. Be creative in your questions.

3. As a single adult, you will usually pay the single room rate (a little cheaper than the double room rate), but the chain hotels usually let kids

under 18 stay free in the room. Each one of my newsletters lists at least one hotel that offers a single parent special. Sign up for the newsletter by going to SingleParentTravel.net.

## HOW TO SAVE ON MEAL EXPENSES

1. As mentioned above, eat breakfast in your room (but not room service, which is very pricey!). It's faster and cheaper.

2. Plan on picnics for lunch. They're cheaper and the scenery is a lot better.

3. Occasionally eat dinner in a Chinese restaurant (usually cheap) or at McDonalds (a fun experience overseas).

4. Eat at local ethnic restaurants. They offer good food at a good price, and are a great place to meet the locals.

5. Unless you have a teen-age son, avoid buffets. They are overpriced and adults tend to overeat. If you must eat at a buffet, buy it for yourself and share with your little ones.

6. Unless you plan to cook during vacation, don't bother to pay extra for a room with kitchenette. Instead, if you need to use a small refrigerator for snacks and milk, order one to be placed in a regular hotel room. There may or may not be a small fee for this service.

7. Train your kids *never, ever* to consume items from the mini-bar; they are triple-priced. I solve the problem by handing back the mini-bar key when I check in. More than once I have been billed for mini-bar items my family never consumed. Giving back the key solves two problems in advance, even though it drives the front desk personnel nuts.

## OTHER WAYS TO SAVE

When hailing a taxi in places where cabs are not metered, walk a block or two away from the high-priced hotel and tourist shopping areas.

When the kids and I traveled to Egypt, I was able to secure an excellent travel industry discount at the Cairo Marriott, a superb deluxe resort-like hotel on an island in the middle of the Nile River. Cairo is a very large city with more than 20 million residents, so every time we went somewhere we had to hail a cab. The first time out, we walked out the hotel front door and inquired about the taxi price — US$10. Bargaining did little to bring it down. Thereafter we always grabbed a cab two blocks from the hotel for about US$5. The same applied in reverse. As we would leave the Khan (the major city bazaar) to return to our hotel, we would walk a block or so away from the bazaar entrance to hail a cab. At the very least it cut down the bargaining time. Using this method, we estimated we saved at least US$70 on cab fares during our three-day stay in Cairo.

When shopping in places where it is customary to bargain for goods, use the one-third formula. When the shopkeeper offers you a price, retort with a price that is one-third of what he or she offered initially. Hopefully, after a period of time you will agree to a price that is some-where between each of your original offers. If you are buying a number of items, bargain again for a lower total. For example, if your total comes to US$52, try bargaining down to an even number of US$50 or an even number in the local currency.

## WHAT TYPE OF "WAMPUM" TO CARRY

We'll talk about *how* to carry money when traveling in Part II, but you should give some thought as to *what* you will carry — credit card(s), ATM card, travelers checks, cash — and what is appropriate for your destination.

1.  American Express is not widely accepted in moderate or budget priced restaurants and hotels. VISA or Master Card is your best choice if carrying only one credit card.

2.  ATM cards are great. They are easy to use in the U.S. and Europe, and provide the best exchange rate overseas. Keep in mind that they are not universally accepted. You may have trouble finding an ATM machine in parts of Mexico and Central America, for example.

3.  Some travelers' checks may come in handy as a back up. Carry some in your child's name and keep them in his or her backpack. Always keep the check numbers in a separate place from the checks themselves. I recommend having teen-agers take their cash in traveler checks, even if it is only US$100 or US$200. More than once I have heard parents tell me how their teen-agers saved money from their after-school job and were pick-pocketed or left money in their jeans or unlocked suitcase in the hotel room, only to return and find the money gone. (Suggestion: AAA does not charge its members a fee for buying travelers checks). Many shops no longer accept travelers' checks, but banks always will.

When traveling in foreign countries, especially third world countries, take 50 US$1 bills. Stash some in your wallet and the rest in your backpack in a small envelope. My mother taught me this trick and it still comes in handy. Here's why:

1.  When crossing borders you may run out of currency for the country you are about to leave. Rather than change another US$10 or US$20, you can use a U.S. one-dollar bill to buy a soda or bottle of water. That way you are only stuck with a small coin or two, which you can use as a souvenir.

2.  Despite the ups and downs of the U.S. dollar on the world market in recent decades, there are still many parts of the world where the U.S. dollar is strong and welcome — Latin America, for example. The one-dollar bill makes a perfect size tip for services rendered or a favor performed. Its value may sometimes be higher than the equivalent amount in the local currency.

3.  In many third-world countries, coins and small denomination bills are scarce. In Egypt we had to keep a daily vigil over our wallets, making sure that each morning we had enough small change to take us through the day. Sometimes we simply ran out of small currency and the shopkeepers and cab drivers often had little or none. In those cases, a few U.S. one dollar bills came in handy.

## FAMILY MEMBER RESPONSIBILITIES BEFORE AND DURING THE TRIP

It is important to assign tasks to each family member no matter how young, and to increase those responsibilities each year thereafter so that they are age-appropriate. If not, the burden will always fall on the single parent, leaving the parent exhausted, stressed and having to worry about every little travel detail. In addition, this teaches your children responsibility. At first it will take time to teach and double-check small children, but after one or two trips, the benefits will pay off handsomely.

## LET'S START WITH SOME IDEAS FOR YOUNGER CHILDREN, AGES 3-9

### Locate the safety exits

From the time my son was 4-years-old I made him responsible for locating exit doors on planes, hotels and theaters. I explained the importance of his job and he took it to heart. Every time we checked into a hotel, he would always remember to look down the hallway and count the number of doors to the fire exit. Although we never experienced a hotel fire, it was nice to have one less thing to worry about when checking in. Kids, less encumbered with responsibilities, are more likely to focus on a single task.

### Learn the name of the hotel

My first trip traveling as a single adult with my two kids was to the Knoxville World's Fair. My kids were then 4 and 11. Fearful of being separated in a large, crowded area, I made sure both of my children knew the name of our hotel and had them repeat it back to me every so often. We witnessed one 6-year-old child get lost, a memorable object lesson for my young son. Thereafter, whenever we traveled, without being prompted, my son memorized the hotel name as soon as we checked in. If you are traveling in a foreign country, have your child carry the cover from a set of matches at all times (Don't give your child the matches; that's inviting disaster).

Big kids benefit from this object lesson, too. While I was working for a major European student tour company, our Philadelphia headquarters received a phone call from the Pan American Airways office in downtown Rome. A high school student from one of our groups to Italy wandered off alone on a free afternoon, got lost in the city, and didn't know the name of his hotel. He did remember that he flew on Pan American, so he walked into their office and explained his problem. After checking his flight information, the airline agent was able to verify his group information and called our office in the U.S. to get the name of his hotel. Although the student rated a poor grade in the memory department, he certainly deserved an "A" for ingenuity.

### Count luggage

Little ones can be responsible for counting luggage every time you make a move — arrival at your destination via airplane, checking out of the hotel, and leaving a train or bus. The first couple of years my little son bordered on becoming "Mr. Annoying," as his sister and I had to stop cold in our tracks while he did a formal luggage count (usually a total of three bags and two small backpacks). But it made the kids acutely aware of the importance of not leaving things behind.

As the years went by and my son reached his pre-teen and later his teen years, he automatically took on more responsibility for the luggage, and I was happy to be relieved of this burden as well. When we did curbside check-in at airports, he would stay outside with the luggage until the porter picked it up and took it inside so I didn't have to worry about curbside theft. When we traveled on buses throughout third-world countries, he watched the porters load the luggage on top or inside, making certain it was tied and secured properly. At times he even got up on top of the bus and helped the young men, making friends along the way. I am sure his efforts saved us from some lost or damaged luggage.

Only once did I challenge my son's "Baggage Master" authority, to my regret. We were in Bolivia and had just disembarked from a hydrofoil, which had transported us from Isla del Sol to another resort hotel on the banks of Lake Titicaca. We had signed up for a four-night package that included transfers, porterage, and a guide, along with the hotels. As my son prepared to remove our luggage from the hydrofoil, the guide stopped him and said, "No, the porters will remove the luggage and bring it to your room." Conscious of his duty, my son then positioned himself to watch the porters do their job. The guide came over to me and insisted we go and enjoy ourselves in the hotel, as our actions were making him lose face and look like he wasn't doing his job. When I told this to my son, he thought it was a bad idea. Torn between offending my son and committing a cultural faux pas, I chose the former. I asked Greg to back off and then told our guide I held him personally responsible for our luggage.

About 20 minutes later my son ran up the stairs to our hotel room, yelling that our luggage was on its way to La Paz. As requested, Greg had left the hydrofoil dock, but returned shortly thereafter, only to see half our bags being carted away in a big red pick-up truck. The two of us, with smoke coming out of our ears, stormed into the hotel lobby to find our guide. He was shocked and did address the problem immediately. Our lost luggage arrived back at our hotel and was delivered to our room at 3 a.m. that night. After that, the guide never questioned my son when Greg stood watch over our luggage. I resolved to do the same.

## Do a final room or compartment search

When you feel your child is ready, let him or her assume responsibility for the final room search before you check out of a hotel or leave a train. Kids are good at this. Once they are shown how to properly search a room for items that are left behind (under beds, in drawers and closets, behind the shower curtain) you can count on them to do a suitable search and relieve you of that burden. Of course, until they are tall enough, you will have to check the shelves in the closet!

## IDEAS FOR CHILDREN AGES 10 AND OLDER

### Doing the research

We talked about how kids can ask their teachers for help finding books on topics pertaining to your upcoming trip. Although you, as the parent, will probably want to do the research on airfares, I highly recommend assigning your child the task of searching the Internet for destination information. Unless you work for a dot-com, your child will probably do a better job than you at the grunt work — finding sites that provide the information you need.

### Map reading

Kids as young as nine or 10 can learn to read city tourist maps. They usually have lots of pictures and tourist sites. Let them navigate the way around the city on foot. Don't be afraid to let them make a mistake or two by heading down the wrong street and then learn how to find and correct their mistake. With a little help and lots of praise from you, they will become accomplished tourist map-readers by the age of 11 or 12. This arrangement allows you to window-shop or keep an eye on a younger child while your older child pores over the map. As the child approaches his or her teens, they can graduate to road maps.

### Navigator

Younger children, 10 to 12, are great Junior Navigators, and can help you read road signs as you weave your way in and out of a city, or help you find the poorly marked exit. Teen-agers can be your Senior Navigator, plotting the route of each day's journey.

## THE UNIQUENESS OF SINGLE PARENT TRAVEL

You often read how single parenthood is a disadvantage for kids. When it comes to travel, I think there are many advantages for the single parent child. In a double-parent family situation it is not uncommon for a teenager to regress as both parents take control of the trip and assume most, if not all, of the responsibilities. Just the opposite happens in a traveling single parent family. The single parent needs to rely on the child to perform more duties and responsibilities than would be common for a child of a double-parent family. This makes the child feel more mature, and they are more likely to learn these travel or life skills at an earlier age. If this is such a good idea, why doesn't every parent do it, even double-parent families? Because it takes training, patience, and parental willingness to give up some control. Single parents are more likely to succeed at this task because they have to. They are forced to rely on their kids for help.

You often see TV commercials featuring Mommy and Daddy in the front seat of the van, while their young son and daughter are kept busy in the back seat with TV or headphones. Often teen-agers are portrayed as reclusive and removed from general conversation. In a single parent travel situation the teen-ager would be in the front seat, reading road signs and playing the role of Chief Navigator. No doubt there will be some arguments between teen-ager and parent, but at least the teenager will be developing map skills along the way, and will feel he or she had an active part in making the trip successful.

## THINGS SINGLE PARENTS MUST REMEMBER

### Be sure to laud the child when they have done well

"That was difficult finding our way out of the city with all that traffic. You were a big help reading the signs so quickly." By reinforcing the positive behavior, hopefully you will get less of the negative.

### Keep in mind the delicate balance between increased responsibilities and increased privileges

Even if a child is responsible for a few more things on a trip than at home, certain rules, such as curfews, and reporting one's whereabouts, still apply. This needs to be discussed in advance of the trip.

### Let go and trust

By the time my daughter reached her teens she was my Chief Navigator on our trips out West. For years I tortured that poor girl, always questioning her judgment on a certain route or a certain turn. Invariably I would say, "Are you sure?" Finally one day she handed me the maps and said, "Mom, if you don't trust my judgment, then you do it!" After that I tried to control my compulsive behavior, although once in a while I let slip the phrase "¿Eres segura?" as we traveled through Central America. I figured foreign languages don't count.

Years later, when my daughter was studying abroad, my son and I took off on a wild and wooly fly/drive spring trip across New Mexico and Arizona. Then 16, it was his turn to be Senior Navigator. He plotted a direct course from Canyon de Chelly, located in the remote northeastern part of Arizona, down to Flagstaff. Concerned about traveling partway on secondary roads, I asked him to double-check with the local Navajos. Assured this was a good road to travel, we took off.

After a series of unmarked turn-offs we progressed from secondary to "third-endary" roads. I grew more and more apprehensive and suggested turning back to take the main highway. My son reminded me that I had promised to trust his judgment, so we continued on. Late that afternoon, still on dirt roads, we had now entered private ranch territory. I was convinced that within minutes, some ranch owner would come roaring down the road on his horse, shotgun in hand, filling us and the rental car with buckshot for encroaching on his property. Back East people threaten you just for treading on their parking space.

Shortly before twilight, we reached the paved part of the road. From there on in, it was gloriously scenic and free of traffic. We felt like we were in a TV car commercial as we drove into the sunset. By the time we reached the Coconino Forest and the switchbacks of Oak Creek Canyon, it was pitch black dark. Not exactly the timing I had in mind, but we had an adventure. My son had kept his promise and became a skillful navigator, and I had kept my promise and allowed him to learn.

## TAKING THE PLUNGE — Assuaging Fears — Your Own, Your Kids'

Will we have a good time? Will things go wrong? What happens if . . .?

These are natural concerns. Traveling as the only adult with one or more children is an awesome responsibility, and if it is your first single parent trip, it can be downright scary. If going away on a one-week trip is too much to handle the first time out, start with small steps. Try a day trip or a getaway-driving weekend. The important thing is to do what you can handle and your confidence will grow.

On my first single parent trip to Europe, we traveled via train non-stop from Paris to Amsterdam, a three-hour journey. Friends urged me to stop en route to see Brussels for a few hours. We were traveling on a Eurailpass so there was no additional cost for the stopover. I spoke fluent French so there was no language problem. I had lived in Europe on a student exchange program so I knew my way around. But when I thought about disembarking from the train with two young children, finding the luggage storage area, and then repeating the process several hours later, I decided I couldn't handle it. I wasn't ready. Europe is the easiest place in the world to get around by train. I laugh about my timidity now, but it wasn't funny to me then.

Sometimes kids will have fears about travel and may have trouble expressing them. Shortly before my son's tenth birthday I attended a travel seminar on Scandinavia and was fortunate enough to win a couple of free air tickets on SAS (Scandinavian Airlines System). My daughter was so excited about the news she immediately pulled out the map and pointed out the fact that we could easily extend our Scandinavian trip to visit the city of Leningrad (now called St. Petersburg), only a few hours by train from Helsinki, Finland. At that time the Soviet Union was still Communist, even though Glasnost was on the horizon. It was an exciting idea.

As we planned our trip I noticed my son was less than enthused. Finally one night he haltingly confessed to me that he was afraid to go on the trip. He was worried that something bad might happen to us in the Soviet Union. Given the media exposure at that time (the Soviets were always the evil guys in the movies), his concerns were understandable. To assuage his fears I said to him, "Greg, think of it this way. When you go into the cellar or a strange room and it is dark, it is scary. You don't know what's there. But when you turn on the light, you can see for yourself what's there and it's not so scary anymore. That's what we are going to do when we go to the Soviet Union. We are going to turn on the light."

## EXECUTION OF RESERVATIONS

### WHEN TO BOOK

The answer is simple: as soon as you can. It is often significantly cheaper to book sooner rather than later, as cheap fares sell out first. If you have decided to make the trip, then book it right away. After 30 years in travel, people still ask me that same question and still look just as startled when I give them that answer. Unless you have a compelling reason to hold off, such as a sick relative or a possible work lay-off or transfer, there is no reason to wait. I have found many people fear commitment and it is frightening for them to commit to non-refundable tickets. However keep in mind the following:

1.  Non-refundable tickets can be changed for a fee.

2.  Non-refundable tickets are often good for a year if you have to change them.

3. Travelers can buy trip cancellation insurance.

4. Deposits placed on resort hotel and cruise bookings are usually fully refundable up to six weeks or less before departure.

Be sure to ask about the cancellation/change policies before buying your ticket. Consolidator tickets may have stiffer rules and penalties. We'll discuss that later in this chapter. Trip cancellation insurance usually covers you for sickness or accident, but not work-related issues or other personal matters.

In 20 years of traveling with my kids, representing more than 30 trips, we have had to change departure dates twice, and each time it was for an unforeseen reason. For our two-week summer family vacation we usually book six or nine months in advance to get first choice of hotels and flights. Not everyone needs to do that, but it worked well for us. I preferred to submit my company vacation request early and my kids, once they were teenagers and had part-time jobs, liked to do the same. Sometimes lower airfares were available after I purchased our tickets, but I didn't beat myself up. On other occasions, when we booked at the last minute for an off-season quick trip, like a winter weekend in New Orleans or London, we struck gold with great airfares. It all evens out.

In my early days in the travel business, people expected me, as a travel consultant, to have a magic answer for when they should book their reservations — that perfect time that will give them the lowest fare and the best choice of accommodations. There is no such magic answer, however there are a few general rules for holiday periods.

1. Christmas week — one year ahead, especially for the Caribbean and major U.S. and Canadian ski resorts.

2. Major U.S. national parks in the summer - one year ahead *if* you wish to stay within the park. (One exception is the mule ride down the Grand Canyon, which I have been told must be booked more than one year ahead for peak holiday dates).

3. Walt Disney World — Orlando — nine months to one year for major holiday weeks, *if* you want to stay in the park at a reasonable cost.

4. Areas with short summer seasons — Nine months ahead, especially for peak summer dates. Examples are Alaska and Scandinavia.

Although you can certainly book your trip later than the above-mentioned, these suggestions will assure a full choice of accommodations. In the case of national parks in the summer, you may have to book your hotel in advance of air flights. Keep in mind all national park bookings are fully refundable, if you adhere to their cancellation policies. Because people have to book so far ahead for these lodges, last-minute cancellations do occur, but don't count on it.

If you are traveling on a non-holiday period or are unable to book many months in advance, be aware that the airlines have a number of advance purchase restrictions on their cheapest fares. These restrictions usually require ticket purchase anywhere from three to thirty days in advance. In addition, there may be a Saturday night stay requirement. This does not mean the cheapest fares will be available when you call. For example, you may wish to travel to the Caribbean during spring vacation and see an advertised special fare of US$300 round-trip to several of the islands, which must be booked 21 days in advance. When you call or check the Web 30 days in advance of departure, you may find that the advertised fare is not available on the dates you want to travel and the cheap fares sold out months ago.

If you are flexible with travel dates, ask the airline agent to advise you of the lowest possible existing airfare during the time period you wish to travel. Then ask the agent to search for the dates those fares are available. For example, the weekends may offer only airfares of US$400 to US$500 per person, but an open date search may reveal that you could travel Wednesday-to-Wednesday for US$300 or Thursday-to-Thursday for US$330. You can also do this search yourself on the Internet, but it is slower and more tedious. (One way to do it is through Travelocity.com. Select the places you want to search and select the "My dates are flexible" option.) The airline agents and travel consultants work with different computer programs and can put in certain search codes that you cannot, which allows them to search for low fare availability much faster.

## LAST-MINUTE SPECIALS

Not all trips need be booked months ahead. I have often taken advantage of some last-minute specials to book a getaway spring break vacation or a long weekend to an off-season destination. Specials can even occur at the tail end of the summer season. Some examples:

### Off-Season Specials, Such as London in Winter

From January to March, (sometimes even November to March), international airlines occasionally offer airfares as low as US$200 round trip from the East Coast. Sure it's chilly, but who goes to London for the weather anyway? At a slightly higher price you can also find specials to Paris, Amsterdam or other European cities, often with a reduced hotel package price to boot. These fares go quickly, so try to book the first or second week of January for travel up until March. Another example is New Orleans in the summer (June to August). New Orleans is a big convention city. Because of the hot, humid summer weather, conventioneers avoid New Orleans in the summer, leaving a glut of hotel rooms begging to be filled. June is a good time to book for the June to August period. Bargains are great if you don't mind the heat.

### Seasonal Tail-End Specials

Although not as low priced as off-season specials, you can find some warm weather destination bargains at the tail end of the winter season, especially if Easter week is late. Some examples are the Caribbean and Mexican resorts. The last two weeks of August can produce some bargains for destinations that are high season in the summer.

### Places Under Crisis

One example is the "hoof and mouth disease" that spread throughout the English countryside in the spring of 2001. Although the disease was not dangerous to humans, places to hike were limited, so room prices plummeted throughout the countryside and stayed that way, even at the beginning of the high summer season. By that time the disease had run its course and the countryside was open, but people were still staying away and prices were staying down.

### Frommers.com

A marvelous source for specials, last minute and otherwise, is the e-mail newsletter from Frommers.com. I can't say enough good things about this electronic newsletter. You can scan the headlines in a minute or two, click on what interests you and get detailed information on the trip, along with how to book. To sign up, go to www.Frommers.com and click on "Subscribe" under the heading "Today's Newsletter."

### Priceline.com and LastMinuteTravel.com

We are all familiar with William Shatner's voice telling us how much we can save by booking our airfare with Priceline.com. These sites are not for the traveler who must book several months or even several weeks in advance. In that case your best bet is to shop around for the best prices with other sources mentioned earlier in this book. These last-minute booking sites work best for people who are forced to make reservations under the airlines' traditional advance purchase time limit. Even then, you are not likely to get a fare lower than the standard cheap advance purchase fare offered by the airlines. In some cases you bid blindly, not knowing what your airline schedule will be; only the dates that you will travel.

*OK, now that you are ready to make your reservations, how do you go about it?*

## BOOKING ON THE INTERNET

Begin here if you have access to a computer.

As with your earlier research, you should visit at least three Web sites that offer air and hotel reservations. Some examples are www.Travelocity.com, www.Expedia.com, and the new kid on the block, www.Orbitz.com. Double-check airfares against the airlines' individual sites, such as www.Continental.com, or www.aa.com. By cross checking you may find lower fares, a better selection of itineraries, or even the same fares, but the airline might offer bonus miles for booking on their site.

There are three types of non-refundable flight reservations:

1. *Instant purchase* — pay immediately, no changes allowed, or changes allowed with penalty.

2. *Reservation only with no fare guarantee* — The reservation is held for 24 hours with no fare protection. Some international airlines will hold the reservation for a longer period of time, but the "no fare guarantee" is still in effect.

3. *Reservation held with fare guarantee* — Some airlines will allow you to make a reservation and hold it for 24 hours with fare protection. In this case you are asked for your credit card number and it is incumbent upon you, the traveler, to call or e-mail back within 24 hours to cancel if you do not want the reservation. If the airline does not hear from you, the ticket is automatically issued 24 hours later and your credit card is charged.

➢ The term "non-refundable" can mean no refund at all (as in some consolidator tickets — consolidators are defined later in this book) or it can mean the ticket may be exchanged within one year for another ticket at different travel dates.

➢ Fare guarantee means just that. There are ten million fare changes a day. (Yes, my friends, that is correct). Having a reservation without a fare guarantee means exactly that. Fares can change, go up, or simply disappear by the next day. When I was in the operations side of the travel business, people often asked me, "What are the chances of that happening?" If I were forced to take an educated guess, I would say about 20%.

## Travel Agents - To Use or Not to Use?

The answer to this question will depend upon the type of trip you wish to take. If you are thinking of a beach resort-type vacation, or a package or escorted tour, by all means consider using a travel agent. However, if you are planning an independent fly/drive trip with moderate or budget-priced accommodations, you may have to search far and wide to find a travel consultant who has the interest and knowledge to service your needs and is willing to take the time to do so.

To find a good travel consultant, begin by asking for recommendations from friends and co-workers in the same way you would go about finding a good lawyer or landscaper. Keep in mind that your tastes and travel budget may differ from your friends'. If so, the travel agent they recommend may not be suitable for you. If you can't get a good recommendation, try calling a few in your local area or stop by and visit if you have the time.

If you work for a large company that has contracted a travel agency to service their corporate travel needs, try calling that agency. No doubt they will refer you to their leisure department. As a corporate client you may get better service than cold calling an agency. Also the agency may consider waiving some of their fees if you are a corporate client.

To help you find a good travel agent, I have compiled a list of travel agents that specialize in single parent travel in the Appendix. Many of them are single parents themselves and understand the single parent family's special needs. I welcome recommendations from readers on the agents listed and new ones that you discover. All reviews will be included on my Web site.

## RESERVING YOUR AIR TICKETS

If you decide to travel on a package tour, escorted tour, or book through a travel agent, you need not worry about reserving your air tickets. However, if you are traveling independently, this will probably be the first reservation you need to make. Here are a few more tips to save money and/or aggravation:

### Sign up for a Web site's low fare search e-mail notification

Maybe you are thinking about a couple of destinations but won't be ready to book for a few weeks or months. Have the travel Web site notify you when low fares are available to your preferred destination. Two sites that offer this service are www.Travelocity.com and www.CheapTickets.com. Airlines, such as United and Continental, also offer e-mail notification. If you have frequent flyer cards with a particular airline, it is a good idea to sign up for their e-mail.

### Check out consolidator airfares

These airfares offer an opportunity to save hundreds of dollars, especially to distant places where airfares traditionally run high. Here's how it works: A consolidator buys blocks of seats on various flights from various airlines at a negotiated low price and then resells those seats at a modest profit, to the general public. I have used various consolidators to buy air tickets to Hawaii, Belize, Japan and especially the Middle East. I saved anywhere from US$150-500 per person in the process. There are drawbacks:

1. Tickets are usually instant purchase, non-refundable, and change fees can be very high.

2. Consolidator toll-free numbers are frequently busy during peak booking seasons.

3. Buyer Beware: Some consolidators have been in business a long time; others come and go.

4. You choose flight itineraries from what the consolidators have available, not always what you prefer.

5. Often there is no frequent flyer credit allowed.

6. You may not be able to switch airline carriers in case of a flight cancellation, forcing you to endure a long delay in the airport (sometimes as much as 24 hours).

For names and contact information for consolidators, check the ads in the travel section of your Sunday newspaper, call your travel agent, or do an Internet search. There is no "one-size-fits-all" consolidator. Different companies specialize in different areas of the world. You have to ferret out the one you want. Be sure to check out the ethnic agencies/consolidators. They may speak English with a heavy accent, but if the majority of their business is sending people back and forth to a specific country or region that coincides with your travel destination, by all means, check them out. They are likely to be good information and booking sources.

## Open Jaw Tickets

These are tickets that allow you to fly into one city and out of another and still have the benefit of a round trip excursion airfare. For example, you may wish to visit San Francisco and Los Angeles and drive the coast between the two cities. Another example would be an itinerary that includes Phoenix and Los Angeles. In this case you may not wish to drive between the two cities but instead purchase an inexpensive one-way ticket from Phoenix to Los Angeles on Southwest Airlines. When you do this type of creative vacation planning, be sure to check rental car drop rates between cities before you buy your air ticket. Just because an airline allows you to "open jaw" between cities at a special rate, this does not mean that rental car companies will allow you to do the same. Even if they do, the "drop" fee can be quite high (a drop fee is a charge by a rental car company to pick up the car in one city and drop off at another). Some states with heavy tourism, such as Florida, have few, if any drop fees.

## E-Tickets

In my opinion, the invention of electronic tickets ranks right up there with sliced bread. E-tickets are paperless tickets. Technically speaking, you only need go to the airline departure gate, show the gate agent your driver's license or photo ID, and you are issued a boarding pass on the spot. In some airports you can even check in your luggage curbside with an E-ticket. I do advise everyone to carry the printout showing flights and confirmation number of their booking. This is great for single parents, since you no longer need worry about carrying tickets for everyone.

When *not* to buy an e-ticket:

1. If you are flying on more than one carrier in your itinerary, it is advisable to stay with a paper ticket, or else, fare permitting, get separate e-tickets.

2. If you are traveling overseas, particularly to a non-English speaking country, it is advisable to carry a paper tickets in case you need to be re-routed to another carrier due to flight cancellations or delays. London is the one exception.

## RESERVING HOTELS

If you are traveling independently, you can book your hotels on a major Web site such as www.Expedia.com. Two good Web sites for domestic and international hotel reservations, including B&Bs, are www.PlacesToStay.com and www.HotelsOnLine.com. Another way to book is to call hotels on their toll-free numbers. For domestic hotels, the moderately priced chain hotels usually have the best family rates, such as Best Western and Holiday Inn. Kids stay free, and yes, you have to pay the single rate, but you may be able to wheedle that down with an AAA card or another membership card such as AARP, Rotary Club, etc.

For overseas hotels, most large travel Web sites tend to offer only the larger, more expensive chain hotels. You will need to be a bit more creative with your Internet searches in order to find some hotel bargains. Many small hotels in the Caribbean, Latin America and Europe now have their own Web sites, which provide ample information and allow you to request hotel reservations via e-mail. These hotels may be a block off the beach or a few blocks from a city's downtown area, but the savings on room rates could be 50% or more off of large chain properties. You can find them by using a search engine such as www.Google.com. For example, type in the key words "Hotels in Rome."

If you are moving about during your vacation, try varying your hotel types. A mixture of B&Bs, jungle lodges, and resort hotels can be fun. B&Bs often do not take small children, so check the minimum age requirements before booking. When traveling in third world countries, we found it helpful to stay at a fairly modern hotel (with modern plumbing and a decent-sized room) the night before we flew home. This gave us ample room to pack our bags and freshen up for the next day's flight. If most of your trip will be in Spartan accommodations in adventurous, remote areas, you may wish to stay in a more modern hotel on the first night as well, as a "break-in" period for you and your kids.

Make *all* hotel reservations before you leave. Arriving at a new town or city without hotel reservations may be a very romantic concept for backpackers and couples with wheels, but for a single parent with one or more kids in tow, it makes absolutely *no* sense. Given the proliferation of travel information available to the public today, if you do your research, you will find an interesting place to stay that can be booked in advance.

### PRE-BOOKING ACTIVITIES AND EXCURSIONS

Naturally you do not want to pre-book every day's activities but where possible, it is a good idea to reserve in advance excursions that will be the highlight of your trip, such as rafting, mountain biking or snorkeling. The less time you have to spend attending to reservation details on your vacation, the more time you will have for fun.

### A FINAL WORD ON FREQUENT FLYER PROGRAMS

If you haven't already done so, enroll your family in an airline frequent flyer plan. Continental's One Pass Program is one of the few frequent flyer plans whose miles do not expire. If you enroll a 5-year-old on a non-expiring frequent flyer plan and take him or her on a fly/drive vacation once a year, your child may have earned a free air ticket by the time he or she reaches the age of 10 or 11. There actually are some things that come free in life... without a catch.

Stay on the prowl for other ways to increase your frequent flyer mileage without additional cost. Each airline has a Web site that lists what programs give you frequent flyer points. Some examples are:

1. Open an online brokerage account.

2. Use a credit card program that offers frequent flyer mileage (If you keep a running credit card balance, make sure the finance charge on the frequent flyer program doesn't offset your savings on the airline ticket).

3. ATM cards offer bonus miles.

4. Check with your long distance phone provider (MCI has a program that pays one frequent flyer mile for every dollar spent and gives a terrific phone rate).

5. Purchasing flowers can earn you frequent flower, I mean flyer, points.

Lastly, find out ahead of time if your hotel or rental car company gives frequent flier points. You may have to enroll in the program (like Marriott's rewards program) in advance. I am sometimes guilty of forgetting this, and if you have a good suggestion for remembering, please e-mail me at Brenda@SingleParentTravel.net.

Now we're ready. Let's travel!

# II

## *The Trip Itself (Realization)*

It's finally here — the long-awaited moment. After all of your research, anticipation, and planning, you are ready to go have fun on your vacation! Excitement levels are running high with your kids while you are running, trying to finish up last minute preparations.

## MODES OF TRAVEL

Some adults face a car, air, or train trip with kids in tow with a sense of dread. With a little preparation and organization, you can make it part of the adventure. It has been my personal observation that single parents or single adults traveling alone with children are pretty good at this. Knowing there is no other adult on whom to rely for help, they come prepared to entertain their children and keep them comfortable. Let's talk about some of the ways to get your vacation off to a good start.

### AIRPLANE TRAVEL

#### Familiarize your children with airplane travel

If your child is young (under 10) and this is his or her first plane trip, familiarize that child with procedures. Flying can be a scary thing for anyone, but especially kids, not because flying itself is scary but because it is unknown. Buy a book about an airplane trip, talk about check-in procedures, explain how you will fly above the clouds and yes, there are bathrooms on board planes. If your child has never seen an airport and you live close to one, drive out with your child for a reconnaissance visit. If you fly frequently and have become blasé about it, be prepared for your young child to ask a godzillion questions. This is exciting stuff for a little kid. Revel in it. Conversely, if you are a nervous air traveler, this will rub off on your child, so be prepared for that as well.

## Take an early morning flight

In today's busy overcrowded airports, I like to be the first one out of the chute. Yes, it is tough to get up at dawn or dark and roust your kids out of bed but if they know what to expect and why you are doing it, you will hopefully get cooperation (teen-agers being the glaring exception). By taking an early morning flight, your flight is more likely to leave on time, you will arrive earlier at your destination, and you will have more flight options available to you that day should your flight be delayed or cancelled. Besides, your kids are all in one place — bed — when it is time to gather them up.

## Arrive early at the airport

This is one of the keys to a pleasant trip. Travel is stressful enough for a single parent without incurring the risk of arriving late and being rushed at the airport due to unforeseen traffic jams. Once you check in, plan to play games with your kids. How often do you have each other's undivided attention?

## Pack games, books, and snacks for a trip

If your child is old enough and able to do so, he or she should carry his own backpack. Fill it with a mixture of old and new games or toys, books and some snacks. Healthful snacks, which I discussed in Part I, are an important backpack component. UNO is a great travel game and was one of my son's favorites. From the age of 5-15 he played that game with French teen-agers, Belizean expatriates, and numerous veiled ladies in the Middle East.

## Allow for physical activity before boarding

Little kids get itchy waiting for a plane and need "runaround time and space" before boarding. Select seats at the far end of the waiting area, hopefully near a walkway against the wall. Tell your kids they can run free within that narrow area as long as they do not disturb anyone. Once the far row starts to fill up, ask them to return. Issuing negative commands such as "Don't run around!" is like asking a bird not to fly. Instead make positive statements such as, "You and your brother can run back and forth between the two poles. Once someone sits in the row nearby you have to stop your game and sit next to me."

## A few things to remember when boarding the plane

If you have small children, do not hesitate to take advantage of pre-boarding. Did you request a window seat for your child? Did you remember to order a kid's meal? Not all flights offer them, but it is fun food for kids if they do.

## Set behavioral parameters in advance

Obviously you cannot do this with toddlers, but pre-schoolers can be taught behavioral limits for flying. Discuss in advance the limits on sodas and trips up and down the aisle. Children should be taught that unpleasant noisiness and kicking the seat in front of them is unacceptable behavior. Remember to praise children partway through the flight when they behave well.

I travel by air at least once a month for either business or pleasure. When I spot a family board a plane and they sit near me, I can tell within ten seconds whether or not those kids will be well behaved or whether they will terrorize surrounding passengers. Sometimes it takes only five seconds to determine if it will be a flight from hell. Screaming babies are often unavoidable given their discomfort from changes in air pressure. I am referring here to children old enough to entertain themselves or be entertained by their parent(s).

When a family sits down and the parent or parents immediately begin to read, completely ignoring a small child, I know my fellow passengers and I are in trouble. Within a few minutes that child will begin to whine. If further ignored, as is often the case, the child will begin slamming the seat back or kicking the seat in front. The oblivious parent continues to read, or occasionally gives the child negative commands such as, "Don't do that."

When you sit down on a plane with small children, familiarize them with the surroundings — the window, the tray table, exit signs, etc. See to *their* needs first. Then relax a bit. Soon after, children will expect you to entertain them, and you must be prepared to do that for the entire flight. If you get some time off to read or doze, consider it a bonus. Yes, you will arrive at your destination a little tired, but you won't be stressed.

## Teach your children good airplane manners

Kids that say "please" and "thank you" to flight attendants, accompanied by an engaging smile, often get extra peanuts. Just ask my son. The same treatment applies to fellow passengers. Once on an overbooked flight from Dallas to Honolulu, my 12-year-old son and I wound up seated separately, rows apart, each in a center seat of a row of five. Seven hours is a long time for a 12-year-old to amuse himself, especially when he is hyperactive like my son. Surrounded by matronly ladies, he was very careful to say, "Excuse me for disturbing you" every time he got up. Finally the hot meal arrived and with it, his favorite dessert, apple pie. After the meal was cleared away, he scrambled back to my seat, expecting to retrieve my dessert. As he saw the sheepish look on my face, he wailed plaintively, "Mom, how *could* you! You know apple pie is my favorite." At that moment a piece of apple pie was passed back to us, mosh-pit style, over five rows. The person seated behind Greg was so impressed with his manners she offered up her dessert in appreciation.

Being respectful of fellow passengers is also good manners. Being in the travel business, my kids and I were occasionally upgraded to first class. When that happened, the three of us were usually seated separately. My children were instructed to be polite and only speak when spoken to, and then in modulated tones. I told the kids business people often needed to work on the plane. More than once a well-dressed businessman would approach me after the flight, hand me his card, and say how much he enjoyed talking with my son or daughter about our travels. And for you single parent dads out there, I can say with certainty that single ladies are very impressed with single men who travel comfortably and easily with their kids, myself included.

## Dress for the flight

I am constantly astounded at how people dress for airplane travel today, in some cases, a half step above beachwear. When flying throughout North America and the Caribbean there are two key words to keep in mind: comfort and neatness. When traveling to any other part of the world you need to add another element: respectability.

Comfort and neatness implies a clean shirt with no holes, T-shirts without offensive sayings emblazoned on them, and clothing that adequately covers one's backside. Diamond-studded belly buttons are another matter these days, given the influence of Britney Spears. Although it is now quite fashionable to show off your pierced belly button in the U.S., bear in mind that in more conservative countries, this is still considered inappropriate.

Unlike the United States, the Caribbean and Europe, the rest of the world will determine your station in life by what you wear. Except for flying directly into resort areas, I recommend adhering to local dress customs when you board the plane for your foreign destination. For example, in the Middle East and in major cities in Central America, men do not bare their legs. The standard "uniform" for men in these places is a lightweight collared cotton shirt with long pants. Once my son reached adult size, I expected him to dress like a young man would in those countries. Granted, we looked like Americans (sneakers are a dead giveaway), but at least we didn't look like *ignorant* Americans. It is my personal feeling that by showing discretion in your personal appearance you are granted more respect when going through customs and immigration upon your arrival. Of course, resort and touristy areas are an exception.

Now this doesn't mean that your teen-ager has to give up his or her individuality. A 15-year-old with green spiked hair and a nose ring is showing his cultural affectations. A firm handshake, a direct gaze, and a polite manner show his respect for the people around him. There's a difference and people will recognize that. My son used to wear his hair in a ponytail down to his waist, but since his demeanor was polite and respectful, his ponytail piqued interest of a favorable kind.

## CAR TRAVEL

Car travel falls into two categories: a long car trip to get to your destination and a fly/drive vacation where you rent a car and drive fairly short distances. In this section we'll address the long car trip.

First consider some prep work on your car.

1.  Get your car thoroughly checked before your trip.

2.  Pack the car with every navigational tool you will need — directions, city maps, state maps — and study them all *before* the trip.

3.  If your kids are not old enough to read and you need to follow complicated directions to your destination, write them out in a big black marker or in bold type on your computer and tape them to your dashboard so you can drive and read at the same time.

4.  Make sure your car has every tool needed to signal a breakdown or fix a flat tire.

5.  Consider investing in a cell phone. (Note that these do not always work well in remote or mountainous areas. Also, beware of roaming charges if you are on a budget and you do not have a national call plan!)

6. Pack everything you need for your children's comfort and amusement — a favorite toy or pillow, a cooler with healthful snacks, plus paper towels and water for sticky hands. A damp washcloth folded into a Ziploc® bag also works well, and can be washed out at stops. Gar games are an excellent addition to your packing list. The license plate game was popular with my son. It can be purchased online at www.loveandlearn.com or at toy and travel stores. Another site for free car game ideas is www.activitiesforkids.com.

The second issue to consider is patience, which is usually in short supply during a long car trip. I have found that the best way to remain patient with your kids while traveling by car is to eliminate in advance as many situations as possible that require your patience. Sound simplistic? It is. Here's how:

There are two common irritating car travel complaints that can drive parents nuts:

1. When do we get there?

2. I'm tired/bored/hungry.

The suggestions I offer are not foolproof, but should reduce the frequency and intensity of complaints so your patience does not wear thin.

### When do we get there?

For a small child who has no sense of time, planning a relatively stress-free long motor trip takes a little advance work. There are the usual car games, such as word games, spotting car colors or license plates, story telling, and the "I'm thinking of (a person, place or thing)." But small children also need time guidance. Several days before the trip, and again the night before, explain how long the trip is and what you will be doing along the way. For example, if it is a six-hour drive, explain that there will be three planned stops, and the lunch stop is the halfway stop. If your children are 10-years-old or older, they can begin learning to read maps and map out the trip.

Years ago a friend of mine had to travel by car several times a year from New Jersey to Maine to visit family, a tedious eight-hour drive with her three small rambunctious boys. She loaded the car with games and nutritious snacks, but found that after six hours nothing worked. On the next trip she added one item to the trunk — a closed box filled with sodas and junk food. After six hours, when the "Point of No Patience" was reached, she pulled over at the New Hampshire border and unleashed the booty along with a supply of airsick bags. My friend arrived at her destination safely and with patience intact. Hey, whatever works.

### I'm tired/bored/hungry

Some of these complaints can be reduced by breaking up the trip with interesting stops and packing the car with nutritious snacks, but if the car drive is a very long one, you may need to look for other solutions.

When my daughter was 5-years-old we drove 12 straight hours from Maryland to the Canadian Laurentians for a one-week ski trip. At the time I was still married, so there were two adults to share driving and child-care responsibilities. Nonetheless it was a challenge to keep a small child content and well behaved for such a long car trip. Here's what worked:

1. First, get buy-in. In this case, the reward for enduring a 12-hour car trip was a Canadian ski vacation.

2. Make it a challenge. "Boy, an all day trip in a car. Not many little kids can handle that. Do you think you can do it?"

3. Review the commitment. Talk about it on and off, especially the few days before the trip. Focus on the positive - the destination, but remind the child of the challenge of the long trip to get there.

4. Prepare the child. Discuss where you will be at lunch, at dinner, and what to expect time-wise. We told our daughter we would cross the Canadian border as it was getting dark, and would arrive at our destination shortly before her bedtime. Once we got into Canada she was then free to ask, "When do we get there?" (But not before).

5. Praise the child for good behavior as the ride progresses.

I know this must sound like an agenda for a corporate meeting or a case of silly over-preparation, but I can tell you from experience, it worked! Not once did my daughter whine about being tired, hungry or bored. However, mindful of the daytime ban on asking, "When do we get there?" she chose instead the phrase, "When will it get dark?" She asked that question numerous times between lunch and dinner.

## FLY/DRIVE

If you are a new single parent mom, unless you travel for business, you may have had little or no experience renting a car. Often that is the domain of the male of the family. (Guys, you can skip to the next section). Renting a car is an easy and liberating experience, but it can be a bit intimidating the first time you do it. Here are the suggestions I have shared with female travel clients in need of a little reassurance:

1.  Before you reserve your rental car, sign up for one of their free membership programs that allow you speedy check-in so you can bypass the long lines at the counter and go to a special lane or directly to your car. This is great when you are traveling with kids!

2.  Pre-reserve any kid's car seats you may need.

3.  Before reserving your rental, call your car insurance and your credit card companies so you know what insurance coverage you have. You may not need to purchase any additional insurance if you are renting within the U.S.

4.  Once you get to the car, *before* you leave the parking space, take all the time you need to familiarize yourself with the operation of the car. Adjust the driver's seat and rear- and side-view mirrors to your comfort, and check out the location of the headlights, window washer and windshield wipers controls. If you have problems with something, ask a local attendant or the gate agent who checks your rental papers as you leave the lot. Determine the use for all mystery knobs and buttons. (I once rented a car in Arizona and couldn't figure out how to remove the key after shutting off the ignition. I had to send one of the kids to fetch a park ranger, who showed me the knob I had to push for the key release).

5.  Collect a local rental car map before you leave and pay attention to how to get back to the rental car lot. (Directional signs are usually excellent when returning cars back to airports but there are exceptions. Years ago in Brussels, Belgium, cars were returned to the indoor public parking lot at the airport and no rental car returns signs were posted until you were *inside* the lot. My daughter and I circled that airport three times before we figured it out. The same thing happened a few years later in San Francisco while the airport was under construction. (That time I was better prepared and circled the airport only once).

6.  Keep the car rental agreement out of sight and in the glove compartment of your car.

7. Remember to gas up your car before returning it. Rental car gas refill charges are stiff!

## A Note on Car Rental in Orlando

The Alamo Rental Car facility in Orlando, Florida is the largest in the world and rather unique in its customer processing, which is not very single parent family friendly. The facility is some distance from the airport, and once the transfer bus arrives at the Alamo terminal, all passengers, other than the driver of the car, are asked to disembark and wait under a canopy outside the terminal while the driver secures the car. This works fine if your kids are older, but not if they are little. I am sure you could bring little kids into the building with you, but the lines were long, I didn't see speedy check-in gates, nor did I see any indoor "wiggle space" for kids. The flip side is that Alamo often offers some of the cheapest rental car rates. It's your call as to whether or not to use Alamo when visiting Orlando.

## International Car Rentals

Many rental companies require that you prepay for all necessary insurance. If not, buy it anyway. Laws are different overseas and the extra cost is worth the peace of mind. Although I have rented cars on three different continents, I don't recommend doing this overseas as a single parent with small children in tow. Driving in third world countries requires a constant watch for road hazards, and European driving can be stressful in some countries, given the different customs and road signs. Once your kids are old enough to not require constant attention, then by all means, go for the adventure!

## TRAIN TRAVEL

In the U.S. long distance train travel is limited, usually expensive, and is not always the most value-oriented way to travel for single parent families. In Europe, however, quite the opposite is true. Unlike the U.S., which is committed to road building, European governments spend huge sums building and upgrading their rail systems, so the trains go everywhere. In addition, European trains offer a smoother ride due to the fact that Europe has two separate rail systems for passenger trains and freight trains. In the U.S., freight and passenger trains operate on the same set of rail tracks, making for a bumpier track.

For a single parent traveling with little kids to Europe or the United Kingdom, train travel offers an ideal way to get around. You can relax and enjoy the ride, bring along a picnic lunch or buy tasty fresh food on board, play games with or read to your kids, and the children can move safely about the train car making new friends. It is not uncommon for young children to travel by themselves on a European train. It is equivalent to a young child in the U.S. traveling across the country by air, quite safe and secure.

On our first single parent trip to Europe, my 5-year-old son and 12-year-old daughter were allowed to move freely about the entire train. There was only one rule: When they heard an announcement, no matter what language it was in, they had to return immediately to me. I explained that in Europe one or more train cars are sometimes disengaged at the next stop, often with only one announcement as a warning. My son, always the trickster, would return to our car after an announcement, then quickly hide behind the last seat or the luggage area, waiting for me to rush frantically by searching for him, heart pumping, as the train would pull into the station.

The babble of languages on a European train is always great exposure for children. I taught my kids a few words in French, Spanish and German, and they grew up in a multi-national neighborhood, so they were acquainted with foreign languages. What I hadn't prepared them for was the range of American accents. Every time my son met someone from Texas, New England or the Deep South, he would tell him or her they had an "accident" (accent), not realizing he had one as well. During one train ride he rushed over to me excitedly, yelling "Mommy, Mommy, I found some girls who speak New Jersey!" "You mean they speak English, honey," I said. "No, no, Mommy, I *mean* they speak *New Jersey*!" Sure enough, when I was dragged over to meet the young ladies, I found my son's new friends lived an hour from our home.

### Eurail Passes

There is a wonderful selection of train passes available throughout Europe and the U.K. You can buy them for multiple countries, single countries, and even in combination as train/rental car passes. Children's rates apply. These passes *must* be purchased prior to departure; they *cannot* be purchased overseas. A comprehensive Web site for European train information and passes, including the U.K., is www.europeonrail.com, or you can call toll-free 877-On-RAIL7. Another is www.raileurope.com. For travel within the U.K., also check out www.britainontrack.com or call toll-free 888 667-9734.

For the best use of your time and money keep these train travel suggestions in mind:

1.  If you plan to travel on long haul train routes on a Eurailpass, consider making advance seat reservations. There is a small fee for this service, but it insures good seating at peak summer travel times. This can be done in the U.S. via the Web sites above, or with a phone call.

2.  The very first time you use your Eurailpass, you must have it stamped at a ticket counter *before* you board the train. Allow at least 40 minutes for this task during peak season. Lines can be long. After that, you don't have to wait in line, just board the train directly for future trips.

3.  If you only need to buy one or two point-to-point tickets, consider purchasing them here in the U.S. and save yourself the hassle of buying them overseas. There may be a small additional fee for the service.

4.  If you will be visiting London for three or more days, I highly recommend you buy a London Visitor Travelcard, which gives you unlimited travel on London's Bus and Underground networks. This *must* be purchased here in the U.S. You can purchase online at www.europconrail.com or call toll free to 877-OnRail7. If you are flying into Heathrow Airport, it will also include your Underground train trip from airport to city center.

5.  There are similar transportation passes for other cities, but often those passes are priced to include travel outside the city, so you should weigh the cost of these passes against your intended city travel plans.

## A Word About Couchettes/Sleeper Cars

For long train trips of six hours or more, consider traveling at night in a couchette. This is a train compartment with four or six stacked fold-down train beds. It sounds uncomfortable, but the beds are quite comfortable and the gentle rocking of the train will put you quickly to sleep. The rail fare is already included in your Eurailpass; you pay the additional fee for the couchette, which is usually less than half the cost of a hotel room. There are drawbacks:

1.  Married couples and families of four are usually assigned to the four bed compartments.

2.  As a single parent family you will be expected to share your compartment with strangers, both men and women, so you sleep in your clothes. More than likely you will be assigned the six-bed compartment, which

means more activity of people going in and out to use the hallway bathroom.

3.  Pickpockets may lurk the hallways hoping to find an unlocked compartment with sleeping travelers who have carelessly left their valuables in plain view instead of tucking them under the pillow or locking them up in a suitcase. Back in the days when I foolishly carried a purse when traveling, our couchette compartment was rifled while everyone was sleeping (The last person to the bathroom forgot to lock the compartment door). My purse was taken from the far end of my bed. I had everything in it: passports, air tickets, train passes, visas for the former Soviet Union, traveler's checks, and US$250 cash in various currencies. The purse was recovered in one of the bathrooms with everything in it but the cash. I was lucky. That was the last time I carried a purse while traveling.

A few things to keep in mind when traveling by train in Europe:

➤ If you are traveling from one major city to another, it is often essential to have an advance seat reservation. These city-to-city trains are very popular and often oversell during high season. If you arrive with a Eurailpass or a train ticket, but no seat reservation, you may be denied boarding. Some high-speed train journeys require advance seat reservations at all times, similar to the U.S. East Coast's Metroliner service.

➤ European trains leave precisely on time. You can set your watch by a train's departure. If you are running to catch a train, the train will not slow down or wait for you, even if it is a local.

➤ If you didn't have time to purchase a picnic lunch before boarding the train, don't fret. European trains usually have restaurant cars and/or vendors selling sandwiches and snacks. (My daughter's first introduction to the French version of a ham sandwich was on board a train. She has been a devotee of the crusty "sandwich de jambon" ever since). This advice does not always apply to trains in third world countries. Better stock up on food before you board the train.

➤ If your budget includes an occasional luxury, plan on eating at least one meal in the dining car of a European train. The atmosphere is white tablecloth, and there is something deliciously decadent about eating a delicious meal and lingering over a glass of fine wine while watching the scenery roll by. You can close your eyes and pretend you are on the Orient Express. Even your kids will appreciate the special experience.

> On a similar note, one of the most reasonable places to enjoy a moderately priced fine meal is in a European train station. Surprised? Although not as common as 10 or 20 years ago, you can still find a few of these white tablecloth bargains tucked away in some of the older train stations.

> Plan on arriving at a train station about 20 minutes before departure (assuming you already have your tickets or your train pass). This will give you enough time to locate your track, your train car, and get you and your kids comfortably settled into your seats. Chunnel trains, which travel between the UK and the European continent, have special check-in times, so be sure to determine what they are from your tickets or verify with a conductor at the station and adhere to them.

> Finding your track and train car in a major European city is pretty straightforward. Electronic signs everywhere indicate track and train numbers. If you cannot find your confirmed seat or are not sure where to sit in an unreserved train, multilingual conductors are both ubiquitous and helpful. First class cars are at the front of the train and second class at the back. Seats with stickers on them are reserved.

> Catching a train in a small town may require a more grassroots approach. In the absence of signs, ask your ticket agent and fellow travelers for track guidance. Verify again with the conductor before boarding the train. Oh, and one more important point, in Europe, unlike the U.S., local trains are announced by what city they are *coming from,* not what city they are *going to.* I learned that lesson the hard way.

## BUS TRAVEL

When traveling overseas, there are two types of bus transportation to consider: long haul and local. Both are cheap, fun and a great way to meet locals.

### Long Haul

1.  The U.K. offers a wonderful network of comfortable motorcoaches that criss-cross the countries of the British Isles.

2.  Many Alpine countries have point-to-point bus service that is frequent, moderately priced, and gorgeously scenic when crossing over the Alps. In Switzerland the buses have the right-of-way on mountain roads. To signal oncoming car drivers to make way, buses use a special horn,

which delivers the first four notes of the William Tell Overture (For those not acquainted with Swiss folklore, William Tell is a national folk hero).

3.  In the Middle East, long-distance buses are a common, safe, and inexpensive mode of travel. In the summer of 2000 my son and I traveled by long haul bus from Amman, Jordan to Aleppo, Syria. The five-hour journey cost US$10 per person.

My seatmate on our Jordanian journey was a charming young Palestinian nun who spoke fluent English and saved me from a document disaster. As we approached our first border crossing, we were asked to surrender our passports to the bus attendant. (Americans loath giving up their passports, myself included, but I had no choice). We were then shepherded inside the immigration building and then back onto the bus. It was only after we reboarded and the bus took off that I realized that I, not the bus attendant, was supposed to take back my passport in the immigration building. My angel in nun's clothing came to my rescue and with her help, convinced the disgruntled bus driver to return back and retrieve my and my son's passports. Thereafter I made sure my new friend was right by my side when we went through two more border crossings. We have since become e-mail pals.

4.  When traveling by long haul bus in Latin America or the Middle East, or any country where there is little or no train service, you should make bus reservations anywhere from one to three days in advance. Advance seat reservations are usually assigned at time of purchase.

**Local Buses**

Traveling by local bus overseas is a wonderful way to save money and have a mini adventure. In London, you should take at least one double-decker bus ride. Elsewhere in Europe you will find clean, comfortable local buses. Many of these run on the honor system; you board the bus and go to the rear and feed your change into a machine. Have plenty of coins handy and beware of local customs. My 5-year-old son got his knees rapped in Holland by a senior citizen wielding a fierce cane. After that episode he was careful to never put his feet on the seat.

During our three-day tour to Leningrad (now called St. Petersburg) we had one free afternoon, so the kids and I were dropped off in the heart of this beautiful (then still Soviet) city. After some interesting shopping excursions we decided to take the local bus back to our hotel. Unable to read the signs in the Cyrillic alphabet, we showed some passers-by our hotel matchbox cover and were guided to the correct bus stop. I had read that bus fare was the equivalent of 10 cents per person, so I was prepared with small change. However when I boarded the bus the driver refused to take my money and kept yelling at me in Russian. (In the Soviet Union a first encounter with a person in authority — a waiter, a bus driver, a museum attendee — always involved a heated discussion. It was part of the Soviet culture. It was also part of the culture never to smile during these encounters). Undaunted, I kept trying to pay, and finally, in disgust, the driver motioned for us to take a seat. At that moment I felt a tug at my sleeve. A sweet-faced elderly lady handed me three bus tickets and refused to take payment. Joyfully I jumped up, handed them to the bus driver, only to be yelled at again. Subdued, but not defeated, I decided I would watch the incoming passengers and learn the Soviet system.

It soon became evident that paying for a ticket was a three-step process. First you had to buy a block of tickets from the driver, then you had to retreat to the center of the bus where you stamped the ticket(s) you needed for that journey in a validator, perched over one of the windows. Lastly, as you disembarked the bus, you handed the validated tickets to the driver. My ten-year-old son validated our tickets and soon became the official "validator" for all of the little old ladies who boarded the bus. In no time at all they adopted him and were clucking away at him in Russian. As I watched the pleasant scene unfold it dawned on me that many of these elderly women had probably survived the infamous Siege of Leningrad during World War II. If only I could speak Russian. What stories I would hear! All too soon our ride ended. I approached the stone-faced driver and handed him our validated tickets with a smile, a flourish, and a loud "Eh voilà!" As the bus pulled away, all of the old women waved at us. I stole a quick glance at the bus driver and detected a slight smile at the corner of his lips.

Traveling on local buses in Latin America is always a hoot and sometimes offers more of an adventure than originally anticipated. On a 1998 summer trip to Peru, we decided to take the local bus from the ancient Inca capital of Cusco (10,000 feet/3,000 meters) up to the ruins of Tambo Machay (over 12,000 feet/3,660 meters). From Tambo Machay it's a spectacular four-mile downhill walk back to the city of Cusco. Along the way you can stop to watch the native Quechua and Aymara Indians weave by the roadside and visit several Inca ruins, including the world-famous Sacsayhuaman, often featured on the Discovery Channel and *National Geographic* magazine. We had arrived Cusco from the U.S. the day before and thought this would be an easy walk to kick start our altitude acclimation.

It was a 10-minute search to find the back street dusty bus station and took almost as long to shoo away all the pesky, persistent cab drivers that wanted to charge us US$20 for the half-hour uphill ride. The bus tickets were the equivalent of 25 cents each, and we were quickly loaded into a compact crowded 20-passenger bus. Seat reservations were mandated and enforced. My son had been assigned a window seat next to a Quechua woman with a lapful of clucking pigeons. As we approached our destination my daughter and I wiggled our way up front and disembarked. To my surprise, the bus immediately took off and I chased after it, banging on the door with my fist and screaming, *"¡Mi hijo! ¡Mi hijo! ¡Tiene mi hijo!"* (My son! My son! You have my son!) Seconds later the bus stopped, the door opened, and my son emerged with pigeon feathers coming out of his shirtsleeves and ponytail. He was *not* a happy camper.

As we walked down the road to join my daughter, we found her sitting on a rock, head down. I felt her pulse, which was beating as fast as a humming-bird's. I knew I needed to get her down to a lower altitude and *fast*. I jumped out onto the road and stopped an old station wagon filled with Quechua Indians heading downhill. They agreed to take us to Cusco. My daughter and I scurried into the back seat while my son squirmed into the rear compartment with several giggling young Quechua ladies, who promptly began stroking my son's long blond ponytail. As soon as we dropped 1,000 feet (300 meters) my daughter felt better and we asked the driver to stop at the ruins of Sacsayhuaman. I gave the driver a couple of dollars and the ladies quickly emerged for a series of photographs with my son, which I later sent them. The next day we repeated our journey to Tambo Machay and successfully walked back to Cusco. This time we negotiated for a cab. We had enough adventure on the pigeon bus.

*Later in this section, under "Health Matters," we will discuss ways to deal with altitude sickness.*

*Author's Note:* When traveling to Andean countries, an easy way to spot a Quechua Indian from an Aymaran is by their hats. Quechuas like to wear brown fedoras, while Aymaras favor black bowlers.

## MISCELLANEOUS MODES OF TRAVEL

Once you arrive at your destination, consider sampling as many modes of transportation as you can. Some of them may not be so exciting for you, but the kids will love it and their enthusiasm is contagious. On our first single parent trip to Europe we sampled trains, double-decker buses, subways, cog railways, ferries, lake steamers and cable cars. Many of these rides are included in your European train pass.

Use the subway system to get around in the cities. In London it is called the Tube or Underground, in Paris, the Metro. Train passes are available in many cities. Unlike some U.S. cities, underground systems in foreign countries are often well marked and easy to navigate even without local language abilities, unless of course you are traveling to a country in Asia or the Middle East, where the Roman alphabet is not the norm.

When arriving at a foreign airport, check out your transportation options to the downtown part of the city. For airports located far from the city, airport transport buses may be your cheapest option. Often they will drop you off close to your hotel or at least a short cab ride away. When arriving at small airports, especially in Central American cities, if it is convenient and safe to walk out of the airport area to grab a cab, do so. Prices will be considerably cheaper roadside.

Two other taxicab savings tips to keep in mind: First, find out the going rate beforehand. Ask your flight attendant or your seatmate. If your first cab does not offer the price you like, continue down the line. Second, in Latin America, learn to say "How much to go to...?" *in Spanish.* (¿Cuándo es para ir a...?) You may not understand the answer, and you may have to ask to have the amount be repeated in English, but by asking the initial question in Spanish, you have taken control and will throw the cab driver off kilter for a moment. That little maneuver can save you a few dollars if you don't know the going rate.

Although it does not always include transportation, you should always ask the local tourist board whether your destination city offers a Visitor's Card. These are convenient money-saving purchases that also make a nice trip souvenir. Each major Scandinavian city offers a two-, three- or four-day card that includes local transportation, museum admissions and other sightseeing features. The Visitor Ticket for Cusco, Peru includes admission to all surrounding ruins and is presented in the form of a colorful certificate, suitable for framing upon your return home. Once you visit two ruins, you have already saved money on the ticket purchase.


## DEALING WITH ISSUES

### TENDING TO "BUSINESS" ON THE TRIP

When raising my kids, I didn't make a lot of rules, but those that I did have were inviolate. From the time they were very little, one of the rules I set was the necessity to remain silent and still during critical occasions. Those occasions were:

1. Business phone calls (which I announced beforehand);

2. Driving around traffic circles, a life-threatening situation in South Jersey;

3. Conducting a "transaction."

I began teaching my children this behavior when they were pre-schoolers. I gently explained what the result could be if they distracted me or misbehaved during these transactions. It took a lot of coaching, but by the time each child turned 5, I knew I could depend upon them during these critical situations. They learned to amuse themselves during business calls, they stopped speaking mid-sentence as we approached a traffic circle, and, even though they couldn't pronounce the word "transaction," they knew what one was and instinctively knew to keep quiet during that time. This last learned skill turned out to be a great benefit when we traveled as a single parent family. With few exceptions, I was able to pay restaurant and hotel bills, exchange foreign currency, and peruse and sign a rental car contract without getting harassed or distracted by my kids (Of course the second I finished they expected my full attention). If I caught the hotel desk or the car rental agent in an overcharge or was able to negotiate a better rate than originally confirmed, I made sure to share that information with my kids, thus verbally rewarding them for their good behavior. Following their Mom's example, they usually negotiated for an extra treat.

## MANAGING CONFLICT

Lest everyone think that traveling with children is always a piece of cake and my trips with my children were always rosy affairs, be assured that was not, and, still is not, the case. Traveling can be stressful and tiring, especially on an active vacation or a trip to a distant, exotic locale. Relaxing vacations can also produce boredom, especially with teen-agers, who, in addition to needing friends their own age, also need lots of activities to work off their high energy levels. During vacation you and your kids are thrown together for longer periods of time than those to which you are accustomed. There is often no place to retreat from one another, other than the far corner of a hotel room or back seat of a car. Family dynamics such as sibling rivalry will often be exacerbated during a vacation. As a single parent you will bear the brunt of your kids' frustration, boredom, anger, and exhaustion. What's a single parent to do?

## Grin and bear it

Be prepared. Arguments and disagreements will occur, even with the best-laid plans and itineraries. This is especially true with teen-agers. My kids and I are all strong-willed people so, on every trip, as wonderful as each one was, there were usually a few mini-disagreements throughout each day, plus at least one big "blow-out" during the trip. As the years went by, I thought we had a system going to diffuse those arguments, and family dynamics would change, sending us back to ground zero. As my daughter graduated from college and matured into a young lady, my son entered college and began to feel "outnumbered" by two adult women as he maneuvered through his changing status in the family. More than once on a trip, he would storm off on his own, only to join us an hour or two later as if nothing had happened. One such argument took place as we approached the Pyramids of Giza on a hot summer morning. The Egyptian cab driver we hired for the day couldn't understand why my son spent the morning doing his pyramid explorations separately from his mother and sister, but my son just needed to blow off some steam. Just remember that no matter how much you argue, years later, if the trip was well-planned, you will remember the good times, not the disagreements, even though you swear at the time you will never travel with your kids again.

## Get buy-in from your kids

In Part I of this book I wrote about ways to get your kids involved in the trip planning and how to prepare a fun-filled, exciting vacation that offers something for everyone. Following these principles will help to eliminate some of the conflict.

## Borrow a kid

Sometimes you need to take an additional step to assure a satisfactory vacation experience. On a three-week fly/drive trip out West, when my son was 12 and my daughter 19, I approached my neighbors with the idea of taking along their 11-year old son James as company for my son. Being a single parent, I had no qualms about asking them to pay for their son's costs, which included airfare, meals and activities. There was no additional charge for rooms, since we would all stay together in a quad. It was a win-win situation. Their son had a wonderful trip at a very reasonable cost and my son had a great travel buddy for three weeks, eliminating stress on the sibling relationship. Since both boys were good friends, we knew James would be a good traveler. He was well behaved, easygoing, and always ready for an adventure. An added plus was that he was an excellent swimmer, which was important for our family. Being Jerseyites born and bred, we gravitate to the nearest body of water like bees to honey when on vacation.

*When you bring a child that is not your own on a trip, even if that child is a relative, you must travel with the following five documents:*

1.  A copy of the child's insurance card.

2.  All necessary medical information about the child — allergies, prescriptions, etc.

3.  A written, signed letter from one or both parents giving you permission to get immediate emergency treatment at a local hospital without having to wait for the parents to be contacted.

4.  A list of all contact information for the parents.

5.  If you are going out of the country, even if traveling to Canada or Mexico, you must travel with a written signed letter from *both* of the child's parents granting you permission to take that child out of the country (The word *both* applies even to divorced parents).

Borrowing a teen-age child is one solution when traveling with teen-agers, especially if you are traveling to an area where there will not be a lot of other young people. Of course you need to exercise caution when selecting a new travel companion and ascertain beforehand that the young person will adhere to your travel rules, even if they are different than those imposed by his or her family.

*Author's Note:* One last note on borrowing kids: make sure they have different socks than the rest of your family. During our three-week trip out West, the word "share" took on new meaning when we did our weekly laundry containing 28 pairs of identical white socks.

### Allow your child some space and freedom

When the kids were little it was understood that we would all stick together, at all times, when traveling. As each of my children entered their teens, we began the delicate dance of when to let go and when to rein in. This is a tough call and an individual family decision. What do you do when your child is asked on a date while you are traveling or is asked to join a group of teen-agers for a few hours? If you are on a cruise ship or staying at a resort hotel, it is somewhat easier to keep tabs on their whereabouts and activities, but what about when you are in a strange town? Teen-agers need to spend some time with kids their own age and learn about different lifestyles, and parents need to know their children are safe. There are times your parental instincts tell you the answer is no and other times when you feel you can let go. This is definitely an arena ripe for conflict.

Allow me to share some "single parent travel with teen-ager" vignettes with you, if for no other reason than to let you know you are not alone.

- The summer my daughter turned 14, we embarked on a fly/drive trip around Arizona. As we pulled into our motel in the early evening in the little town of Show Low, the woman at the front desk greeted us enthusiastically. "Oh I am so glad you are here. One of our guests has a daughter the same age as yours and her mom is a single mom too. She is here on location, heading up a county engineering project. Would it be all right if the two girls went to a dance tonight? " "Sure," I said. My daughter went to look for her new friend and by the time my son and I had taken the luggage into our room, my daughter and her new friend were gone. Concerned and annoyed, I confronted the front desk lady. "Where is my daughter?" I asked testily, "and where is this dance?" Coming from a populous suburban environment I was suspicious and not prepared for the quick disappearing act. The hotel lady chuckled. "It's all right, Ms. Elwell," she said. "The dance is a mile down the dirt road and it is sponsored by the Mormon Church, which means there is no smoking, drinking, or drugs. This is a small town and everyone knows everyone else. Your daughter is perfectly safe." With that I went back to my room to enjoy small-town life.

- Two summers later, when my daughter was 16, we spent a couple of nights in Cooperstown, New York en route to Niagara Falls. Besides the Baseball Hall of Fame, this delightful town has many fine museums, including an indoor/outdoor Farmer's Museum showing what life was like in that part of the country in the mid 1800s. The kids had a ball trying out the popular games of that period including the stilts. A local guide, a mannerly and poised young man of 18, soon joined us. About 20 minutes later he walked purposefully over to me. I knew at that moment he was going to ask permission to take my daughter out that night. I also knew at that moment I would say yes. There were three reasons:

1.  He was respectful and looked me in the eye when he introduced himself earlier.

2.  He was attending a state university in the fall on a full scholastic scholarship. I doubted he wished to do anything that would jeopardize that.

3.  My daughter and I needed a few hours away from each other. That year had been the most difficult and traumatic in our parent/teen relationship.

I advised the young man of my daughter's midnight curfew and he nodded. Much to my surprise, he returned my daughter to our guesthouse shortly after 11 p.m. (She *never* came home before curfew). The party they attended had ended at 11 p.m. Her escort explained that in a small town like Cooperstown, he was expected to come straight home when a party ended unless he was willing to risk a search party and his relatives' ire. It was an educational experience for my daughter and a big (quiet) chuckle for me.

- When my son turned 15, we spent an overnight in an historic mining-camp-turned-hotel in the town of Ester, Alaska. I had reserved tickets for the show at the Malamute Saloon. Shortly before the show began, my son ran over to our table, told me he made some new friends, wasn't attending the show, and took off. I shot out of my seat and caught up to him and his small group of friends. Doing my motherly thing, I pulled out my memo pad and proceeded to ask his friends where they lived and was next prepared to ask for phone numbers. One young man gave me a strange look and pointed to six houses down a dirt road. "That's the extent of the town, Ma'am," he said. "I live in the brown house at the end, but we will probably move about all the houses tonight." At that moment, I couldn't decide whom I had embarrassed more, me or my son. Tucking away my memo pad, I simply said, "Have fun!" and trotted back to the Malamute Saloon in time for the show.

- Not all of our single parent/teen travel experiences ended so pleasantly. During the difficult summer when my daughter was 16 we spent an overnight in a remote ski resort in the Canadian wilderness. A DJ played music at our hotel that night. I went back to our room at 11 p.m. with my 9-year-old son after giving my daughter permission to stay on the dance floor until her midnight curfew. When my daughter did not return by 12:30 a.m., I went downstairs to investigate, only to find a darkened dance floor and an empty front desk. Since it was off-season, the hotel was sealed shut and the phone system turned off for the night. I couldn't call anyone and I couldn't leave the hotel without getting locked out. I went back to my room and lay awake the entire night, floating between white-hot anger and extreme distress. It was the darkest moment of my single parent travel experiences. At 6 a.m., when the hotel reopened, my daughter knocked at our door. Seeing the look on my face, she wisely chose not to say a word. If she had, I think we would have come to blows. We immediately checked out of the hotel and drove to Toronto. Twelve hours passed before I was even able to speak to her. I later found out she stayed up all night talking to the DJ in the parking lot. Knowing that I would not leave her little brother alone in the hotel, she took full advantage of the situation. Did I mention there would be times you will swear never to travel with your kids again?

## MAJOR LIFE DECISIONS

There is something about getting away from it all that makes us think more clearly about things. Travel enables us to do that. Deeper discussions can take place between parent and child or between siblings. Thoughts seem to bubble to the surface more easily when you are far away from home. Sitting atop a cliff in Sedona, Arizona one spring, the three of us became engaged in a deep discussion about my son's college education. Greg was unsure if his chosen major would provide steady employment opportunities. After tossing around some ideas, his sister suggested he consider a double major. I assured him it didn't matter how long it took him to finish his education as long as it was what he wanted. The light bulb came on. That fall he changed his course schedule to accommodate a second major.

Discussions may take place between siblings and, as a parent; sometimes you need to be "invisible." While seated at a restaurant, my pre-teen son began querying his older sister about drugs, as if I was not there. The discussion continued between them throughout the meal and well past dessert. Not wanting to disrupt the moment, I kept re-ordering coffee. I spent the evening wired to the hilt and running to the bathroom, but my son had gained information at the time he needed it from a person he trusted.

Non-parental single adults, traveling with a youngster, often fall into the role of confidante. During those times it is important to be non-judgmental and just listen.

## EMERGENCIES AND HEALTH MATTERS

In Part I, I wrote about the importance of vaccinations. In spite of these preventive measures, there may be times you or your child may get sick or have an accident. The following are some suggestions for the treatment of common travel ailments. Since I am merely an experienced single parent traveler and not a doctor, I recommend you verify these suggestions with your family physician.

**Ear Infections**

Since ear infections are common with small children, I recommend traveling with antiseptic over-the-counter eardrops. Insert a couple of drops in your child's ear before and after any swim in a body of water — lake, pool, ocean, Mexican cenote, whatever. If you are concerned about your child contracting an ear infection while you are out of reach of a local doctor, such as on an overnight train trip, consider asking your children's pediatrician for a small supply of medication for just such as emergency.

**Motion Sickness**

Since early childhood my daughter has suffered from severe motion sickness. Until her early twenties, the only way for her to conquer it was to take Dramamine® and sleep through 90% of the scenic rides by train, plane, boat, car, and bus. About five years ago she tried ginger tablets, a natural substance with no drowsy side effects, and has never used Dramamine® again.

**Altitude Sickness**

For sea level folks like our East Coast-based family, traveling to a high altitude destination may require an acclimation period of 24 hours or more. Problems can occur at 8,000 feet (2,440 meters), or more commonly, at 10,000 feet (3,000 meters) and above. Some common symptoms are dizziness, headaches, upset stomach, rapid pulse, sleepiness, nosebleeds, or inability to sleep. Your reaction to high altitude can be different on each trip. Just because you were symptom-free the last time does not mean you will be symptom-free the next time. Back in my twenties and thirties, when I frequently skied the high Rockies, I would literally fall asleep in my soup (actually alongside it would be a more accurate description). Later in life my symptoms changed from no reaction to mild headaches and dizziness. My poor daughter had the severest symptoms during our trip to Cusco, Peru, but years earlier it was my son who was bothered when we flew into the high altitude of Quito, Ecuador.

*There are a few things you can do to ease altitude discomfort for you and your child:*

1. Drink lots of water. The body needs oxygen and water is an excellent provider.

2. Avoid alcohol and caffeine, at least until you are acclimated.

3. Have some Mate (*pronounced Mah tay*) de Cocoa, which is tea made from coca leaves. (This is often served in the high Andes of Peru, Bolivia, and Argentina. It is not a medically proven cure, but it sure does give you a psychological boost. And yes, it is legal).

4. Try to sleep at an altitude that is the same as, or preferably lower, than the highest altitude you reached that day.

5. Ask your doctor for a prescription for altitude sickness before you leave the U.S. and take the medicine as soon as you feel the symptoms coming on.

6. If you experience severe symptoms, especially a very rapid pulse, coughing blood, or severe nosebleeds, get down to a lower altitude as soon as possible. Often you only need to drop a thousand feet (300 meters) to feel immediate relief.

*Two other things of note:*

1. The Spanish word for altitude sickness is "Soroche," (*pronounced sō RŌ chay*) handy in the Andes.

2. Oxygen levels in the high altitude atmosphere drop at night. Do not plan on driving a car late at night in altitudes over 12,000 feet (3,660 meters) as the motor may sputter and die for lack of oxygen. While staying overnight at 13,000 feet (4,000 meters) in Lake Titicaca, Bolivia, the kids and I regularly woke up in the middle of the night gasping for air. The first night it was frightening until we realized the cause. Also be prepared for weird dreams, which we presumed were caused by oxygen deprivation.

3. Keep glasses of water by your beds. High altitude climates are very dry, and this helps you keep hydrated through the night as well.

## Intestinal and Tummy Problems

When traveling in countries where the water is not safe to drink, avoid salads, fruits you cannot peel, and wipe off soda and juice cans that are "sweating." If you do contract Montezuma's Revenge, so aptly named in Mexico, the best thing to do is let your system ride its course and remember to keep yourself or your child hydrated. However, while traveling that is not always practical. Our pediatrician recommended Pepto-Bismol® as the first course of action. If that doesn't do the trick, then bring out the stronger stuff like Imodium®.

Known to have a cast-iron stomach, I never experienced intestinal problems until we went to Egypt. One morning, in the middle of our Nile Cruise, I was unable to leave the bathroom and sent the kids scurrying off to find something stronger than Imodium®. They had never seen me sick on a trip and didn't know what to do. (Our cruise had provided a superb Egyptian guide, a history professor from the University of Cairo, and I was determined not to miss the morning's excursion). "Knock on every cabin door," I said, "until you find our new English-speaking friends that live in the Middle East. They will have something, I am sure." Within minutes my cabin was buzzing with a committee of do-gooders trying to decide what medication to dispense. "Just gimme the top of the line," I yelled from behind the bathroom door. My daughter appeared with a small white pill in her hand. "The lady said just take one, Mom, then wait 30 minutes and take a second if you need it. She said not to take anymore after that or you will never go to the bathroom again." The first one worked like a charm. I wish I had remembered to ask what it was.

My daughter suffered from severe tummy problems after a recent trip to Thailand and Cambodia. She now swears by Acidophilus or a branded version, Culturelle®. A nutritionist friend told her it could be used as a preventative measure to ward off tummy and intestinal problems while traveling, or to help recover after a problem.

## Accidents and Other Illnesses

There are times when travelers need to see a local doctor or visit a local clinic. Often your hotel or cruise ship will have a doctor on staff. If the illness or accident is not serious, visiting a local hospital or clinic can be an interesting cultural experience, especially in a third world country.

While in the Ecuadorian Amazon, my daughter became quite dizzy the last day of our stay. Fearful that she had contracted some tropical disease we arranged for a visit with the doctor at the Flotel (an Amazon floating "hotel") on our way out of our remote tourist camp. The doctor wasn't certain of the origin of her dizziness, but he was able to determine quickly that she had no tropical disease, but did have an ear infection. The cost for his visit, including some medication was US$15. We found out upon our return home that my daughter's electrolytes were out of balance, which, along with her ear infection, had exacerbated her dizziness. She had consumed enough water during our trip but not enough salt.

While on a business trip to Guatemala, my colleague developed severe stomach cramps during a weekend visit to the delightful colonial town of Antigua. We walked to the local clinic where she was diagnosed and treated for an intestinal bug. The total cost for the doctor and the medication came to US$30.

While she was being examined, I waited in a pleasant canopied outdoor waiting room, which was filled with a broad spectrum of people from town — Yankees, Europeans and local indigenous people. I played with babies, chatted with tourists, and enjoyed a card game with a local teen-ager with a broken arm. The clinic was immaculately clean and the floor under our feet was wiped twice during my one-hour wait.

I am not recommending you have surgery in a third world country. You need to go home for that. And many third world clinics are not so sanitary as the one in Antigua. But you needn't feel that a visit to a local clinic or hospital will be a horrific experience. Just get the vaccinations that are recommended for your destination and you will have done all you can to be prepared for emergencies. In addition, American doctors may not be familiar with diseases seen in third world countries and will not be able to quickly diagnose you. By all means visit a doctor after returning home, but if your symptoms are serious while in another country or state, don't put off a visit there until returning home.

When we first began to travel as a single parent family, our policy was that if one of us got sick, we all stayed together until that person got well. As my children got older, we loosened that policy somewhat. If my daughter wasn't feeling tip-top and we were staying at a classy hotel in a nice part of town, my son and I would leave her in the hotel room to nap or rest while we visited a nearby park for an hour or so.

On one trip my son had tummy troubles. It was the last day of a one-week stay in Hong Kong. Some of the corporate travel accounts I managed did business with the Peninsula Hotel, so I was able to secure two complimentary hotel nights. The Peninsula in Hong Kong is ranked as one of the top ten hotels world wide for its fine service. We were greeted like family and assigned a beautiful mini-suite. The bathroom was all marble, and music was pumped into every room (with a selection of everything from classical to rock), and the TV offered first run movies in about six different languages. Our floor butler was a kindly dignified gentleman who had been with the hotel for nearly 40 years. I decided it was safe to leave my 13-year-old son alone for a few hours while his sister and I did some last minute shopping. After five days of intensive sightseeing around Hong Kong and the Outer Islands, we were woefully short of gifts for friends and family back home.

When my daughter and I returned to the hotel room a few hours later, my son had a concerned look on his face. "Is something wrong?" I asked. "Well, Mom," my son said, "I watched a movie and then I took a bubble bath. I felt better and wanted to get something to eat, so I went downstairs and bought a box of four little chocolates in the hotel store. I charged it to the room like you told me, but when I saw the bill it was for US$7.50 and I didn't know what to do since I had already signed for it." "That's OK, honey," I said, "as long as you enjoyed the chocolates." "Well, the chocolates were delicious, but that's not all, Mom," he said. "When I got back to my room, the butler checked in on me and when he saw I was feeling better he brought in a bowl of fruit and three boxes of the same chocolates, all for *free*. I'm sorry, Mom." I laughed and said everything was fine, but my daughter turned to my son and said, "So, where are the chocolates?" After she found out he had eaten them all, it took me several minutes to pry them apart.

## CARRYING YOUR MONEY AND VALUABLES

1. Keep your cash, passport and credit cards in a safe place, preferably spread about your body. For women this means discarding the purse in favor of a fanny pack or money pouch, or pinning some emergency cash to the inside of your bra. For men it means keeping extra cash in a money belt rather than the back pocket wallet.

2. Once your child is old enough to carry a backpack, stash some traveler's checks in his or her name in the backpack (good for emergencies).

3. Always keep copies of passports, credit card emergency numbers, and traveler's check numbers in a safe place other than your person.

## KEEPING YOU AND YOUR CHILDREN SAFE

When a single adult takes a child on vacation, one of the primary concerns is safety — safety for oneself and safety for one's child. This concern is particularly acute for a single mom with young children. As a woman traveling alone with one or two kids, there is a tendency to feel especially vulnerable, especially in an unfamiliar or foreign locale. This needn't be the case if you follow a few simple procedures that will make your family look more confident, knowledgeable, and less like potential victims.

1.  Walk with confidence. Know where you are going and how to get there before you leave your hotel room. If you have to stop to consult a map, get off the street corner and do it inside a store or away from the crowd. (Locals often assumed we were residents because of the way we walked. Even tourists asked us for directions).

2.  When traveling in third world countries do not wear expensive jewelry. You are inviting theft. Everyone in your family, including your children, should wear only cheap plastic watches.

3.  Don't openly display your expensive camera in a crowded area. Keep it in a backpack or camera bag.

4.  Trust your instincts. If you feel an area is unsafe, leave it or duck into a restaurant and have someone call you a cab.

5.  Learn the local customs and dress codes in advance. You may look like a tourist, but at least you won't look like a dumb tourist.

6.  Before you go out at night, ask where it is safe to walk. Keep in mind areas that are very safe in the daytime may not be so after dark.

7.  When traveling in a rental car, keep your windows up and doors locked when stopping for traffic lights in the city, especially if you are traveling in a jeep. Jeeps are great targets for quick-snatch thefts (My sunglasses were ripped off of my face in San Jose, Costa Rica while waiting in a jeep for the traffic light to change, and yes, the windows were down).

8.  Caution your children against bringing in any drugs into a foreign country, even a small amount of pot. Even if your destination country is rather loose about drug usage, caution them against buying anything. Punishment for foreigners who buy drugs can be more severe than for locals. It is one way for these countries to earn a little extra money from tourists. In some countries, possession of drugs means an immediate jail sentence (My teen-age son, with his long ponytail, was sometimes approached on the street to buy drugs. In Belize City the dealer did it with me standing right there!)

9.  Have a plan if you get separated in a crowd. Make sure your children know the name of your hotel or are carrying the hotel name with them (matchbook covers do the trick).

*The following is an excerpt from my article on Single Parent Travel Safety published on ParentsWithoutPartners.org. (September 2001).*

When my kids were 12 and 5, we took our first single parent trip to Europe. It was impractical to hold them both by the hand in a crowded area, especially walking down city streets, so we devised a method of walking together that we dubbed "The Triangle." My daughter and I would walk close together, side by side, with my son tucked in front of us, leaving all of us hands-free. This method worked beautifully as we traveled for years throughout the cities of Europe, the Orient, and Central and South America. None of us felt confined and I could always keep an eye on my young rambunctious son.

In the summer of 1995 we planned our first single parent family trip to the Middle East traveling to Syria and Egypt. We were going to visit Damascus and Palmyra on our own and then join my daughter's college friend, Karim, in his hometown of Aleppo, Syria. Upon arrival in Damascus our first order of business was to purchase our pre-reserved air tickets from Aleppo to Cairo, something we were unable to do in the United States. I knew that Syria was a cash society but I was unprepared for the fact that Syrian Airlines would not take my credit card as payment for the air tickets. Not only that, payment had to be in Syrian Pounds, not traveler's checks or U.S. dollars. We were forced to go to a bank about four blocks away to exchange our money (ATMs are non-existent in Syria).

Banking in Syria is done outdoors. The bank teller sits behind a caged window and you, the customer, stand outside, completely exposed, to complete your transaction. Unable to find a bathroom, my daughter and I stepped aside to surreptitiously unpin cash from our bras while my son shielded us from passers-by. We then approached the bank teller, cash in hand. In the Arab world, people do not form neat lines when they await service. They noisily crowd around the focal point, each demanding attention. It is part of their culture. Jet lagged and nervous, my daughter turned to the men crowding around us and yelled "Back off!" The teller, seeing our distress, reinforced our command in Arabic and we had a few moments of peace to complete our money exchange. As we turned away from the teller with nearly US$800 in cash nervously clutched to our bosoms, we prepared to resume our triangle position to walk back to the office of Syrian Air. As I looked at my 18-year-old son, it suddenly dawned on me that my little boy had become a six-foot-tall, lean, mean, muscle machine.

It was time to flip the triangle.

Turning to Greg, I hastily whispered, "From here on, walk behind Monique and me. You keep watch for our backs and if anyone approaches us, stare them down, and if they still keep coming, shove them away and ask questions later. I am not about to lose all this money."

We successfully purchased our Syrian Air tickets and after a wonderful stay in Damascus and Palmyra, we met up with Karim in Aleppo and told him our banking story. He laughed so hard the tears rolled down his face. He patiently explained that Syria is such a theft-free society we could have dropped our money on the street and people would have stopped in their tracks to scoop it up and return it to us.

*Author's Note:* In a July 2001 article in *National Geographic Traveler,* Control Risks Group, a London-based consulting firm, rated 14 large cities throughout the world as having an insignificant or low security risk. Damascus, Syria was one of them.

*2002 update:* In April the U.S. State Department just issued the first warning against travel to Syria in many years. Please consult U.S. State Department warnings before planning a trip to any destination. They can be found at http://travel.state.gov/travel_warnings.html.


## BREAKING THE ICE

There are many ways to break the ice and make new friends on your vacation, whether it is here in the U.S. or far from home. Making friends with people traveling with you as part of a tour group is easy. However, when you travel on your own, you need to put in a little extra effort to "reach out and touch someone." The mere fact that you are traveling with a child will break the ice. I have yet to find a country where people are not drawn to children. Being a single parent can be an advantage. People will view you as a person who is competent (You got there!), caring (You are traveling with your kids), and adventurous (You are doing it as a single adult!). They may reach out to you as a person who appears interesting, a bit of a curiosity, and therefore someone they would like to get to know. Besides, being a parent bestows upon you a little extra dignity, especially in foreign cultures. Enjoy and reap the benefits.

Let's talk about some things that you can do to enhance your ability to make friends overseas.

## LEARN LOCAL CUSTOMS IN ADVANCE

Earlier in the book we talked about being respectful of local dress customs. Once at your destination you should also be aware of local behavioral customs. I taught my kids that in Latin America people stand much closer to one another when they speak than they do in the U.S. When traveling in Latin countries they were respectful of this smaller personal space and refrained from a natural reaction to step back. In Japan I cautioned my young son to avoid sitting next to elderly women in the subway or bus. If the only seat left was next to an elderly or pregnant woman, then he was to stand. Unlike Russia, where the little old bus ladies clucked over him, elderly Japanese women are often very uncomfortable in close proximity to a "gaijin" (foreigner), especially a male (Of course in major tourist and resort areas you may not see these behaviors, but when you get off the beaten track, you do).

Just before our first trip to Syria, I briefed my teen-age son on Arab male behavior. "In conservative countries in the Middle East, men cannot show affection toward women in public. However, according to what I read, it is quite common for men to show affection toward other men. They may sit very close to another and put their arms around each other. So if that happens to you, don't go homophobic on me. It is part of their Arab culture." "Yeah, OK, Mom," my son replied.

Shortly after our arrival in Damascus, we strolled around town to stretch our legs. I deposited my son at a café table while my daughter and I checked out a nearby shop. When we emerged from the store about 10 minutes later, I found my son surrounded by several men, arms around him, mint tea in front of him, and a water pipe at his side. He had a Buddha-like grin on his face and was obviously enjoying the attention. I wasn't too thrilled about his smoking the water pipe, but I was glad he had paid attention to my lecture. "Leave him be, Mom," said my daughter, "and don't worry about his smoking. He's just doing his male bonding thing with the Arabs, like you told him." With that, my daughter and I ducked into the next shop.

## LEARN SOME WORDS OF THE LOCAL LANGUAGE

Have you ever visited a foreign country, learned a few words of their language, and watched someone's face light up when you used them? Once you have tried it, there is no going back, only forward. Of course, Americans have grown up hearing horror stories of how the French make fun of you if you don't pronounce their beautiful language just right. There is a modicum of truth to that, especially in Paris, but only a modicum. Through-out the rest of France, people are appreciative of any effort you make to speak their native language. Spanish-speaking countries are an entirely dif-ferent matter. I have witnessed linguistically challenged Americans absolu-tely murder the Spanish language and those wonderfully sweet people will express genuine, unabashed enthusiasm for any effort, however mispro-nounced, to speak their language. So go ahead, give it a try. Rent some lan-guage tapes and books from your local library. If you can afford it, take a crash language course. If not, have a student tutor you for cheap. If you can speak one or more languages, teach your kids some key words and phrases. And if your child is studying a language in school, have him or her do the same for you.

When my daughter spent a semester at Temple University Tokyo, I made arrangements for my son and I to join her for a two-week Christmas/New Year's vacation in Japan and Hong Kong. I was able to secure a free air ticket for myself, purchased a moderately priced consolidator ticket for my son, and wrangled some freebie hotel nights. Given the extremely poor exchange rate of yen to dollars that year, I knew we would be hard-pressed to buy meals in Japan at a price I could afford. Nonetheless, I was not about to pass up the fabulous opportunity for the three of us to spend the holidays in the Orient. Either we would go hungry now and then or eat a lot of noodle soup. We did both.

Determined to learn a little Japanese before we left, I gathered up my friends and formed a small class so I could get a group rate for a crash course at our local Inlingua School. The teachers were all Japanese and refused to speak English in class. It was mighty painful at first, but after a few lessons, my son and I began to pick up a few phrases in Japanese, along with the ca-dence of the language. I urged my son to write down some statements about himself and ask our teacher to say them in Japanese. He was reluctant at first but eventually consented to the idea of my writing down these phrases on 3x5 cards to take on the trip.

Several days into our trip we headed by train up to Koya-san to stay over-night at a mountaintop Buddhist monastery. As we chugged into one of the small countryside towns, three adorable little Japanese girls boarded the train, dressed neatly in pigtails and plaid skirts. They looked to be about 12 or 13 years old, the same age as my son. Predictably, about five minutes later, I heard a series of giggles behind me and with a shy smile on his face, my son quietly asked me if I had those Japanese cue cards handy. He slipped out of his seat, cards in hand, and then I heard in Japanese, "Hello, my name is Greg. I am 13 years old and I like to skateboard." More giggles.

The girls had learned some English in school, so conversation quickly flowed in both broken English and Japanese. At the next stop, in a typical Japanese gesture, one of the girls jumped off to buy a disposable camera and spent the rest of the train trip taking pictures of all of us. Greg had some new pen pals and I got my money's worth out of the language lessons.

## DO WHAT THE LOCALS DO

Even if you are traveling in the U.S., it is fun to join people on their every-day and social activities to discover regional differences, and maybe even make new friends. The kids and I are big movie buffs. In our local suburban town, which has many multiplexes, opening night at a blockbuster movie is often sold out 15 minutes in advance of show time. While vacationing in Key Largo, Florida one summer, we showed up at the local theater 40 min-utes in advance to catch the opening night of Arnold Schwartzenegger's "True Lies." No one was there and the movie house was dark. Certain I had read the show time wrong in the newspaper, the kids chastised me. "Let's wait and see what happens," I said. About 15 minutes before the show, everything came to life. The movie house lit up, the patrons arrived in one bunch, and the manager turned on the popcorn machine. As we grabbed our seats and I returned to the lobby to wait for the first batch of popcorn, two stragglers came in to buy tickets. "Are you sold out yet?" they inquired. "Wait, I'll go check," said the ticket seller. And he *left* his booth to go *hand count* the people in the theater as well as those of us buying popcorn. "Nope," he replied, "room for two more." He sold them the tickets. For a Jersey girl, that was a story to bring back home!

*When traveling overseas it is more of a challenge to create opportunities for meaningful interaction with the local populace. These tips offer some field-tested suggestions, some of which may require you to step out of your usual "foreign comfort travel zone," but the results will be worth it!*

## Suggestion #1 — Go to the movies

Most movies are produced in Hollywood, the movie capital of the world, and usually are in English with subtitles in the local language. It's a fun way to learn a few foreign colloquialisms. In many countries, the feature film is preceded by elaborate and entertaining commercials rather than movie trail-ers, offering a chance to gain cultural insight. Overseas movies often have an intermission, which offers patrons a chance to have a smoke and buy food. While waiting in line to buy the local version of popcorn, the locals are more likely to start up a conversation with you, since you obviously are not a typical tourist.

Since movie theaters are usually in residential neighborhoods, there isn't a concern for safety. In fact, you are probably safer in a local movie theater than strolling along the usual tourist routes at night, which are pickpocket heaven. In a few rare cases, it may not be safe to attend a movie at night, because of the neighborhood or local customs. Your hotel front desk or tourism office can help you select a sub-titled English-speaking movie and advise you on the safety of the neighborhood. Enjoy!

### Suggestion #2 — Take the local bus or subway to get there

This is another great way to interact with the locals and save money to boot! Once again, check with your hotel or local tourism office for routes and safety advisories.

### Suggestion #3 — After the movie, celebrate with a beer at the local pub

Sound shocking if you are traveling with young children? Not necessarily. In some countries, pubs are social centers frequented by entire families, especially in areas not frequented by tourists. While waiting in line to buy your movie tickets, ask the person next to you to recommend a nearby place for snacks or a beer. Who knows? Maybe he (or she) and his friends may join you afterwards for a lively discussion about the movie you just saw.

### Suggestion #4 — Step back to student days

One fun and educational way to interact with the locals is to visit a school. During our vacations when my kids were little, we often visited grade schools and middle schools. As they grew older we expanded our repertoire to include high schools and universities. Having grown up in a large suburban environment where high school graduating classes can number as high as 1,000 students, my children have had some lively schoolyard discussions with kids their age from small towns in remote areas of the world, including the U.S., where one-room schoolhouses are still in existence.

During one summer trip to central Alaska, the custodian of a local school was kind enough to give us a tour of the facilities. The school, which serviced grades kindergarten through twelfth grade, had a stunning colorful mural in the central hallway depicting Alaska's indigenous peoples. The custodian explained that the student population usually totaled about 200, never enough for a sports team or debating team, so schools were "bundled up" regionally to form teams and provide competition. I was surprised to see that the student lockers were quite narrow, thinner even than those found in our home state of New Jersey. "Where did the students find room for their heavy coats and boots?" I asked the custodian. He chuckled as he responded, "Oh, the kids here usually just wear a parka when it is cold. Once the temperature goes above freezing they come to school in cut-offs."

Two years ago, while hiking around Moon Island in Lake Titicaca in Bolivia, we asked our guide if we could visit the one-room schoolhouse in the distance. The teacher was happy to oblige and chatted with us during recess as we sat down cross-legged in the schoolyard. We learned that in Bolivia, due to their steady year-round climate, the school year has two separate one-month breaks rather than a long summer vacation. We also learned that in Bolivia, English teachers are in great demand but in short supply. On Moon Island the students are taught scholastic subjects in the morning and the afternoon is spent teaching life skills, such as farming and weaving. This method, rather than a full-time scholastic schedule, seemed to have greater support from the parents, and insured 100% student attendance. Within minutes the students cast aside their shyness and clustered around us. Engaging smiles and curious looks soon engulfed us. Everyone was eager to pose for pictures, including several formal poses of the class in front of the Moon Island schoolhouse, which I later sent to the school. Fortunately we had just enough pens, paper tablets, and bookmarks in our backpacks to hand to the teacher so that each student would receive something. That day we all learned a little something about each other.

**Suggestion #5 — Check out the local supermarket and pharmacy**

Whether vacationing in the U.S. or overseas, I always make it a point to stop at the local supermarket for picnic food, water, and other daily essentials. It is a great way to save money, learn about regional foods, and mingle with the locals. Checkout procedures can sometimes be an adventure. In some Scandinavian stores you are required to weigh, price, and tag your own produce on a pictorial scale. With some help from our fellow Norwegian shoppers, we soon became "pictorially" familiar with the nuances of the dozen local varieties of berries (It was a good thing, since all of them looked light green to me!). My kids had a fun time with the scale and wound up buying every type of berry in the store. In Belize the local supermarkets carry packets of wonderful Belizean spices, complete with recipes — a lightweight and inexpensive gift for the folks back home.

All throughout Central and parts of South America you can find small pharmacies with personalized service (now almost non-existent in the U.S.). Many pharmacists speak some English and will assist you in finding an over-the-counter local salve for itchy mosquito bites acquired during your jungle hikes. These salves are made from local herbs and have been used by the indigenous peoples for centuries. We found them to be cheaper and sometimes more effective than U.S.-produced ointments. If nothing else, your sojourn to the supermarket will at least teach you how to say "Cheerios" or your favorite cereal brand in the local lingo!

**Suggestion #6 — Don your soccer shoes**

Love to play sports? Enjoy going to sporting events? Soccer (or fútbol), as it is known throughout Latin America, is the number one sport worldwide. One of the best ways to immerse yourself in local culture is to get involved in sports. Soccer stadiums are found in every medium to small sized city in Central and South America. Attending a soccer match and rooting for the home team is a fun way to spend an afternoon while endearing yourself to the local denizens.

Soccer fields are ubiquitous in the small towns of Latin America, and games often spring up spontaneously. Just hang loose on the sidelines, soccer shoes in hand, and look hopeful. I guarantee within 10 or 15 minutes someone will stroll over and ask "¿Quiere jugar?" ("Wanna play?"). Broaden your smile and answer "¡Sí!"

*People are less likely to treat you as a tourist, and more like a guest in their state or country, when you "go local."*

In 1999 when my son and I returned to Hawaii for a second time, we decided to cram in four islands in two weeks. Renting a jeep on each island, we sampled many beaches, sightseeing and hiking like crazy from dawn 'til dusk. Early one morning in Maui, we spent an hour body surfing at one of the local beaches before driving the famed Hana Road. About a mile short of the Seven Sacred Pools, the usual Hana Road turnaround point, we stopped to admire a beautiful waterfall. I walked closer to get some photos and when I returned to our jeep I found my son talking to a truckload of local men and women. They had noticed his bodysurfing earlier that day and called him over to find out where he was from. Telling someone you are from New Jersey is always good for a laugh (and that was *before* HBO's show "The Sopranos!"). When the teasing died down, we asked for some hiking suggestions for our next day's excursion to

Haleakala National Park. Pretty soon we were invited to visit their home down the road.

"Home" was an extensive tented commune set in the midst of an enormous flower, fruit, and vegetable garden with a million-dollar-view of the mountains and the sea. They grew what they needed. Our hosts, a Polynesian woman and her mother, owned the land, and told us developers were putting pressure on them to sell the parcel, which had been in their family since Polynesian settlers arrived on Maui. The young men served a wonderful meal of freshly prepared fish soup, fresh fruit juice and, for dessert, a melon husk filled with fresh fruits topped with a flaming sweet sauce, which was absolutely decadent. People of all ages, interests, and ethnic backgrounds stopped by throughout the evening to chat, and we were greeted as visiting family. It was truly an enchanting evening in paradise.

Finally, well after dark, we took leave of our new friends, promising to return some day. Rather than drive back via the winding Hana Road, we decided to complete the loop back to our hotel the opposite way, via the lonely, pitch-black dirt road. Always the Nervous Nelly Night Driver, I gave my son the wheel, assuming the rental car police wouldn't catch us at that hour of the night (He was under 25). After a few unnecessary motherly directions about watching out for potholes, I finally settled in to enjoy our bumpy ride home with the moonlit ocean on our left and the dark looming volcanic peaks of Haleakala on our right. What a night!

## COME BEARING GIFTS

When you are making new friends, think about carrying tokens of appreciation to have at the ready. I am not talking about gifts for those people you contacted ahead of time and anticipate meeting, I am talking about unexpected encounters. We always carry small, lightweight items in our fanny pack or backpack. Things that look ordinary to us may be thrilling to someone from another country or climate. Some examples are:

### Pens and Pencils

Collect all of the colorful pens and pencils you can during your business meetings, conferences, and hotel stays and bring them with you on your trip. Children all over the world love to receive a colorful pen. In many third world countries pens are in scarce supply and therefore make a welcome useful gift. In the outlying areas of Syria we encountered many people, adults included, who would approach us, asking for a pen. Unprepared for the numerous requests, we ran out of them early in the trip, but came prepared with 50 of them on our second visit.

## Bookmarks

I am a bookmark collector. Every place I travel, I pick up a few as gifts, especially when I visit a U.S. national park. Just before a vacation overseas I run down to my local bookstore and buy scenic ones, encased in plastic, so they will travel well.

1. Remember my Palestinian nun friend? As a thank you for her services I offered her a selection of scenic U.S. bookmarks. She immediately chose a dreamy scene of the California coast.

2. On the semi-barren Sun Island in Lake Titicaca, Bolivia, our young hotel waiter noticed my bookmark of Redwood National Park sitting on the table. He had never seen trees that tall so, forgetting his shyness, he asked about them and where they grew. At the end of my explanation I handed him the bookmark as a gift. His face lit up and he ran back to the kitchen, where I saw him explaining the scene to his friends.

3. While on safari in Kenya I was befriended by an engaging Masai warrior. I think he was particularly fond of me because I was genuinely interested in his lifestyle and was the only one in our group who bothered to learn his Swahili name (Olaykeerohray). Everybody else called him John, his English name. As a token thank you for answering my endless questions, I rummaged through my "gift selections." What do you give a Masai warrior who lives outdoors, travels light, and has everything he needs? He was well educated and I knew he liked to read, so a bookmark seemed an ideal gift. I chose a picture of an Alaskan timber wolf with a dusting of snow on his back. The picture seemed a fitting contrast to the plains of Africa. When I handed it to him and heard his squeal of delight, I knew I had made the right choice. This time *I* was the one answering the questions. Where did this animal live? What did he eat? How did he hunt? All good warrior questions and I was prepared with the answers.

## T-Shirts

Although bulky to pack, these are a popular gift with young people overseas, especially if the shirt includes English sayings. If you don't have the opportunity to give them away, they make great packing material for fragile gifts that you plan to carry home.

## Tschotchke

While my daughter was living in Manhattan I asked her to buy a dozen or so cheap tourist gifts, commonly called "tschotchke," by our Yiddish-speaking friends, to take on our overseas vacations. Little rubber Statues of Liberty and erasers shaped like the Empire State Building made a big hit at the little one-room schoolhouse on Moon Island in Bolivia.

## Postcards

Bring a few which show the tourist attractions and scenery in your hometown area.

## Make-up

In some countries cosmetics are quite expensive and selection may be limited. I have a friend from Shanghai, China who travels to the U.S. on business once or twice a year. He always arrives with a long shopping list of cosmetics for his wife and all her female relatives.

On our first trip to Syria, the kids and I spent an overnight in the fabulous desert oasis town of Palmyra. Once a crossroads of the world, the place is full of caravan and Roman history and is almost completely devoid of tourists. After an early morning hike up to an ancient citadel, we arranged for a camel ride with one of the local Bedouins. At the end of the ride, as I reached into my fanny pack to pay the camel driver, he approached me and pointed determinedly at the lipstick next to my wallet. "Pour ma femme" ("For my wife"), he pleaded gently in French. It was an extra lipstick, which I bought for the trip and had not yet used. Without hesitation I handed it over to him. After that, we added lipsticks to our stock of travel gifts for the Middle East.

## Nature Gifts

Is there something unique near your home you can bring with you? Pinecones and seashells make great presents for someone who lives in the desert. The Navajos of Arizona make beautiful jewelry from seashells.

## A FEW MORE FIELD-TESTED SUGGESTIONS FOR MAKING FRIENDS

### Offer to take photographs of a person or family and send copies

Note the key word here is "offer." If they say no, accept their decision. In some cultures, people believe their spirit is stolen if you take their photo, or they may consider it an invasion of their privacy. My offer has never been refused once I had the opportunity to chat a bit with a person. If you don't speak the local language, try sign language, or have someone write down the question in the local language for you so you can read the words from the paper. Don't hand people the message to read — you read it. In third world countries, people are often illiterate and you will embarrass them by handing them a message they cannot read. Cameras and film are luxury items in many countries, and the offer to take photos of a family may result in several relatives and friends being called to join the photo session. I have yet to find a grandparent who refuses to have his or her photo taken with a beloved grandchild.

### Always carry a memo pad to write down names, addresses, and yes, e-mail addresses of new friends

If you are sending new friends photographs and their native language is written in something other than the Roman alphabet, have them write down their address in Chinese, Arabic, or Greek for you. When you send the photos, make a copy of the address and tape that to the envelope along with the English version of the address, thus insuring delivery.

### Carry photos of family, your house, your pet, or something personal about your life

If you are a teacher, carry a photo of your school or classroom. Showing these pictures to new friends helps them understand your way of life. We always had a photo of our house with autumn leaves as well as one of our home covered in snow. Family photos cross all cultural borders. You may think these photos will make you appear "rich" to native peoples in poor countries. You are already considered rich by the mere fact that you had the money to travel to their country. Sharing a bit of your life and family with someone does not make you a braggart.

**Once your children reach young adulthood, don't be surprised
if you are approached first by their young admirers**

In many foreign countries it is considered quite respectable for young adults
to travel with parents and other family members. More than one young Latin
lady approached me first, introducing herself, so that she could then be
introduced to my son. His height and blond good looks caught the eye of
many a pretty lady, but the fact that he was traveling with his mother and sister was the clincher. It didn't get more respectable than that.

## FINAL GOAL

If you follow my suggestions, with a little practice and a few trips under
your belt, you and your child or children will soon begin to function as a
cohesive unit. It will happen sooner than you think. One day you will board
the train or load up the rental car with a minimum of fuss and you will notice that everyone is "in tune." You are going with the flow. If you unexpectedly miss a train, you won't panic and feel the trip is ruined. Maybe there
will be a new friend waiting on the next one.

During our December trip to Japan we had planned a full day visiting the
beautiful temples of Kyoto. The day dawned cold and rainy. By the time we
visited the second temple on a hillside outside of town, my normally good-
natured young son was getting crankier and crankier. I soon discovered that
he had a hole in the sole of one of his sneakers and his foot had become
completely wet and cold inside, making him miserable. "How could you let
this happen?" I wailed. "I asked you before we left the States if we needed
to buy any new shoes and you said your sneakers were fine." "I know
Mom," he said, "but I patched it up before we left and I thought it would be
OK." My anger began to build for two reasons:

1. I knew we had to attend to his shoe problem immediately, and that meant
   heading into town to find a department store, missing seeing the other
   Kyoto temples.

2. Given the poor rate of exchange at that time between the yen and the
   dollar I was expecting to pay up to three times more for a pair of sneakers than I would back home. It was a very expensive trip to begin with,
   and now I would incur a bill of US$150 for shoes that cost US$50 in the
   States.

I fussed and I fumed all the way to the store but, as we entered, I decided to relax and enjoy the experience. Service in a Japanese department store was reputed to be legendary. Once we reached the shoe department we sat on a comfortable bench and were immediately approached by a crisply dressed young lady who gently removed Greg's wet sneakers and socks and quickly brought over a selection of sneakers and socks and a towel to dry his feet. Greg was in his glory with all of the attention. To our delight we soon found a pair of Japanese-style sneakers that cost only US$70. They were black high-tops with a huge Velcro flap over the front that made them look like Japanese rocket boots. The shoes were "way cool" and surely would make my son the envy of the schoolyard upon his return home.

Just as the salesgirl was placing the shoes on my son's feet, a middle-aged Japanese man came over to her and tapped her on the shoulder. Without a word, he ceremoniously sat down with his young son on a nearby bench. I saw a fleeting look of consternation flicker in the salesgirl's eyes. She quickly got up, bowed graciously to everyone, and then sped away like a Japanese bullet train. My daughter leaned over to Greg and me and said, "Do you understand what is happening here?" "No," I said. "Please clue me in." My daughter replied, "Well, in Japan the man is served first, before a woman. Since we are foreigners I don't know how the salesgirl is going to handle this situation. I think we just threw the detailed Japanese social structure for a loop." Soon thereafter our salesgirl returned with a serene look of triumph on her face. She had borrowed the salesgirl from the nearby men's shirt department to serve the newly arrived customer.

Now it was time to pay for the shoes. Our salesgirl motioned for me to stay seated while she took my credit card. As she departed I said to my daughter, "Only in Japan would I trust someone to walk away with my credit card. According to the tour books, it is supposed to be safe." My daughter chuckled, "The average Japanese person is very honest, Mom, however many high-ranking executives have recently been accused of white collar crime. I often read in the papers about some high-level financial scandal in a large Japanese company. It is one of the many dichotomies that exist in Japan."

So we missed seeing a few temples that day, but we had a first-hand cultural experience, and my son secured some primo "Show and Tell" sneakers. Some of the best travel stories emerge from circumstances that go awry.

Vacations won't go smoothly all the time, but when they do, you will all be relaxed and having fun. Even when they don't, you still might have fun. When that happens and you are open to new adventures, people will be drawn to you. This doesn't happen magically and it does take practice. Athletes train daily so they can be "in the zone" (at peak performance) as frequently as possible. Travel is a bit like that. The more you do it, the more polished you become. We hope the recommendations in this book assist you in your journey to becoming a confident well-traveled single parent family.

Oh, and one last bit of advice: Remember to wear a bright smile. It speaks a universal language.

# III

# *Storing and Reliving the Memories*
# *Recollection and Pay-Off*

## RECOLLECTION

Now that you have returned from your trip, several tasks demand your immediate attention: laundry, restocking the fridge, and paying your bills. Then there are the projects at work that demand your attention after a one or two-week absence. The responsibilities of being a single parent weigh heavily after a long vacation trip. Once your vacation photos are developed, it is tempting to shove them in a drawer as their final resting place. Don't! Make the time to create a special memory of your trip, something that you and the children can refer back to frequently and share with friends and family.

### PHOTO ALBUMS

Photography is one of my hobbies, so I take a lot of pictures. I create a photo album for each major vacation. Through the years I have learned a few things that make our photo albums visually interesting as well as informative:

➢ Tuck a copy of your itinerary inside the front of the photo album. This will help you remember what you did and the places you visited, even after the details fade from memory.

➢ Tape a simple map inside the front cover showing where you traveled. I usually cut out a map from a tour brochure or tourist literature. It is a big help to all of your geographically challenged American friends.

➢ Trash *all* repetitive or poor-quality photos. No one wants to see them. Exceptions might be a rarely seen animal that you snapped so that you can claim bragging rights.

During a trip to the Amazon we spent one evening caiman hunting in canoes. Caimans are the Amazon version of an alligator. Our guide shone a powerful spotlight across the river until she spotted a baby caiman hiding in the rushes. Only the caiman's eye was showing through the reeds. We paddled in right next to it. Not knowing if the caiman would "spook," I kept shooting photos until we came within inches (7 to 8 centimeters) and I got the perfect shot. When I returned home, I posted the final shot in my album, labeled it "The eye of a caiman," and discarded the eight shots that preceded it.

➤ Shoot a variety of photos, some with scenery and some with people. Whenever possible, take photos that tell a story or portray a sequence of events.

While in Bolivia we visited a magnificent outdoor museum that housed an exhibit of reed boat making. Presiding over the exhibit was José Lamachi, the youngest of the three brothers who assisted Thor Heyerdahl in building the reed boat for one of Thor's famous voyages. With a series of close-up and distant shots I was able to portray how the reed was woven by hand to make a bundle tight enough to withstand an ocean voyage.

➤ At each significant or scenic spot, have someone take a picture of everyone in your family. Pick out the best shot and make it the signature shot of your trip. Enlarge it, frame it, and put a copy of it on the front cover or front page of your photo album.

We learned from experience that the best photographers are the Japanese. Without exception they take a photo that is properly centered and focused. When the Japanese economy was hot, we had no problem finding them at scenic spots around the world. When their economy spiraled downward, we began searching for German tourists to take our signature photos, and failing that, we asked anyone holding an expensive camera to take our signature photo.

➤ When you prepare your photo album, tape a typed or handwritten title onto the photos that have special significance that need to be identified. This allows your viewer to look at your album at his or her own pace, asking questions only as needed. Nothing is more annoying than having someone standing over your shoulders showing photos explaining every detail at *their* pace.

➢ When storing your photo albums, tape the title of the trip on the side panel as well as the front of the album for easy retrieval.

➢ Make it a point to prepare the photo album as quickly as possible after your pictures are developed. Get the kids to help. I did this religiously when the kids were little. When both of my kids were in soccer, I was so pressed for time after our summer vacation I fell behind on this task and consequently there are still five years worth of travel photos sitting in a box waiting for a home. After my Soccer Mom period was finished, my son volunteered to help with the photo albums, and since then we have kept them up-to-date.

Photography is an expensive hobby. One way to save money on film development is by using an online processing service, such as www.Snapfish.com. I have used their services and was pleased. At no cost they will develop and scan your photos, post them on their Web site, and mail you the prints and negatives. You only pay regular first class mailing costs. The scanned photos are quite good, and you have the ability to send them to friends and family over the Internet. The prints are sometimes not as good as the professional photo service I use locally, but in that case I take a few negatives to my local photo service and have them reprinted. I recommend enrolling online for these services several weeks before your departure so your mailing envelopes are in hand when you return from your vacation.

## SLIDES AND VIDEOS

The advice I gave about editing film or slides to deliver a nice storytelling presentation also applies to these two media. Label and store your slides and videos with an itinerary copy attached. Slides make a wonderful tool for school presentations.

## DIARIES

Earlier in the book I discussed how children should ask their teachers for research assistance. The teachers always volunteered to do so, but in return they asked my son or daughter to keep a diary of the trip and deliver a class presentation upon returning to school. The diaries turned out to be a great idea. When the kids were too little to write, I wrote down their impressions for them. This only need be a paragraph or two each night. Rather than write down what we did, which was already on the itinerary, I asked my kids for their impressions of the people, the things we did and saw, and what they did or didn't like. You needn't spend the money for a leather-bound diary; any secretarial pad or theme book will do just as well.

The summer that my children turned 10 and 17 we traveled throughout Denmark, Norway, Sweden, and Finland, with a side trip to Leningrad (now called St. Petersburg, Russia). That summer I decided to keep a three-way diary. Every time we boarded a boat, ferry, or train I pulled out my steno pad and asked my kids for their impressions of the last 12 hours. I wrote down their unedited comments. By the end of the first week it was interesting to see how each of us viewed the trip from an entirely different perspective. Although there were commonalties, each of us had noticed things the others had not. We learned from each other.

I began paying more attention to the conveyances that fascinated my young son. He happily dragged me all over the deck of the ferryboats, showing me how the pulleys and ramps worked, and told me why he liked to talk about them in the diary. My teen-age daughter was focused on the lifestyles of the young people she met and observed. She pointed out to us that teen-agers in Scandinavia seemed to be more mature and much more outdoorsy. They were unaffected by the frequent showers and not always perfect climate; outdoor activities continued, rain or shine. The local young people were not so concerned about getting muddy or wet or being a bit physically uncomfortable.

Being the frugal Single Mom, many of my diary entries focused on the rate of exchange in each country and the value of the goods or food we purchased. By the time we reached Sweden, the third country on our itinerary, my son said to me, "Mom, I don't really understand this rate of exchange thing. Can you explain it to me and tell me why it is so important?" I explained in simple terms how our dollar has different values in different countries and the importance of being aware of the fluctuations should one decide to work or go to college in a foreign country. I knew he wasn't grasping the abstract concept, so I gave him an example he could understand. When we travel to a foreign country we always stop once in a local McDonald's. It's fun, cheap, the food is familiar, and the paper menu in all of those foreign languages makes a great souvenir. So I whipped out my calculator and said to my son, "Greg, you and I and your sister always order exactly the same things when we eat at McDonalds. At home that meal for the three of us costs US$7.48 (These were 1988 prices). When we had that meal in Denmark it cost 55 Danish Kroner, but the value of that meal in U.S. dollars was US$13.38. When we ate that same meal in Norway, the cost was 55 Norwegian Kroner, but its value in U.S. dollars was US$15.56. Here in Sweden, the same McDonalds meal cost 68 Swedish Kroner, but its value in U.S. dollars is a whopping US$21.45. So, as you can see, things in Denmark and Norway cost twice as much to buy as they do in the U.S., but in Sweden food cost us three times as much."

About seven years later, when my daughter had finished college and launched a successful financial career on Wall Street, she called me from her office one day. "Mom," she chuckled, "I am sitting here reading *The Economist*. The article talks about the value of the dollar against the major economies of the world. They use about a dozen barometers to measure the dollar's value. Right up on top of the barometer list is the Big Mac! You were way ahead of Wall Street, Mom."

## SCRAPBOOKS

For small children, this may be the answer to storing their memories. Little kids love to save things that we as adults consider inconsequential, but years later, they provide sweet memories of a trip. Recently I pulled out an old scrapbook and photo album from my summer as an exchange student in Switzerland. I spent a weekend at a reunion with the other exchange students who lived in nearby villages in Switzerland. We hadn't seen one another in more than 30 years. We all enjoyed the photos and slides, but the scrapbook brought back some interesting memories we had forgotten.

## PAYOFF

Besides the obvious — precious time spent with your children in joint activities — travel gives your children a wonderful pay-off in terms of education and sophistication, whether you travel overseas or within the borders of the U.S. Children at any age benefit from travel, and the benefits are sometimes unforeseen and often unexpected. Some examples:

A few months after our return from our first single parent trip to Europe I took my 5-year-old son to my office one evening so I could catch up on work. At that time I was managing a suburban travel agency located in a corporate high-rise building. While we were there, a couple came in thinking the office was open. It became obvious they were looking for some free information and had no intention of making reservations. When my normally shy son heard the word "Paris," he emerged from his hiding place under the desk and cheerily chirped, "We were in Paris!" The woman turned to him and said, "What did you think of it?" My son replied, "I liked it. There were lots of things to do and plenty of good things to eat." As I opened the map of Paris, my son pointed to the section of town where we stayed and said, "That's where we stayed. That's the eighth ... what do you call it, Mom?" "Arrondissement," I said. "That was a good place," my son said. "We were close to everything." By this time the woman and my son had built a rapport. She asked him how long he spent in Paris. "Three days," he replied. "And was that enough time?" she queried. He replied. "It was enough for us." Then my son remembered his shyness, retreated under the desk, and the couple left. The next morning the husband came in and booked a two-week trip to Paris and Amsterdam. He told me his wife was so impressed with what my son knew that they felt they could trust me with their vacation reservations.

On that same trip my 12-year-old daughter gave my son and me a wonderful guided tour of the Château de Chillon in Switzerland. She had just studied castles in school and wanted to guide us around the château. Within minutes she warmed up to her role and was leading us around with an explanation for each room's purpose. After that she was appointed the "Castle Expert" of the family.

Years later, in the summer of 1995, my kids and I visited Syria for the first time. Our Syrian friend, who is a superb guide, took us to visit a Kurdish village up in the hills outside of Aleppo. We learned from our friend that the Kurds, with a population of about 20 million, represent the largest ethnic group in the world without a country to call their own. The Kurds prefer a simple lifestyle, are spread over five countries, and differ from their fellow Middle Easterners in that they are of Aryan origin. As we drank from a pure Kurdish well that was more than 1000 years old, I said to my son, "You know Greg, the next time you hear about the Kurds in the news, it will have some meaning to you."

The next day we flew home, and the day after my son started his first day of college. His first class was World Politics, and the newspaper headlines that morning featured Sadam Hussein's confrontation with the Iraqui Kurds. The teacher asked if anyone in the class knew anything about the Kurds. My son raised his hand. After he spoke for a few minutes, the teacher asked my son how he knew so much. Greg explained he had visited a Kurdish village. "When was that?" queried the teacher. "The day before yesterday," answered my son. The teacher shook her head and said, "Why don't you get up here and teach this class?" After that sterling start, my son had no problems getting a good grade.

Not all payoff stories are that dramatic, but you will find travel helps children become more confident of their abilities and knowledge. Encourage your child to give school presentations to share their experiences with classmates. Everyone will benefit: the students, the teacher, and most of all, your child.

# IV

## Single Parent Dads Tell Their Stories

I observed that a sizeable percentage of my Web site readers on www.Single ParentTravel.net were single dads. Judging by the content of their e-mail messages, their concerns about traveling as a single parent with their kid(s) were identical to those of single moms — including finding activities that appealed to both parent and child, bonding with the child, and safety concerns. Many single dads planned to travel with very young children, and their needs were rarely addressed and their voices were not heard.

Some people have the misconception that men can't perform as well as women when it comes to nurturing and caring for children, and they cannot multi-task or handle children's needs as well as women, especially in stressful situations or environments, such as traveling to unfamiliar places. Based on feedback I receive on my Web site, I knew this was not true. So, I decided to put a call out requesting travel stories from Single Parent Dads. I placed no restrictions on their stories. I simply asked them to write from the heart, and that is exactly what they did.

I present to you seven delightful, informative, and entertaining travel stories. The dads range in age from 20s to 70s; the children from pre-school to post-college. Each story is very different, but each has a common theme of love and caring coupled with strong doses of humor. The stories remain intact as originally written, and were edited only for clarity.

Readers are welcome to send in comments or questions about these stories and their authors to Brenda@SingleParentTravel.net. All comments will be forwarded to the respective author.

## THE ORIGINAL STAIRMASTER: A TALE OF MUNDO MAYA
### By LEWIS FLINKMAN

*Lewis is a 44-year-old real estate broker living and working in West Los Angeles. He spends his free time mindfully planning his next trip. Lewis writes, "After taking an art history class at the local junior college I took several trips to Europe and saw the sites I had studied. Studying the places I am traveling to, the cultures, antiquities, flora and fauna, really adds to the overall experience. I now try to take my son to interesting places every summer. After the Maya trip we went to Thailand last year, and are now off to the Peruvian Amazon and Machu Picchu. My hope is that is that his outer experiences in this world gained from traveling at a young age will enrich his inner world so he has a desire to give back in the future.*

Having traveled abroad only once with my son to the self-contained world of a Mexican Club Med when he was 5, I pondered where to take him when he was 7. He requested a trip to the pyramids in Egypt. Egypt just didn't feel safe to me at the time, and I knew I would not have a good time if I went somewhere where I have mixed feelings. I thought he might have gotten the idea for Egypt from a Wild Thornbury's cartoon episode on Nickelodeon TV, but he told me it was actually a Discovery Channel show on mummies. That same week I stumbled upon a book about the Mayan Civilization in the neighborhood bookstore/coffee house, and the beginnings of an idea for a trip came to me. There were pyramids in the Mayan Empire, lots of them, and soon my son was quite excited about the idea of traveling there. The period of the Mayan Civilization known as the Late Classic Period appeared to have some of the most interesting sites. The place known as Palenque in southern Mexico seemed to be something special. Tikal in Guatemala, along with Copan in Honduras were also well represented in the book, and all had been significant Mayan cultural centers.

If all of these places had been in one country, booking an organized tour would not have been my first choice, but given the extensive international border crossings, plus traveling with a child, the use of a formal tour seemed a good idea. A company called Mayatour, which I found on the Internet, had the exact itinerary I wanted, and the travel agent said we could even visit the Children's Museum in Guatemala City the first day.

To keep my son involved, I kept talking to him about the trip and reading to him about the Mayan Civilization. He was particularly excited about the prospect of climbing the pyramids. We even practiced for our adventure by walking up many flights of stairs as the opportunity presented itself.

He wouldn't take his malaria pills, but the Center For Disease Control Web site didn't list these areas as major threats. Figuring that the same pills were also the cure if he got malaria, it seemed that we'd cross that bridge if we had to. We both got our other required shots, in this case, Hepatitis and Typhoid, and were on our way. It's a good idea to get these shots way ahead of time, since they are not effective unless taken a certain amount of time before traveling.

This trip ended up being one of my all-time favorites. Traveling with my son let me see things from an entirely different perspective, as well as do things that an adult alone wouldn't do, like going to the Children's Museum in Guatemala City. He wasn't as thrilled with the other museums in Guate-mala City, Palenque, or Copan, but hey, he's a kid. When I was a kid I just wanted to have fun, and boy did he ever. He climbed pyramids, saw lots of wildlife, flew in a variety of different airplanes from seven-seaters to 707s, and got to stay in the Holiday Inn in Guatemala City. For some reason he likes Sheratons and Holiday Inns a lot. This worried me, because I knew most of our lodgings were going to be a bit more modest, and wouldn't have things like the hospitality rooms he so covets. But it worked out OK.

He didn't take up our guide's request in Palenque to see a boa constrictor that had just finished eating in the jungle. The jungle in general scared him a little, but I know he has my genes so he'll grow out of it. He finally fi-gured out that most of the things there didn't want to eat him (except the mosquitoes) and started to enjoy our little treks through the rain forest. The howler monkeys in Tikal were really something. They roar like lions or some other wild beast from the depths of your imagination, and if you didn't know they were monkeys you definitely would walk quickly in the oppo-site direction. Costa Rica didn't have anything on that place as far as the wildlife goes! My son took a liking to the Mayan rain god Chac, and enjo-yed venturing into his crypt, where he met the rather large spider guarding it. He composed a very spooky melody in honor of the place.

Sitting on the top of the Pyramid of the Sun in Palenque we witnessed hun-dreds, maybe thousands, of dragonflies hovering at eye level for what seemed an eternity. They appeared from nowhere, and disappeared just as suddenly. It was such a magical moment — awe-inspiring. Then they vanished, just like the Mayan Civilization. No one is sure exactly why the Mayans vanished. Their descendents are the indigenous peoples who still populate the area. These people seem to be always smiling, like they know some deep secret about life and all its mysteries. The Mayans were also expert astronomers, far more advanced than Europe during the same period. It's now months after our trip, and my son has decided he wants to be an astronomer.

In Copan, on the way back to Guatemala, we stopped at a butterfly farm. It was priceless to watch my son seeing butterflies being born.

The only major problem occurred at the airport on the way from Flores, Guatemala to Palenque, Mexico. There was a huge airport tax that had to be paid, in cash, on the spot, or they wouldn't let us get on the plane. At this point we were on our own, and were not scheduled to meet our guide until we arrived at the Palenque site. Fortunately I had the cash to pay the tax, but I pity the soul who thought that the tour agency included this in the price of the trip. Having paid so much for a custom trip, since the tax wasn't included, it should have at least been mentioned beforehand.

Thankfully I purchased a Sony digital video/still camera before the trip, so I have hours and hours of video and a hundred photos to document the trip in the event my son ever accuses me of not taking him to really cool places when he was young.

## CAMPING AND CANOEING THE ADIRONDACKS
### By MARDEN ELWELL

*Marden (Mardy) Elwell is a lifelong outdoor enthusiast currently residing in South Jersey. His past activities, besides canoeing, have included hiking, skiing, and camping. As a former infantry officer, Army aviator, and Alaskan bush pilot, he is as comfortable in the air as he is on land or water. Mardy writes, "Being a teacher I am able to pursue my love of the outdoors for several weeks each summer. Looking forward to retirement in the near future, I recently bought a camper. My children are grown so I travel alone now, but I treasure the memories of time spent with them doing outdoor activities, which they enjoy as much as I do."*

*Author's Note:* Readers may have noticed Mardy has the same last name as the author of the book. Yes, Mardy is the author's ex-husband and father of Monique and Gregory.

My son Greg was 11-years-old and I was 59 when we ventured forth on our first canoeing and camping trip in the Adirondacks of upstate New York. I was out of shape, so we didn't get very far, nor did we go very fast. The canoes that we rented are heavy. A 15 or 16 footer is about 60–65 pounds, and it gets exponentially heavier with every step that you carry it, especially in the heat, with the mosquitoes and the black flies competing for your attention. The first "carry" was a little over a mile long, some of it uphill. Believe me, that was a long, long, painful afternoon. It was also educational in the sense that I now know the precise definition of pain. Never again did I go on a canoe trip without first getting in shape. I mean in *good* shape. I continued to carry those canoes well into my middle 60s. Now that I am in my 70s, it gives me great pleasure to let you know that Greg, who is now in his 20s, does all the carrying. I want you to know that when he complains about the pain, it gives me even greater pleasure to remind him of what he can expect in the next 40 or so years. Life is sweet.

On our first trip, Greg was a passenger in the front of the canoe, and relished the discovery of all the birds and butterflies and bears and beavers that crossed our path. At the campsite I sent him to gather firewood and showed him which was good wood and which was not, and how to arrange it by size. He was fascinated with constructing a fire and the fact that it could be started with one match. Just as important, I taught him the difference between a cooking fire and a roaring campfire. He learned that a roaring campfire is more fun.

Each day of our trip he learned a little more. Now as a young man, he does most of the paddling and steering and some of the navigating. Certainly there is no navigational challenge in a small lake or river, but it is a different matter on some of the larger lakes. Although the shores are visible in the distance, it is very difficult to see clearly from water level, even when the lake is smooth. Sometimes, when the wind blows, the waves try to get into the canoe with us. At no time did I ever get the urge to stand up in the canoe in the middle of the lake to get a better look.

Nowadays, when we cut across some of the large lakes, we discuss all the aspects of navigating and the logic behind making those decisions. We both constantly hone our skills and share the enjoyment and satisfaction of solving these problems. Our positions in the canoe are now reversed. I sit in the front and when there is a need to go faster, all I have to do is to shout "TURBO BOOST!" Did I say life is sweet?

It was on one of these trips in the Adirondacks that we saw our first set of beaver dams, which are really very large piles of twigs and branches. It's astounding to see the sheer mass of these piles. They look much more porous than I originally imagined. It appears that they do not totally block the water but slow it down so there is buildup of water. At any rate, it sure does the trick. I was fascinated to see that each dam raises the water only a few inches. However, after we had passed over several dams, we saw that the overall effect raised the water high enough to cause flooding.

I remember how difficult it was trying to get a fully loaded canoe over those dams. Actually, it was *damn* tough (Sorry, I hate when I do that). The bottom of the canoe would hang up on the top of the dam and we had to push and pull while trying to keep our footing on the pile of twigs and branches. Our passing caused no damage to the dams at all. It was quite pleasant as we used the opportunity to stand up, stretch our legs, and savor the sights of the wild flowers, the sky, and the clouds. We only saw dams on that river one year and have been through there many times since, but, alas, they are all gone now. I don't know why.

We were also surprised to find out that beavers are active at night.

*Things we learned from our trips:*

➢ Bring plenty of water and a pot to make tea or coffee when the fresh water runs out. Lake and river water should never be considered safe to drink unless boiled.

➢ Bring an old pair of gloves to reduce the chance of blisters forming from paddling all day. I found that they are also handy around the fire in place of a potholder.

➢ Take along a good water repellant hat with a wide brim and a string. It's better than a baseball cap, which can't protect the back of your neck when the afternoon sun is bearing down on you.

➢ Do bring a few of the very large thick candles to use in the lean-tos at night. Believe it or not, one or two will be more than adequate. This creates such a restful and soothing ambiance; you'll always remember it with pleasure. It may just be the highlight of your trip. (*Author's Note:* Forest-fire phobic Westerners will take issue with the preceding statement. Please note that Adirondack forests are most and frequently wet from rain or snowstorms. Readers should use their own best judgment or bring a flashlight with batteries).

➢ Bring a couple of large sponges to keep the bottom of the canoe dry

➢ When the canoe on your shoulders gets so heavy that you want to drop it, *don't!* The most strenuous aspect of carrying a canoe is getting it from the ground up to your shoulders. One remedy is to angle it with the back end on the ground and the front end resting up on the limb of a tree. It saves a lot of effort. Trust me!

➢ Keep your menu simple.

Remember that the object of the first few trips is to have fun with your child. I never felt that this was an endurance test or an imperative to get from Point A to Point B at all costs. About six days into our first canoe trip, my 11-year-old son woke up one morning and said, " Can we go home? I miss Mommy." Without hesitating I assured him that we would pack up first thing and go right home and that Mommy missed him too. Up until that time he was thoroughly enjoying the pleasures of the trip, and that's what I wanted to have him store in his memory. It worked. We have gone back canoeing many times and plan to again for many more.

*If you would like to canoe the Adirondack Waterways, here are some facts and procedures to get you started:*

➢ There are more than 2000 lakes in the Adirondack Wilderness Region, all of which are beautiful. On a one- or two-week canoeing trip it is possible to see several dozen. New York State maintains the Adirondack Canoe Route, which connects lakes and streams and rivers by well-marked trails. The first summer we covered 35 miles, and now cover up to 100 miles on a seven to 10-day canoe trip. It is necessary to carry the canoe and luggage over the portages, which are called "carries" in the Adirondacks. Surrounding the lakes are softly curved mountains with lots of pine, hemlock, and balsam trees. The scent is intoxicating, especially after a fresh rain.

➤ The Adirondack Canoe Routes start at Old Forge, New York and lead to the East. You can branch off into the wilderness or choose to go right through populated areas. A night in the wilderness by a crackling fire could be followed by a night in a motel. Three-sided log lean-tos are located at frequent intervals. Grocery stores are about two to three days apart and out-of-staters will be happy to learn they stock beer. Provisions such as canned goods may be "cached" (hidden along your planned canoe route) so you don't have to carry them between lakes.

➤ Maps are indispensable for the trip. No trip should be attempted without them. For maps, rules, and data on DEC campsites write to:

The New York State Department of Environmental Conservation
Albany, New York 12233

➤ Another handy brochure entitled "Canoe Franklin County" may be obtained by writing to:

The Director, Department of Tourism
63 West Main Street, Box 5
Malone, New York 12953

➤ Lastly, be sure to pick up the large, multi-colored map called the Adirondack Canoe Map. It is a topographical map with lots of excellent detail. Having this in your canoe with you will make your trip more enjoyable and your navigation a lot more precise. There is plenty of space in the margins for keeping a diary of time and distances. Store it in a large clear plastic Ziploc® bag to keep it dry. This map is on sale in grocery stores, diners and anywhere postcards are sold in the Adirondack Region.

➤ Your preparation at the start of the trip can set the tone for the days and nights to come. We start our trip at the Old Forge Marina and make arrangements with the proprietors to leave our car there and to pick us up at our canoe trip termination point. (Depending on car traffic and the distance you canoe, it may take several hours for your "ride" to arrive once you make that phone call for pick-up service). Experience has taught us to keep the first day's travel short. We use the first day to make any necessary campsite reservations and store our canned goods along our planned route. This is where the multi-colored "Adirondack Canoe Map" comes in handy.

*If readers would like to contact the author of this article for further information on the Adirondacks, they may do through the Web site at www.Single ParentTravel.net or e-mail Brenda@SingleParentTravel.net.*

## PACIFIC NORTHWEST TRIP 2000
### By DON BAHAM

*Don Baham is a 23-year-old network administrator residing in the Seattle area. Don writes: "After living in California my entire life, moving to the Pacific Northwest in January of 2001 was quite a change. The move brought me closer to my beautiful 3-year-old daughter, Taylor. She is the best part of my marriage, which ended three years ago. Miles had separated us for almost a year. Each month I would fly up north to bring her home for a long weekend, but I just couldn't imagine living so far from her anymore. Now we are only five minutes apart, and we get to see each other regularly. She is such a joy! We enjoy going to church, playing at the park, taking walks, riding our bikes, and doing anything that allows us to spend time together."*

It was almost midnight, and I still hadn't finished packing the minivan. "Well, we are only going to be camping for a couple of days," I thought. "I guess I have everything." The next morning my 2-year-old daughter, Taylor, and I would begin our trip from the San Francisco Bay Area to the San Juan Islands off the coast of Washington State, via the Oregon coast.

Our route took us north on Interstate 5 to Grant's Pass, where we drove on Highway 199 to coastal route US 101. Once we reached Highway 199 outside of Grant's Pass, Oregon, Taylor drifted off to sleep, and I was able to survey my surroundings. I had never seen a place so green and alive with flora. The 100-mile stretch between I-5 and US 101 was one of the most beautiful drives I have ever taken!

We spent our first night camping at Harris Beach State Park near Brookings, Oregon. Unfortunately, it was raining. I had the bright idea of getting a canopy for the picnic table so that we could eat and stay dry. As I started to assemble my canopy, I read, "Requires three adults for assembly." Oh, wonderful! One adult and a 2-year-old fall a little short of three adults. After about 30 minutes of futility, I gave up.

The next day, we packed up our wet gear and headed to Beverly Beach State Park, about six hours north, to camp for the night. We started up the coast of Oregon, ready for fun and adventure. Beautiful weather followed us all the way up the coast for the next two days. What a great drive!

We discovered a Wildlife Safari Game Park near Bandon, Oregon. We were able to see wild animals up close and play with seven-week old tiger kittens! That was an experience that Taylor and I won't forget.

Along the way keep your eyes open, because there is a vista point that is a great place to take a picture of Heceta Head lighthouse.

I decided not to brave the great outdoors another night, so instead we spent the night in a motel in the small town of Newport, Oregon. Newport has a small bay dotted with fishing trollers traveling back and forth from the Pacific, and sea lions relaxing on the docks. We visited an underwater aquarium, where tanks were filled with all kinds of creatures from the deep. After the aquarium we walked across the street and had dinner at the Rogue Ale House (home of — you guessed it — Rogue Ales). They had a good kids' menu, crayons, and toys for Taylor to play with, and good food and beer for me. Perfect!

The next morning we left Newport and continued up the coast to Tillamook to see Cape Meares Lighthouse. Just south of Tillamook, we took a detour to Munson Creek Falls. It is about a half-mile drive off US 101 on a gravel road. The quarter-mile hike from the parking area to the base of the falls is well worth the view. Just a side note, Munson Creek Falls is the highest falls in Oregon.

After entering Tillamook, we quickly made our way towards the coast to the Cape Meares lighthouse. It took about 40 minutes to get there after getting off US 101. I recommend this spot to everyone! It isn't a tall lighthouse, but it is rich in history and has a spectacular view. Visitors are able to climb the spiral staircase to the top of the lighthouse and explore. We enjoyed our lunch at the one of the many picnic tables on the grounds. 'The Octopus Tree' grows on a walking path near the lighthouse. This Sitka Spruce has eight "arms" that split off from the main trunk. Great picture spot! I took several with Taylor standing in front.

After leaving the lighthouse, we headed back towards Tillamook where we toured the Air Museum. After leaving the air museum, we headed North on 101 for about five miles, then headed inland on Highway 106 towards Portland. That ended our journey up the Oregon Coast. Next, we would head for the San Juan Islands in Washington.

The next morning we drove to Anacortes to catch the 2 p.m. ferry to Friday Harbor on San Juan Island. We spent two nights in Friday Harbor. This busy little town is lined with shops and restaurants. Taylor's favorite meal is "skab etti," so we dined that evening at Bella Luna, a great family-style Italian restaurant. After enjoying our meal, we drove to a neighborhood park so that Taylor could stretch her legs before going to bed. We arrived at the Discovery Inn ready for a good night's sleep. The Discovery Inn is a pleasant and affordable place, and we were happy we had made the choice to stay there.

The next day we went whale watching with San Juan Excursions. We were fortunate enough to spot an Orca whale from one of the local pods and a Minke whale during the trip. Taylor probably would have appreciated whale-watching more had she been a little older.

After whale watching, we drove around San Juan Island. First, we headed for Roche Harbor, on the opposite side of the island, about 15 minutes away. Roche Harbor's main attractions, besides a place to dock boats and seaplanes, are the boardwalk, a few shops, and the old Roche Harbor Hotel.

Shortly after leaving the harbor we came to an interesting historical site, the British Camp National Park, once occupied by both the British and the United States. There are several restored buildings on the grounds, which used to be a fort. We had ice cream melting in the ice chest, which I purchased at the boardwalk in Roche Harbor, so after a short stay we headed off again in search of Limekiln (Whale Watch) State Park.

After arriving at the park, we found a lookout with a half wall surrounding several picnic tables, perfect for snacking and watching the water for whales or porpoises. A short walk meandering through the trees next to the shore led to a rocky open area next to Limekiln lighthouse. What a beautiful setting! Taylor played and collected rocks (one of her favorite pastimes) while I recorded the sunset over Victoria, British Columbia and watched porpoises jumping out of the water nearby. It was picturesque, to say the very least.

Late the next morning we left the San Juan Islands, taking I-5 south to Seattle. Taylor was going back to her Mom's this day, so this was the last day of fun. We arrived downtown in the early afternoon, grabbed a quick bite to eat, and headed for the Space Needle. Taylor's admission was free since she is under 5 years old. The Space Needle affords a beautiful view of the city and its surroundings. Snowcapped Mt. Rainer towered to the south, and Mt. Baker stood majestically to the northeast — a great end to a wonderful day spent together.

As I headed to the place where Taylor's mother and I had agreed to meet, I reflected on the past two weeks that Taylor and I had shared, and couldn't imagine time better spent.

## TRIP TO UNIVERSAL STUDIOS AND WALT DISNEY WORLD FLORIDA
### By VICTOR KATZ

*I am 39 years old and divorced. I care for my children 50% of the time. Lauren will be 9 in July and Michael was 6 in March of 2002. I am a veterinarian with an office in Gaithersburg, Maryland. My children and I have a great relationship. We love to do things together and travel. I consider vacations with them as what they are — fun vacations with my family. The trips are never chores if planned accordingly. We call them adventures.*

A few people definitely thought that I was crazy taking two small children to these places by myself. They thought I might need intensive therapy when I got back from the trip. Or was it intensive therapy for wanting to go in the first place? Good question! Anyway, the trip had its challenges, but with good planning, the challenges were met and handled easily.

Challenge One was the plane trip. We flew from Washington, D. C. to Orlando, Florida. How was I going to keep an 8- and a 5-year-old entertained without finding myself wanting to practice sky diving somewhere over Georgia? My children both love music. They both have individual CD players. They chose their CDs to bring on the trip. They also had Game Boys®. This also helped entertain them. All right, I am cheating. I let electronic gadgetry baby-sit my kids on the plane, but I was able to relax and plow into one of my own novels. This was a plus because I hate flying. Of course I brought the endless supply of juice boxes, snacks, and munchies for those hungry tummies at 29,000 feet. We had many compliments from the flight crew and several passengers about how "well behaved" we were. Thank you, Nintendo®.

Challenge Two was waiting in line for rides. This was easy to take care of. If you ever go to Universal Studios/Islands of Adventure, STAY ON THE PROPERTY! We used the Hard Rock Hotel for our lodging. This is one of the hotels on the resort. Your room key gets you to the front of the line of just about all of the major attractions. This is well worth the extra expense. My son loved the Spider Man ride at Islands of Adventure. There were times when this ride had a two- to three-hour-wait. When we showed our room key to the ride attendant, our wait was never more than 10 minutes (Disney has a fast pass system. You can get a ticket for a specific time for certain attractions. This also helped, but was not as convenient as the Hard Rock Hotel room key at Universal Studios).

Universal also does the "Eat Breakfast with The Tunes" thing (AKA Disney clone). The kids loved eating breakfast with Woody Woodpecker and Scooby

Doo, among others. I will say that the Tune Breakfast at Universal was far less crowded than Disney's. My kids were the only children in the restaurant at one time. They got a lot of individual attention.

Challenge Number Three was "Potty Breaks." What to do with Lauren when she needed to go and what to do with Lauren when Michael or I needed to go? For Lauren's calls to nature, it was easier. We walked up to the bathroom and I indicated which door to go in and out. You need to be careful. Some bathrooms have multiple entrances and exits. You may be waiting by a door and find out your little one exited on the other side of the park. It isn't that bad, but you can get nervous. We discussed all of this ahead of time, before the need for speed. Lauren was told what door to go in and out of. Michael and I waited patiently until she was done. When it was Michael's or my turn, it was a little more stressful. I had Lauren wait by the door while Michael and I went in. She was always within earshot if she needed me. It really is very safe. Park attendants watch closely for lost children or children in distress either at Disney or Universal. I felt very safe with the kids at both parks.

Challenge Number Four: How to eat at the parks without running up the national debt? I will say two words: Kids Meals. Kids Meals. Kids Meals. Oh, did I forget to mention Kids Meals? Kids meals at both parks are large. You can often split a children's meal between two. Sometimes an appetizer is necessary. The parks are great with these meals. They usually come with a hat or some toy. I was able to get the meal I wanted, i.e., tuna burger and a beer at Margaritaville at Universal Studios. Michael and Lauren had their grilled cheese sandwiches. Lauren is also hooked on Virgin Piña Coladas. The children's meals are not that expensive, either.

Both parks will let you carry in bottled water. This works out well. You can refill the water bottles at many fountains to carry around the park with you. You need to keep hydrated while walking around in the summer heat.

Overall, the challenges were very minimal. Both parks were a blast. We all had a great time doing the attractions. Disney is Disney. It is always special. Universal Studios was a pleasant surprise. The days were long. We hit the parks in early morning, took a break by the pool at midday, and then went back to the parks in the evening. The pool at the Hard Rock Hotel was huge. They had a sand beach around the pool, a huge water slide, and even showed movies by poolside at night.

Checking into Disney was always a treat. When we checked in the "Disney Cast Member" gave each of us a pin for trading. The children could go up to "Disney Cast Members" at the parks and trade pins. This, of course, necessitated buying a few more pins to trade. A child cannot trade just one pin, can they? What a wonderful capitalistic country we live in. Disney is very good at this.

A neat trick I devised so we would not go into every gift shop and spend, spend, spend was this: I gave each child $10 in cash at the beginning of the trip. They could buy what ever they wanted. When it was gone, it was gone. My son spent it in two days. He did try a few more "Daddy, can I have that's." I mentioned that he already spent his money. He understood and really did not give me a hard time. Lauren actually kept her money until the last day at Disney. Hey, why not teach them money management while on vacation?

I go on vacations and travel with my children often. The Universal/Disney trip was one of the best.

## A TRADITIONAL BRITISH SEASIDE ADVENTURE
### By COLIN BENNETT

*Colin Bennett, age 31, is from the UK and wrote this with inspiration from his daughter Victoria, age 4.*

To cover the June 2002 term holiday I decided to take Victoria (VB) on a traditional British seaside adventure. This coincided nicely with VB's schoolwork, which was centered on insects, creatures, and nature at the time. Normally the "family" would have packed up and visited Minorca in the Balearic Islands (where my now ex-wife was born). We have visited Menorca for the last ten years and this was our first holiday away together without mum.

I felt a little apprehensive about taking VB on holiday as I had so many negative comments from other parents, such as "you're brave," and so on. Some people obviously do not realise how capable dads are and that we are not all the same! I have always thought that Victoria has missed out on the things that are best about British holidays; e.g. rock pools, kites on an over-cast day, boating, crab-catching, making sand castles in the rain, and so on and that she would not have the same memories I had from my childhood holidays. Menorca is so hot that it isn't possible to "play" on the beach without applying cream every 30 minutes.

I discovered that there are some great beaches in Tenby, Pembrokeshire, South Wales, and we set off. I booked a family-orientated hotel, which really paid off. The room we booked was small, with just two small beds and a small bathroom, but the view was good and we were right at the top of the house, which added to the adventure. The journey was more than four hours to Tenby, and we stopped a few times going, but not at all on the way back.

Luckily there were many restaurants to choose from, and we dined on sea-food and traditional meat dishes all the week we were away. We ate shellfish on the beach and fed the Sea Gulls our leftovers. The Pubs were family-friendly as well, which helped.

The first day or so VB seemed to be a little reluctant to join in my enthusiasm, but she soon got into the swing of things as we started to visit local attractions. Pembrokeshire has many children's attractions, which was another reason for going. We arrived Sunday and didn't do much at all except settle in and walk around town a bit. The next day we had a large breakfast and set off for Folly Farm where there are events all day indoors and out. VB fed goats, sheep, held rabbits, and generally took part in the whole farmyard experience. Tuesday we had another large breakfast and then headed of to the local indoor aquarium, followed by the Dinosaur Experience Park. Again both had coloring activities, play areas, shows, talks and more for children. Wednesday we visited Pembroke Castle and Pembroke Town. Thursday was a beach day making sand castles, swimming and paddling, digging holes, seeking out creatures in rock pools, and generally messing about by the water. Friday we set off for home after visiting the beach one more time.

The whole experience was glued together by ice cream and Candy Floss as VB's reward for eating all of her food. VB learned many things on the holiday, including more about meal times and what they are called (breakfast, lunch, tea, dinner). She also made great progress in reading speed limit signs. The whole week was a great bonding experience for us both and our friendship has grown. VB was really happy and content at the end of the holiday, and she was laughing and positive about everything. I usually only see her three out of four weekends from Friday evening to Sunday afternoon, so it was a pleasure to be with her for six days in a row.

## THE POISON CONTROL AFFAIR
### By PETER KOZA

*Peter Koza says, "I can barely remember my first airplane flight, since I was experiencing sensory overload at the time. But I was hooked for life. I still remember some of my earlier trips with my father. These were long flights through the western deserts. More important than just logging travel memoirs were the lessons I learned about the joys and discipline of traveling that I am passing on to the next generation. I have given well over a hundred other kids their first airplane rides through the Young Eagles program (www.youngeagles.org). My donation of flight time to other people's kids is my repayment of the time and effort that other people put into me. Helping other kids experience their first flights is being part of the tradition of the last (almost) 100 years of flight that started with Wilber Wright (USA pilot license #1). At the end of the day, I know I have succeeded in passing on the tradition while I take the glass cleaner to the greasy nose prints on the inside of the airplane windows."*

*Peter Koza*
*USA pilot number 1,962,145*
*pkoza@aerosoftusa.com*

My flight logbook entry for the flight simply states, "Kids to Grandpa, 4.7 hours." The flight in a single engine Cessna from the Seattle area to Northern California was supposed to be an adventure, but how was I to know that before the weekend was over, I would have had a long conversation with Poison Control and would end up on my knees tasting suspicious-looking white flakes off the floor.

My twin girls had just turned 2, and my confidence as a single parent had been recently boosted by several small trips and a venture through the crowds at the county fair. By this date, I had already given several dozen other kids their first ride in an airplane and felt comfortable with the natural combination of kids and airplanes. My kids were pretty used to travel in a light single engine airplane, and even the weather cooperated on this early fall weekend. The three of us got an early start and they slept for most of three-and-a-half hour duration of the first leg to Oroville. They were glad to get out for a fuel and dry diapers stop. The operator at Oroville Aviation was tolerant as the kids disorganized the lounge and left food debris behind.

We climbed out of the haze of the valley and over the foothills of the Sierra Nevada range. Placerville is on the highway between Sacramento and South

Shore Lake Tahoe. This old gold rush town is nicknamed "Hangtown" after its methodology of establishing civility. We headed to a private airfield to the north of town called Swansboro, across the American River. The cell phone barely works out this far in the country, but a bit of experimentation got it to work by standing on a tree stump near the aircraft tiedown ramp. Grandpa was there before we got the plane unloaded. Travel with kids is a paraphernalia-intensive sport.

Grandpa was a bit dubious going into this weekend, and you can't really blame him. Well-behaved for a 2-year-old is a far cry from his usual quiet, well-ordered home. The kids were still pretty wound-up the next day and a bit manic from the missed napping schedule. I put them down for a nap in the spare bedroom, and as a precaution, duct-taped the pill drawer closed. The sight of a couple young children quietly napping is very close to the physiological calm experienced while viewing a sunset over a beautiful rural landscape. Unfortunately, this was not to be the case, as the kids were not settling in. My father and I had a good talk for a while, with only a few peeps coming out of the back bedroom.

Perhaps it was an inappropriate giggle or maybe the absence of noise that caught my attention. I quietly opened the bedroom door to a scene of complete devastation! All of the sheets and blankets were on the floor, with scattered underwear and dresser drawers piled on top. Every drawer had been pulled out and/or emptied! This included the formerly duct-taped pill drawer. The girls were sitting on the floor with this drawer between them. Every bottle had been opened, and the contents were scattered. Several capsules and pills showed definite evidence of mastication. I'm not too sure what came out of my mouth at this moment, but it certainly got everybody's attention. I gathered up the pills off the floor, straightened up for a few minutes and announced that it was time to call Poison Control.

My father came up with a list of his friend's medications who had had recent angioplasty. The person who answered at Poison Control (PC) answered right away with a calm, reassuring voice. I quickly explained the situation and stated that I had a list of the pills and what was left of the pills in front of me. We started with the first drug on the list and PC dismissed it as not hazardous, and asked for the next one. I explained that I needed to match up the drugs with the bottles and asked for him to describe the pill's appearance using the Physician's Desk Reference. The PDR contains a section of photographs of the pharmaceuticals; something that I remembered from my pre-parent days. We continued down the list and collected and eliminated each of them as being of significant concern. "That one is a diuretic," "This one lowers blood pressure and is not of concern unless they ate a whole bottle.

In which case they might pass out"... That idea had some merit at this point in time. We finally got down to one colored pill and an unlabeled pill bottle. It was a coated aspirin, and was the only one of concern. It turned out that aspirin overdose in kids is a major problem and can be a killer. We discussed the symptoms: ringing in the ears, and in extreme cases, vomiting accompanied with blood. We could not determine how many aspirins had been repackaged in the bottle, how many were missing, and the owner was unavailable by phone. Poison Control strongly recommended that I take the kids into the hospital for observation.

This was obviously time for a "Pilot-In-Command" executive decision. On one side of the equation, at least one of these pills had definitely been in and/or out of a mouth. Fortunately the coating, while an attractive primary color, was not sweet. Since the innards are bitter, perhaps there would be some evidence of spit-out pills on the bedroom floor. I decided to stay put and watch the kids for a while.

The geographical logistics complicated the decision. We were several miles/kilometers out of town with the American River between civilization and us. One route, Mosquito Road, is the hundred-year-old original horse and buggy road with 180-degree switchbacks carved into the cliff face and a one-lane suspension bridge over the chasm. The other road is wider and longer, but still a 45-minute drive away from town, especially the way my father drives his old vehicles. On the other hand, I had an airplane sitting about 10 minutes away, ready to go, and complete with child seats installed. Plan C was to call 911 and have the medics meet us at the Placerville Airport. I declined their recommendation to head into the emergency room. We agreed that I would keep a close watch on the kids for symptoms, and PC would call back in a couple hours for a follow-up.

The next step was to look for evidence of chewed-up aspirins at the scene of the crime. I got down on all fours in the bedroom and found some white flakes in the carpet. I tasted a couple samples with the intensity of a food connoisseur evaluating a five-star restaurant. It turned out to be only a one star meal, "This doesn't taste like aspirin. It tastes more like plaster." "Oh, yeah," my father replied, "It probably is, I was fixing the light in the ceiling last week." Hey, after changing the first thousand diapers, eating plaster off the floor hardly rates even close to gross.

Having paid my dues as a dad, and feeling more or less back in command, I diverged from the kids' mom's dietary regulations and let them eat what they wanted, "junk food." They ate a bunch of crackers and some sweets, which are definitely near the low end of the junk food hierarchy. The September afternoon was warm enough to play outside in the sprinkler. It burned off some of their energy and gave my dad some personal time to recover. Poison Control called back to check up. I explained what had transpired and the operator agreed with my decision. All of us slept well that night.

My father is closer to the far end of the touchie-feelie spectrum. The next day, as we were getting ready to head back north, he gave me a sincere compliment, "I appreciate the way you handled the Poison Control incident." To this day, he remains leery of my showing up with the kids. I can't blame him a bit.

The twins and I have had many an adventure since that trip almost three years ago. We have camped in the wilds and stayed dozens more times in hotels. We have come to mutual understandings about limits, and the three of us have many adventures under our belts. Travel with the three of us is now a very natural experience for these kids. Since they are naturally accommodating, they cooperate when they need to stay close, and when they can they get a longer leash.

On that trip, on the way back to Seattle, we stopped for gas in Salem, Oregon. Oregon does not have self-fueling, even at general aviation airports. The horizontal stabilizer on the airplane, (i.e. tail-feathers), makes a great changing table (not while in motion, of course). I set the first kid back on the ground with dry diapers and let her loose around the plane after verifying that no other planes were moving around the fuel ramp. While changing the second child, the gas jockey was somewhat shocked and exclaimed, "What are you doing? Running an aerial day care center?" What more could I wish for? My times as a single parent have been some of the best of my life. Seeing my kids grow and develop is worth more than anything to me, and we have many more adventures yet to come.

## GROWING DOWN A RIVER
### By GREGG P. BOERSMA

*Gregg graduated from Babson College in Wellesley, Massachusetts in 1982. Since then he has worked in advertising sales for various magazine publishers, including Outside magazine. There, his interest in the outdoors was heightened as he had the good fortune of taking adventure trips with the staff and clients for "work." Among others, these trips included kayaking in Alaska, horse-packing in Colorado, and mountaineering on Mt. Rainer. Upon his departure from Outside, Gregg vowed to keep exploring the world outside on his own and is committed to exposing his only child, Chelsea, to the beauty and excitement of similar outdoor adventures. His most recent adventure was a month-long photo safari in Namibia, Africa.*

*Being a self-taught award-winning photographer, images of his travels hang throughout his home and act as a daily reminder of the places he has been and the dreams he has yet to fulfill.*

*Gregg is divorced, single, and lives in South Salem, NY.*

They say that it's the unexpected surprises that make traveling fun, but this was one surprise I could have done without. It was 7 a.m. on a Saturday morning in August. I was at LaGuardia airport, ready to attempt my first vacation alone with my 7-year-old daughter, when I discovered that my driver's license was missing from my wallet. We had planned to rent a car to make the five-hour drive east from Salt Lake City to Vernal, Utah, where we would begin an adventurous vacation — a professionally guided, four-day, family-oriented whitewater rafting trip through the Gates of Lodore and Dinosaur National Monument on the Green River in Utah. I tried desperately to remember where I'd placed it or why I'd taken that license out of my wallet, but I could not remember ever doing so. So there we were, one hour into a weeklong vacation, and we had a huge problem. No driver's license, no rental car. No rental car, no way to get to the river. No river, no vacation. Much to my dismay, we were suddenly off on an adventure of a different sort.

I called the rental car company and they confirmed, strongly, that I would not be able to take the car without showing them some proof of a valid driver's license. I speculated that in today's world, with technology, there must be a way for the rental company to check and see that I did in fact have a valid license. Theoretically, we should be able to do this. But, in a situation like this, one quickly realizes that theory is irrelevant. The only thing that counts is the reality that is staring you in the face. And in reality, we were already up the river without a paddle.

Next I hoped that American Express Travel Services might have experience with a problem like this and know the solution, but I was wrong. Try as they might (and they did try) they could offer no real solution short of going home and getting a new driver's license issued. I really couldn't believe no one else had ever done this and they hadn't found a solution, but it seems I have the dubious distinction of being the only person ever to make this foolish mistake (and I did it with the dreams of a beautiful 7-year-old girl relying on my ability to fix the problem).

Unable to reach the Department of Motor Vehicles at that hour, I made the decision to board the plane (this was before 9/11, when one could still talk their way past the airport security using just credit cards for I.D.). This was a risky choice as it meant that we would possibly arrive in Utah, discover there was no way to get a duplicate license, and have no choice other than to spend the week in Salt Lake City without transportation or be forced to return to New York, dejected. We were traveling on frequent flyer miles and I was concerned that if we missed this flight we might not get ticketed on another flight anytime soon. Without any real evidence, I assured my daughter that we'd be able to work it out when we got there, and we stepped on the plane.

During a layover in Chicago I made several more desperate phone calls, this time to the DMV. Suffice it to say; when you're having a crisis situation, the *last* organization you want to be dealing with is the DMV. For a variety of reasons that seemed perfectly logical to them and completely insane to me, they could not (or would not) do anything to provide the rental car company with confirmation of my valid license. I was told I would have to come there in person to purchase a duplicate license. I persisted and finally I reached a man who must have children himself. He listened to my plea to save my daughter's vacation and agreed to allow another person to pick up a document that would provide sufficient verification of my valid license. Now all I needed was to find a friend to go to the DMV voluntarily on a Saturday morning and become entangled in this mess. No easy task. I called a friend back home and, after explaining my predicament and promising to be indebted to her for life, she agreed to go.

Now, I haven't mentioned much about my daughter, Chelsea, but that's not to say she wasn't involved during this whole process. As any 7-year-old would do, she produced an endless stream of questions, asking what was going to happen. When you're trying to navigate through helpless service representatives, suspicious airport security guards, bureaucratic government employees, liability-minded rental car executives and guilt-wielding friends, it's not easy to maintain your composure, no less have the patience needed to deal with a curious and concerned child. But I did and as a result, this story is one that we can tell together with smiles and fond memories.

By the time Chelsea and I arrived at the rental car desk in Salt Lake City, they already knew us well. My friend Carolyn had already had several conversations with them and they had received a fax from her with a copy of the verification they needed. We loaded up the car with our gear and set off for the originally planned adventure. Three years later, I'm still buying drinks to repay that favor.

We broke up the five-hour drive to Vernal with a stop in Park City. We ate, shopped a little and then discovered the land luge at the mountain's base lodge. We took several trips down the course riding tandem, each run a little faster and a little more daring than the last. It was a blast, but be careful. These "sleds" can flip in a turn and cause severe road rash. With hours still to drive, I dragged us away from the fun and back out onto the road. We arrived in Vernal with just enough time to check into our modest hotel room (modest by my business traveler taste, but "really great" by Chelsea's) at the Lamplighter, call Mom to inform her of a safe arrival, take a quick dip in the pool, grab dinner and fall into bed.

Our guided trip began on Monday, so we had Sunday to do some exploring. After breakfast we visited a dinosaur museum in town and then went to the see the archeological exhibit at Dinosaur National Monument. The monument was originally established to protect an area that was one of the most productive sources of dinosaur bones in the world. The Quarry Area contains approximately 1,600 exposed bones from 11 different dinosaur species. Chelsea and I both found the bones and accompanying fossils truly fascinating. That afternoon we drove through parts of the Monument and found a river with a sandy beach, where we spent much of the remainder of the day playing in the sand and river mud like, well, kids. We returned to the hotel and cleaned up so that we could attend a mandatory briefing held that evening by our river guides/outfitters, a non-profit organization called ARTA (American River Touring Association; 800-323-2782; www.arta.org).

ARTA was founded in 1963 and runs river trips of various lengths on rivers throughout the western U.S. I selected ARTA because they were running a river canyon which I'd discovered from my research was one of the most spectacular in the U.S. (second, perhaps, only to the Grand Canyon), and the cost was less than other profit-oriented tour operators. I surmised that all the river guides have to go through the same certification process and that, despite the lower cost, our experience with ARTA would really be no different than it would be with any of the other companies that also run the Green River through the Lodore Canyon. By my observation of the river guides and the equipment used by other groups we saw on the river, I think I was right. ARTA was just as professional, perhaps more customer friendly, and less expensive. I'd highly recommend ARTA.

The next morning we met at a designated spot (our ultimate take-out point), loaded our gear onto a bus and took a two plus hour drive to our put-in, just across the state border in Colorado. The bus trip gave us a chance to get to know the other families on the trip. Chelsea and I were the only single parent/child pair but it wasn't all traditional families consisting of Mom, Dad and the kids. There was one family that included their grandfather and another group that included a married woman, her daughter, Alison, her daughter's friend, Patty, and the woman's sister. In all, there were eight kids ranging in age from 7 (Chelsea) to 16; 12 adult clients and six adult guides (one woman and five men).

Finally, we were on the river and after only a few hundred yards of calm water we were thrown into a series of rapids. So much for warming up to the challenge. The fun and thrill of crashing through whitewater was everything the brochures had promised and, when you dared look up from the water, the scenery was spectacular. This is true wilderness; during our four days on the river, we saw only one building, a small hut that had been erected by the park service. The Green River consists primarily of Class II and Class III rapids, which is plenty of excitement for kids and not so hairy that parents will be (too) concerned about their child's safety. First traversed by Major John Wesley Powell in 1869, the river winds its way through three distinct canyons: Lodore, with its red rock walls and famous rapids; Whirlpool, which features Jones Hole Creek and echoing cliffs that come straight down into the river; and Split Mountain, which contains geological curiosities and exciting whitewater. A part of the rock that is exposed in Lodore Canyon is estimated to be one *million* years old. Our minds struggled to grasp the concept of that much time.

Speaking of age, Chelsea turned 8 the first day we were on the river. That night, having been informed of this event beforehand, the ARTA guides did a superb job of surprising her with a German chocolate cake freshly baked in a Dutch oven (a cast iron pot buried under hot coals) and topped with candles so that everyone on the trip could sing her happy birthday and celebrate. Afterwards, we lay side-by-side in our tent, looking through the mesh windows into a sky filled with more stars than Chelsea had ever seen before, and I had to fight back the tears. After a difficult start, this was turning out to be the special trip I had hoped it would be.

A little education at this point about the camping facilities and some other things on this trip might be helpful. ARTA supplies all the major equipment you need, you really only need to bring the right clothing and your personal gear. But, being an experienced backpacker, I choose to bring our own tent to insure Chelsea and I had a non-leaking roof over our heads (nothing turns new campers off more than sleeping in a wet sleeping bag). In hindsight, this wasn't necessary. The guides also prepare all the meals. The ARTA literature says they keep costs down, in part, by not serving fancy, gourmet meals. But I found the cooking to be wonderful, outdoor dining fare. Everything always tastes better in the wilderness anyway, and besides, on a family trip, who's worried about fine dining? Any fine dining experience that the other outfitters might have provided would have been ruined anyway. Why?

The answer lies in something Chelsea and I both learned on this trip: Utah is called "The Beehive State" for good reason. While the official explanation for the appearance of a beehive on the state's emblem is that it represents industry, we think it simply represents bees! Every time we stopped for food, honeybees would magically appear from nowhere. At no other time were they present during the trip, but each meal became an act of bravery. The bees were only interested in the food, and if you could convince yourself that they were crawling all over your plate for that sole purpose, you could proceed to eat as normal. But, needless to say, that's easier said than done. Those "damn bees" would have been the one thing I would have changed about this trip if I could have changed anything. So you've been forewarned, but know too that I don't recall anyone being stung during our entire trip.

Now, because everyone always wants to know but is too embarrassed to ask, I'll tell you that the rest room facilities consisted of a wooden box with a toilet seat on top, placed over a hole that had been dug in the ground. All of this was located well out of sight from the camping area and everyone, kids included, easily followed a system of using the toilet paper roll in order to know whether or not the facility was "occupied" without having to look and see. It was really not bad at all. In fact, in one location I commented to Chelsea that this particular "bathroom" had a million dollar view and she would probably never see anything nearly this beautiful from any house she would ever own.

The second day on the river was filled with more fun and excitement. ARTA floats three types of boats on these family trips. Oar boats are used primarily to move the gear and are paddled by just the guide, but small children or anyone not interested in paddling can sit up front and get a very wet and exhilarating front row view of the whitewater and scenery. Next are the classic paddleboats — three paddlers per side and a guide sitting on the back giving instructions and steering. Lastly, they bring along a couple of "duckies." These are inflatable one-person open kayaks. I'd only recommend experienced paddlers or athletic types run the rapids in one of these. I fall into the latter category and, still, when I got my chance in a ducky, I was quickly tossed overboard by the first rapid. They are designed to fill with water, and then drain quickly. I stuck with it and got the hang of it, but I can still close my eyes and see how large those Class III rapids looked while approaching it in one of these small boats. The ride makes you feel like Stuart Little when he is trapped in the washing machine.

During the course of the trip Chelsea and I spent time in each of the boats. In stretches of the river that were flat, we went tandem in the ducky or tied it to the back of an oar boat and towed a couple of kids behind. In some stretches that included only Class II rapids, we tried our skills in the paddleboats. I felt it was important to give Chelsea an opportunity to be a participant rather than just a passenger in order for her to get the fullest experience. Despite the occasional complaint ("My arms are too tired") and a few wild moments when she took my advice and fell to the floor of the raft and just hung on, I think this was a good decision. In the most aggressive water we sought the safety of an oar boat and the expertise of our favorite guide, Brendan.

Brendan had grown up with divorced parents and could easily relate to Chelsea's situation; he subtly reassured her that everything would be fine. Beyond being "really cool," Brendan possessed a ponytail, good looks, and a body that was sculpted and tanned by a summer spent working on the river. In no time all the young girls were lobbying to get on his boat.

Brendan was a skilled and very capable river guide, but he made one poor decision that week that led to the biggest fear — and now the greatest memory — of the week. With three small girls — Patty, Alison and Chelsea — and me in the front of his boat, we were running as the sweeper boat through "Hell's Half Mile," the biggest rapids of the trip. Brendan spotted another boat from our group that was hung up on a boulder and, not thinking about his cargo, he purposely steered our boat into the other, hoping to bump them off the rock. Normally this might have been the correct thing to do, but considering the age of his passengers at the moment, he should have been less heroic. The bump worked, sort of. The other boat was bumped free and quickly disappeared down the river, but our boat immediately got hung up on the same rock. The girls had been thrown forward by the sudden stop. Fortunately, I had been sitting on the very bow of the boat facing backwards to take their photo, so I was able to spread my arms and catch all three of them to keep them from going overboard.

The oar boat turned perpendicular to the current, and within seconds, literally tons of water poured over the bow and stern. The boat was quickly wrapped and partially submerged around the upstream side of the rock. I lifted the girls out of the water and onto the only part of the boat and rock that wasn't underwater. Brendan and I shared glances and I instantly knew this was no laughing matter. Instinctually, Brendan and I divided responsibilities. My sole task was to keep the kids as safe and calm as possible. I let them know that we were fine, that shore was just a little distance away and we could sit on this rock for hours if we had to and we wouldn't be hurt. Initially they were all frightened and Chelsea was on the verge of tears. Most kids her age probably would have cried at this point, and justifiably so, but she remained strong. Patty and Alison, who were only a year or two older than Chelsea, quickly assumed the role of big sisters and added their own comforting thoughts to mine and everyone remained calm. A wonderful dynamic quickly evolved. The older girls showed strength to ease Chelsea's mind and Chelsea worked hard to impress everyone that she could be as brave as the "big" girls. Soon there was nervous laughter as we joked about what a great "What I did on my summer vacation" story they all were going to tell when they returned to school the next month. Meanwhile, Brendan worked to free the boat, but the downward pressure of the rushing water was too much for one man to overcome, and I wasn't about the leave Chelsea and the other girls alone in order to help him.

The other boats were down the river, around a bend, and out of sight. About 15 minutes had passed when we spotted another one of our guides walking back upriver along the shore. We had been expected to meet them downriver for lunch and our absence caused obvious concern. Additionally, several of the children's items that had not been lashed down were swept overboard and had been spotted floating downstream by other members of our group. Imagine how those parents felt when they saw that!

The roar of the river made it impossible for us to talk to the guide on shore, but using hand signals the two guides devised a plan to free the boat using a system of ropes tied to trees on the shore. Assembling this rigging took another 20 minutes or so and once it was complete we spent another 20 minutes working to free the boat without any success. About that time a group of firemen on a kayak trip came down the river. They had stopped above the rapids and were walking down to scout them when they spotted us. Finally, we had the manpower we needed. It had now been an hour since we landed on this rock and the girls were running out of bravery. Brendan immediately agreed with my suggestion that we just focus on getting them to shore.

An adult could have just jumped into the river and had some fun riding the remaining (small) rapids feet first to calmer water, where they could have easily swum to shore. But that was too much to expect — and too dangerous — for the kids. Instead, one of the experienced kayakers used one of our duckies (it had been carried upstream from the lunch site by another guide) and paddled into the calm water just downstream of the rock. Once there, we lowered a child into his lap and he ferried them one at a time to dry land. All three made it to shore without further incident and I stayed with Brendan to help rescue the boat. Ultimately, we ferried much of the gear off the boat, just as we'd done with the kids. Then, we deflated one side of the boat and, using the ropes that had already been rigged, the shore crew was finally able to pull the boat free.

In all, nearly two hours had elapsed. Finally, we were all standing on firm ground, unharmed, with a story that'll last a lifetime. To his credit, Brendan freely admitted afterwards that he'd made a poor decision to bump that other boat and promised he had learned a valuable lesson. Honestly, the manner in which he handled this crisis and the experience and skills he demonstrated on the river only impressed me more. I wouldn't hesitate one second to place my child or myself into another boat with Brendan at the oars (or any ARTA guide for that matter). In fact, we did just that after lunch.

The remainder of the trip consisted of more great whitewater rafting, drifting in and out of the boat down lazy stretches of the river, wildlife sightings, hiking to see petroglyphs, showering in natural waterfalls, and making our own waterfall at a spot dubbed "Butt Dam Falls," a favorite among the kids because of both its moniker and the activity.

One other note, especially for Dads traveling with young daughters: Don't forget the girly stuff. One item we packed in our gear bags was one of Chelsea's favorite Beanie Babies, "Blackie." Blackie provided a source of comfort for her in the sleeping bag at night and we joked a lot about him while we were stuck on that rock. A female guide brought the other item, and I now make it standard gear for all trips: nail polish. One of my favorite photos from this trip is of the three girls getting a pedicure while sitting in a raft that is pulled up on a beach in the middle of wilderness. No guy would have thought of painting toenails on a rugged trip like this, but Chelsea loved that. On subsequent trips we've also used nail polish for natural arts and crafts projects, like painting rocks to make decorative tablecloth holders that look like ladybugs.

I teased Chelsea frequently that she'd be a different person after this rafting trip. After all, she began it as a 7-year-old in Colorado and finished it as an 8-year-old in Utah. But those were mere changes in time and place. Over those four days I saw more significant changes. She met kids from different parts of the country, learned about their way of life, and broadened her perspective. She faced some fears before and during the rafting and overcame them. And with each day on the water and around the campsites she became more independent and confident — I could practically see her self-esteem growing as a result.

We've taken other adventurous trips together since this one and we always come home with great stories and a closer bond after each of them. We plan to continue to travel together for many more years to come. As a result, I hope that one day, when she has her own driver's license, we'll have fewer obstacles to overcome, literally and figuratively.

# V

## Alternate Vacation Ideas

### KID EXCHANGE

There are times when a single parent cannot afford a family vacation. Perhaps a recent job change or financial or personal matters prevent you from going away. As summer nears, you are concerned about keeping your restless pre-teen or teen-ager occupied and happy. One novel, inexpensive solution to consider is a kid exchange. I am not talking about a local exchange for the day, but rather a full-fledged out-of-state experience for a week or more. This is a very different experience than sending your child off to visit his or her out-of-state grandparents.

The summer my daughter turned 10 we were unable to take a family vacation. I wanted her to have something to look forward to that summer, so I arranged for a kid exchange with my former college roommate who had a daughter the same age. The family my daughter was to visit lived on a farm in central Florida, a very different atmosphere from our large suburban hometown in New Jersey. My friend and I agreed that we would each pay the round trip airfare for our child and would host the visiting child and pay all entertainment expenses. We made plans for what each child would see and do during their visit. I typed up an itinerary and sent it to Florida so 10-year-old Traci and her family could begin anticipating all the things she would see when she flew up north.

The idea was a bit of a gamble. Traci and my daughter had never met, but I knew Traci's Mom and Dad would take good care of my daughter and show her a good time. My daughter flew down to Florida first. This was the first time Monique had flown by herself, so that was exciting for her. The first couple of days were spent tending to the farm animals and baling hay, all novel experiences for my daughter. Traci had a go-cart, which she and Monique could drive around the farm. Monique learned how to stay alert for alligators, which can inhabit any standing body of water in central Florida. Unfortunately, the weather turned bad as the week wore on and many of the local outdoor fun activities had to be cancelled or postponed. The girls began quarreling and my friend had concerns about sending her daughter to New Jersey. I realized we had been too ambitious in our planning. We had scheduled a two-week visit in each place for the girls, and now realized that a week or 10 days would have been more appropriate. Unfortunately, back then, non-refundable air tickets did not allow for any changes.

Eventually the weather improved and the girls enjoyed a few excursions to local central Florida attractions. They flew together to New Jersey and the good weather held. We took Traci on day trips to New York City, Philadelphia, the Jersey shore, our local amusement parks and enormous shopping malls. Traci particularly enjoyed visiting the historical sites. She explained that at the end of each summer vacation when kids had to "show and tell" about their summer, she never had much to say, since most of the summer was spent working on the farm, which was their busy time. "Now," said Traci, " I have plenty to talk about," and beamed as she held up her recent purchases of the Declaration of Independence, the Liberty Bell, and a colonial quill pen.

## BLENDING FAMILIES

Please note the title is "Blending Families," not "Blended Families," and the subjects are different.

When I began writing my monthly Single Parent Travel newsletter in early 2001, subscribers frequently e-mailed me saying how happy they were that I had started the newsletter. They found it to be both informative and entertaining. After a few months, the content of the e-mails changed. Subscribers began offering suggestions from their experiences to stretch the travel budget of a single parent family, or to find ways to make their vacations more enjoyable for themselves and their children.

One frequently shared suggestion was to blend families for vacation. Single parents approached other single parents about traveling together in order to cut down on hotel expenses and provide companionship both for the adults and children in each family. This arrangement works particularly well for camping and road trips or vacations at the shore, lake, or mountains where a property is rented for a week or more. In this case you have two or more adults sharing the day-to-day cabin or cottage maintenance responsibilities and rental costs.

If you would be interested in sharing a vacation with another single parent family but do not know of one, check out www.ParentsWithoutPartners.org. The chairman of your local PWP chapter can help you post notices or e-mails to potential candidates. You can also visit my Web site, www.SingleParent Travel.net, and post a notice on the Bulletin Boards section. If readers have other suggestions for sources, please contact me via my Web site or e-mail me directly at Brenda@SingleParentTravel.net. All suitable suggestions will be posted in a future newsletter.

## THE ADULT TAKES A BREAK — THE DELICIOUSNESS OF TRAVELING ALONE

The custodial single parent, or even the single parent with shared custody, often plans vacation time to spend with one's child or children. This was certainly true in my case, especially when my children were little. I wanted to provide a strong sense of family after my divorce, and I wanted to spend as much pleasure time as possible with my children, given that there is so little allotted vacation time in corporate America. However, it is also important to nurture oneself and spend time traveling alone.

Once a year I slipped away for a getaway "Ladies' Weekend" with my dearest friend. Sometimes it was as simple as a weekend to a nearby metropolitan city, such as Washington D.C. Other times we traveled to London for a long weekend on one of those fabulous US$200 winter airfares. We were happy to be "just girls" for the weekend, not moms, daughters, wives, or girlfriends, and indulged ourselves with museum visits, window-shopping, and people watching, along with a leisurely cup of afternoon tea.

When family circumstances prevented us from continuing this practice on a yearly basis, I began traveling by myself for an occasional weekend. At first my trips were a one-day extension of a business trip. Instead of returning home on a Friday night, I would stay at my destination an extra day to visit an interesting museum or do an exciting hike. I began treasuring this "stolen day" even though it only occurred a couple of times a year. Of course, this limited the weekend time I had to do chores, and compressed everything into one exhausting Sunday. In spite of that, I felt spiritually refreshed and renewed as an individual.

Wanting more, I took the jump and planned an entire weekend for myself. I had a free standby domestic airline ticket  What better place to travel alone than New Orleans? I needed a break from my teen-age daughter and needed to finish my paper for my CTC (Certified Travel Consultant) degree. The deadline was fast approaching. Fortunately I was able to complete the paper on the plane. Like most people, I work more quickly under stress. Having set aside all parental guilt, I took off for a wonderful mid-December weekend. Traveling alone was, as I rediscovered, quite delicious. I walked the city until my feet hurt, engaged in interesting and lengthy conversations with the locals, and lingered over numerous cups of café au lait. To my surprise New Orleans gets very involved with pre-Christmas celebrations. Fragrant boughs of evergreen hung from every balcony, stores were filled with unique hand-made Christmas gifts, and restaurants featured festive, moderately priced, mouth-watering menus.

By now you are thinking, "Well, it's easy for her. She is in the travel business and can afford a sitter." It's true that I have had opportunities to travel to some exciting destinations at an affordable rate, but any person can plan a driving trip to a nearby destination that offers moderately priced B&Bs or inexpensive motels. Consider going during the off-season, such as to Cape Cod in the fall or New Orleans in the summer or mid-December. Please note as well that you do not get rich in the travel business. Like most single parents I had to find creative ways to secure a free sitter. In most cases it was my children's father. So get out there and ask a friend or relative to take your child for the weekend while you go away. If they look at you askance because you are going by yourself, just tell them you need it and you are great company! Then walk out the door and don't look back!

# VI

## Recommended Destinations & Activities

One of the most common questions that I get from single parents is where to take their kids on vacation. Once they have "done" the shore, the mountains, camping, and, of course, Walt Disney World, they are not certain where to go next. Readers of my Web site, www.SingleParentTravel.net, and subscribers to my monthly newsletter have e-mailed their suggestions to me. They have enjoyed delightful single parent vacations on a Caribbean cruise, or at a Club Med, or by purchasing one of those all-inclusive Caribbean or Mexican resort vacation packages. These are all excellent value vacations and are easy to budget for and plan, important considerations for the single parent.

In addition to those above-mentioned vacation destinations, I have suggestions for other destinations. It is not my intent to make this chapter a comprehensive travel destination guide for single parent families, but rather a list of a dozen or so places, from familiar to exotic, which, I hope, will help you think "out of the box." The list is by no means complete, but has been field-tested by my family and is suitable for single parent families or any adult traveling alone with kids. Each destination provides:

➤ A selection of accommodations, from moderate-priced on up.

➤ The ability to travel around independently and safely.

➤ Once you arrive, ease of travel by car, local transportation or on foot.

➤ Family fun activities *without* an emphasis on the "romantic couples" atmosphere.

➤ Appeal for all age groups, both on the adult and child level.

➤ Opportunities for you and your kids to mingle and make new friends.

➤ Cultural diversity and opportunities to have a fun-filled, adventurous and educational vacation.

I divided the vacation destinations into four groupings:

### Group #1

These are more moderately priced vacations and are a driving or fly/drive vacation, depending on where you live in the U.S.

### Group #2

These vacations will definitely require a flight (unless you live at or near the destination) and tend to be more exotic and expensive than those in the first group. In this group you will find international as well as domestic (U.S.) destinations.

### Group #3

These are "Trips of a Lifetime" suggestions. All are thrilling places to visit and can be financially achievable if you budget and shop properly according to the suggestions set forth in the first part of my book.

### Group #4

The Special Mention Destinations fall into their own category requiring a separate discussion.

If you have questions about a potential vacation destination that is not discussed in this chapter, please feel free to send me an e-mail at Brenda@Single ParentTravel.net or consult my Web site, www.SingleParentTravel.net, to find information on numerous other destinations. Don't forget to sign up for my free monthly newsletter at www.SingleParentTravel.net. I write about new destinations as I visit them and also publish a list of single parent travel specials.

Keep in mind a general note about booking: Most, if not all, of these trips can be planned and booked with the help of a travel agent. All agents listed in the Appendix are specialists in single parent travel and are aware of my book. Give one a call and tell them you read the book and are interested in a trip.

Ready? Put your dream cap on and let's get started...

## GROUP #1 - DRIVE OR FLY/DRIVE VACATIONS

### NIAGARA FALLS

Oh, I can hear it now. "Niagara Falls? You've gotta be kidding! That's *sooo* commercial and full of tourists." Think about that statement for a moment. Why would a place always be full of tourists unless it had something very special to offer? What makes Niagara Falls so special is not merely the falls, but the fact that you can get so up close and personal with the falls in many different ways. Before I was married, I traveled throughout Europe and South America. Every time I would visit some spectacular array of falls on these continents, the brochure would compare them to Niagara Falls — twice as high, three times as wide, four times as much water. No matter what was said, the comparison was always with Niagara. After I became a single parent, I decided I would visit the Mother Lode. Our trip turned out to be lots of fun.

Niagara Falls is a long drive from anywhere on the East Coast, and there are many interesting attractions along the way should you have the time to do a "circle trip" of New York state. If you are flying in from a distant state, the entry airport is Buffalo, New York or, if you prefer, you can also fly into Toronto, Canada, about an hour-and-a-half drive by car. If you are renting a car, make sure the rental car company will allow you to drive the vehicle over the border.

To see the major attractions in and immediately around Niagara Falls requires three full days. Here are the "must see" attractions unique to Niagara:

- ➤ *Maid of the Mist Boat Tour* — This fantastic ride, slickers and boots provided, has been enjoyed by presidents and kings alike, and is the most famous and popular attraction at the falls, next to the falls itself.

- ➤ *Cave of the Winds* — This attraction allows you to walk along the side of the falls, on wooden steps, to within 25 feet (7.6 m) of the base of the falls. Slickers provided. The force of the water spray dislodged my daughter's contact lens onto her cheek. She was impressed.

- ➤ *Table Rock House* — A series of tunnels leading to the backside of the falls. I think this was where Marilyn Monroe had her "illicit kissing tryst" with her boyfriend in the movie "Niagara."

- ➤ *Daredevil Gallery* — Displays the contraptions used by the crazy people who survived a trip over the falls. Not to be missed!

➢ *Goat Island* — Here you can stand only a few feet (1 m) from where people have gone over the falls, either to their death or to permanent fame. It is from this area that several people have also been rescued.

➢ *Fort Niagara* — Only 30 minutes from the falls, this scenic fort offers a history lesson and a musket power demonstration.

➢ *Artpark* — This was a surprise hit. The kids absolutely loved Artpark! This large park, in a lovely setting, offers outdoor sculpture and lots of crafts. My 9-year-old son kept busy playing "mason," building a stone wall with real concrete blocks and mortar. My teen-age daughter was enthralled with the opportunity to get hands-on opportunities with pottery-making and other crafts. This is a free attraction and combines nicely with a visit to nearby Fort Niagara. Bring hats and sunscreen. Except for the canopied crafts area, much of this park is exposed to the outdoors.

For more information on attractions and accommodations, contact the Niagara Falls Convention and Visitors Bureau at www.nfcvb.com, or phone toll free, 800-338-7890.

*If you are driving to Niagara from the East Coast or want to do a circle trip of New York State, here are some major attractions that merit at least an overnight or day's visit.*

### Cooperstown, NY

This delightful small town looks like it belongs in a Norman Rockwell painting. Besides the National Baseball Hall of Fame, which is fun even if you are not interested in baseball, there is a fabulous Farmer's Museum. This indoor/outdoor museum depicts farm life in this area in the 1800s. There are lots of hands-on displays for the kids. My son learned the origin of the name Cooper and my daughter was surprised to learn that the most dangerous occupation for women's health at that time was doing laundry (Long-term exposure to lye was quite harmful). There are other smaller museums as well, so you may want to consider buying a special combination museum pass if you plan to visit more than two. There are several restaurants serving home-cooked food in a family-style atmosphere. To save money, you can stay in a tourist home rather than a motel. The town maintains an excellent Web site for information and booking accommodations via e-mail at www.cooperstown.com.

## Erie Canal Village

Located in Rome, NY, this attraction offers a quaint village and the opportunity to ride a mule-drawn barge down the historic Erie Canal. It is located one and a half hours from Cooperstown and three hours from Niagara Falls. Call 888-374-3226 or visit www.ErieCanalVillage.com.

## Finger Lakes Area

Besides all types of boating and outdoor activities in this scenic area, there are many local wineries. Watkins Glen, at the south end of Seneca Lake, is famous for being a gliding and auto-racing center, and nearby is the not-to-be-missed hike up the Great Gorge, where you can walk by 11 waterfalls, culminating in the bridge walk over the Gorge. At night there is a sound and light presentation at the Gorge called Timespell, which explains the geology and history of this glacially carved area. Visit www.FingerLakes.net.

## Corning Glass Works and Museum

Near this interesting museum is the beautiful campus of Cornell University. Call 800-732-6845 or visit www.cmog.org.

For information and accommodations in the above areas, try the New York State Web site www.iloveny.state.ny.us or call 800-CALL-NYS.

*If you are planning to visit the Canadian side of Niagara Falls, some attractions are:*

## Welland Canal

This is Canada's "up close and personal" version of the Panama Canal. We all enjoyed watching freighters and ocean-going vessels drop down or go up over some of the eight locks that span the 300-foot drop of the Niagara Escarpment. For information call 800-305-5134 or visit www.infoniagara.com/d-canal.html.

## Tivoli Miniature World

Located in the town of St. Catherine's, this attraction recreates the world in miniature. For information call 416-562-7455.

**Toronto**

Often billed as the cleanest city in North America, this multi-cultural metropolis offers a myriad of attractions for families. Among them are:

➢ *CN Tower* — the largest free standing structure in the world and hallmark of the Toronto skyline.

➢ *Ontario Science Center* — a fantastic hands-on place of fun and learning with more than 800 exhibits, one of which will literally make your hair stand on end. The museum is also an architectural wonder, built right into the side of a ravine.

➢ *Ontario Place* — a man-made island of fun and excitement.

➢ *Toronto Harbourfront* — with more than two miles (3.5 kilometers) of waterfront area containing shops, restaurants, theaters, cultural events, boating and street entertainment.

➢ *Canada Wonderland* — a major theme park located a half hour from Toronto.

For further information on Toronto attractions, check out the city's official Web site www.TorontoTourism.com, or call 800-499-2514.

**Georgian Bay**

This unique area offers white sand beaches and crystal clear water that stretches out as far as the eye can see before becoming deep water. No sharks to worry about here! A good place to visit is Collingwood, at the south end of the bay, which is three hours from Niagara Falls or one and a half hours from Toronto. We explored a series of unique and fascinating caves once used by the Native Americans. Our favorite was the "refrigerator" cave used to store foodstuffs. In addition there is the Blue Mountain Pottery Center, a good place for some quality souvenirs.

After your vacation, we hope you, too will come away saying, "I LOVE NEW YORK."

## MID-ATLANTIC HISTORICAL TOUR

When you live in one of the Mid-Atlantic States, it is easy to visit one of its major cities on a long weekend jaunt. School trips to Washington D.C. are often *de rigueur.* However if you are traveling from outside this area, a family-driving trip of a week or more requires advance planning in order to avoid "Big City" overload. The "Big Three" cities of New York, Philadelphia, and Washington D.C. all offer good local transportation and opportunities to walk to many of the most famous tourist sites. Having a car can be a hindrance, especially if you are not familiar with these cities. If you are planning a fly/drive vacation, you may wish to consider flying into one city and out of another and using bus or train transportation to get from one city to the next. You can always rent a car for a day to drive to an attraction outside the city. Your final decision will depend on cost and your willingness to drive in big cities. For transportation schedules and rates, check out the following Web sites:

*Long haul buses/trains*

| | |
|---|---|
| Greyhound | www.greyhound.com |
| Trailways | www.trailways.com |
| Amtrak | www.amtrak.com |

*Local transit authorities*

| | |
|---|---|
| New York City and surrounding areas | www.mta.nyc.ny.us |
| Philadelphia | www.septa.org |
| Philadelphia/Southern NJ | www.drpa.org |
| Washington DC | www.wmata.com |

## New York City

Everyone is familiar with the major attractions of the "Big Apple" and everyone assumes the city is frightfully expensive. It certainly can be, but if you hunt around for bargains you can find a reasonably priced (by New York standards) small hotel or B&B for under US$150 a night in Manhattan. Another option is to stay at an inexpensive motel on the Jersey side and take the train into the city for day trips. For this arrangement you will need a car. Meals need not be expensive in Manhattan. There are many wonderful little (and I mean little, as in three or four tables) ethnic restaurants all over the city that provide great atmosphere and food, from Tibetan to Thai.

Manhattan is quite safe; there is constant activity day and night and you can walk around town at any hour and see people out enjoying themselves. Neighborhoods change their look and character every three to four blocks, so you have to get out and walk. If this is your first trip to New York, the babble of languages and cultural diversity will astound you. You will need three days to "sample" New York. There is so much to do and see in the city that I would never presume to tell anyone what they should do, but after years of traveling there on day and weekend trips, and by asking my daughter (who lived there for years and loved it) for suggestions, we have compiled a list for first-time visitors:

➤ Carry a map of Manhattan and learn to use the subway, the local bus, and walk as much as you can. *Riding the subway* is an experience and will expose you to the cross-cultural and socioeconomic panorama that is New York City. If you plan to ride the subway a few times, purchase a 10 or 20 ride Metro pass that saves you 10%. Buses require exact change.

➤ *Ride a taxicab* at least once. A New York cab ride is considered to be one of the great thrill rides in the U.S.A. If your destination is located on an avenue, be prepared to give the cross street to the cab driver. He may be annoyed if you don't have that information. Pay the cabbie *after* you have retrieved all of your belongings, or risk the cabbie driving speedily off to his next fare with your suitcase in his trunk!

➤ Visit *Central Park* on a weekend to see how New Yorkers enjoy their leisure time. They pursue it with a vengeance. Watch out for roller bladers.

➤ Stroll through *Greenwich Village* at any time of day or night. You will find an array of interesting shops and great little ethnic restaurants here. The people watching is unparalled. St. Marks Place is where you will find some of the cheapest restaurants and the best people watching in the world. My daughter's favorite is the French crèperie called the Crooked Tree on St. Marks place between Ave. A and 1st Aves. Don't like crêpes? Not to worry. On (or one block off) St. Marks you have Japanese, Afghani, Chinese, Spanish, and Tibetan cuisine and more, and all for a song. (NOTE: Eighth Street becomes St. Marks Place as it crosses over Broadway.)

➤ Ride *the Staten Island ferry* for a great view of Manhattan for just a few cents or take the Circle Island Ferry Tour for a few bucks.

➤ You could spend a month in Manhattan and not see all of the museums, but do see at least one or two. *The Natural History Museum and the Metropolitan Museum of Art* (the MET) are outstanding, as well as the MOMA (the Museum of Modern Art). Another of our favorites is the Ellis Island Museum. You have to ferry over, which is exciting. Allow a half-day for Ellis Island, as there is a lot to see.

➤ Go to the top of the *Empire State Building* for a fabulous view.

➤ *The Statue of Liberty* is a big drawing card, but lines usually are three hours long in the summer if you plan to climb to the top. There are so many other things to see and do on your first trip that I recommend you spend those three hours visiting some other attraction. If you still want to climb the lovely lady, lines for the ferry are much shorter if you embark on the Jersey, rather than the New York side.

➤ Seeing a *Broadway Show* is everyone's idea of a visit to Manhattan. I recommend you order your tickets ahead of time if you have a particular show in mind. Visit the Theater Development Fund online at www.tkts.com, or you can order discounted Broadway tickets in advance by visiting www.playbill.com. You must sign up for Playbill membership, which currently is free of charge. Discount tickets can also be purchased the day of the performance (See "Author's note" below). If your budget does not include a Broadway show, don't give up. There are many interesting and funky shows performed on the off Broadway scene that are a lot less expensive and also give you a "New York" experience.

➤ My favorite "splurge" item is *lunch, brunch, or afternoon tea at the Waldorf Astoria* Hotel. This Grand Old Dame still offers old world charm, excellent service, and a memorable, albeit very expensive, dining experience. You will need to dress up a little or you will be out of place among the smartly dressed New Yorkers that dine there.

The official Web site for New York City is www.nyc.gov. Scroll down for the section on tourist attractions.

*Author's Note:* The above section on New York City was originally written prior to the events of September 11, 2001. As of August 2002 the city is still recovering, but tourism is coming back. There is no doubt in my mind that this is a temporary situation and the vibrant spirit of New York City will eventually return in full force. At this time, plans for a memorial for the World Trade Center and its victims are uncertain. My heart and my condolences go out to every one of my readers who suffered the personal loss of a friend or loved one. I was fortunate that my daughter had moved out of Manhattan two weeks prior to the attack and she was fortunate in that all her friends were out of harm's way on that fateful day.

One of the many institutions destroyed on September 11th was the TKTS ticket booth at 2 World Trade Center. The main ticket booth, which offers discounted tickets the day of a performance for a wide range of live entertainment on and off Broadway remains open at Times Square at 47th and Broadway.

## Philadelphia

The "City That Loves You Back" is also known as the Cradle of Liberty, and rightfully so. Here you can visit sites that herald back to the birth of our nation. Make your first stop at the Visitor's Center. If time is limited, you can "do" the main historical sites in one day. They are:

➤ *Independence Hall* — where the Declaration of Independence was signed. A "broadside" copy of the Declaration, as well as the Articles of Confederation and the U.S. Constitution, are in the West Wing of Independence Hall.

➤ *The Liberty Bell* — It will get a new home in 2003, one block closer to Independence Hall.

➤ *Betsy Ross House* — a charming colonial home where our first American flag was made.

➤ *Old Christ Church* — a beautiful peaceful church in a lovely neighborhood, where most of our country's forefathers worshiped. It contains the baptismal fount of William Penn, founder of the city of Philadelphia.

Everything in downtown Philadelphia is within walking distance. After you have filled your cup with colonial history, you can:

➤ Walk down to *the waterfront* for more attractions.

➤ Stroll down *South Street* to eyeball the funky shops and passersby, some with green and orange hair — "must do" fun activity, especially for teenagers and older kids. Nearby Old City has lots of moderately priced ethnic restaurants.

➢ Little kids will enjoy the *"Please Touch" Museum,* a great hands-on attraction, which is both fun and educational.

➢ *The Franklin Institute* is a superb museum where you can walk through a heart.

➢ A popular favorite is the *Philadelphia Museum of Art,* where you can pose, Rocky Balboa style, on the top of the steps. Don't look for Rocky's statue in front of the museum. It was long ago moved to the Sports Center, but his bronze footprints are engraved into the top of the steps. The Museum of Art has one of the most extensive collections of suits of armor I have ever seen.

➢ The imposing *battleship New Jersey* is on display in Camden, New Jersey, right across the Delaware River. Ferry service runs between the two cities.

The official tourism Web site for Philadelphia is www.gophila.com. Scroll down the home page for visitor information.

*To avoid "Big City" overload, weather permitting, you can do the following:*

➢ Spend a day at *Six Flags Great Adventure Theme Park* in Central New Jersey. In addition to an incredible selection of amusement rides, it has the largest drive-through safari outside of Africa. Visit the safari park in the morning when the animals are active. The Web site is www.sixflags.com/parks/greatadventure/home.asp.

➢ Spend the day at *Ocean City, New Jersey,* just south of Atlantic City. Billed as "America's Greatest Family Resort," this lovely seaside family resort offers great beaches and waves, a long boardwalk with many attractions and fun rides, and a safe and friendly family environment for all ages. Founded by Baptists, there is no alcohol sold on the island. Like most New Jersey beach resorts, there are beach fees. The Chamber of Commerce Web site is www.Ocean CityVacation.com.

➢ If you have little kids, head out to *Oxford, Pennsylvania,* less than an hour from downtown Philadelphia, and spend a day at "Sesame Place," an amusement park with no mechanical devices. The kids generate all energy. The only sound you hear is laughter. For information visit www.SesamePlace.com.

➢ Another attraction outside of Philadelphia is *Amish Country,* also known as Pennsylvania Dutch Farmland. The Amish live a simple family and community-oriented lifestyle, eschewing all modern conveniences such as electricity and motor-driven vehicles and appliances. The Web site and phone number are the same: www.800PaDutch.com.

## Washington D.C.

Unlike Manhattan and Philadelphia, Washington D.C. is not laid out on a grid, so driving around the city can be confusing. It is a wonderful walking city and everything is easily reachable by metro. It will take two or three full days to see most of the major sights in downtown D.C. Allow an extra day to cross over into Virginia to visit George Washington's beautiful estate and visit Arlington Cemetery. Be sure to watch the Changing of the Guard at the Tomb of the Unknown Soldier.

Here are the major downtown attractions. Keep in mind *all* national museums are free:

## The Smithsonian

The three major museums are:

➢ *The Air and Space Museum* — the most visited museum in the U.S.

➢ *The Natural History Museum* — this is the one with the dinosaurs.

➢ *The American History Museum* — containing the collection of the inauguration gowns of the first ladies.

Some suggestions: If you only have time to visit two museums, go to the first two. Don't try to do two Smithsonian museums in one day; it's too tiring. When you visit the Air and Space Museum, get there in the morning just before it opens to beat the crowds. As soon as you enter, go immediately to the Imax Theater and buy tickets for one or more of the film presentations. In the summer the Imax presentations often sell out within an hour or two of the museum's opening.

## The Memorials and Monuments

There are four of them located within easy walking distance of one another. The Washington Monument often has a long wait to take the elevator up for the grand view. You will need to decide whether to have your photo taken in front of the monument and just move on. From there it is an easy stroll to the Lincoln Memorial, which has a great museum under the memorial. Next in line is the Vietnam War Memorial, a memorable experience, and from there it is another easy stroll to the Korean War Memorial.

## Other Attractions

➤ *The White House* is open to touring groups only certain days of the week, and you must be in line early in the morning.

➤ *The Capitol Building* is interesting to see, especially if you can gain entrance to a congressional session and get to watch our government at work.

➤ *The Holocaust Museum* is a somber, stirring experience. Should you decide to visit this museum, expect a lot of questions from your children, especially the young ones. Afterwards I recommend strolling around Washington Basin and visiting the nearby Jefferson Memorial.

➤ *The Roosevelt Museum,* situated entirely outdoors, is one of Washington D.C.'s newest, and worth the visit if you have the time.

➤ *The National Gallery* contains famous works of art and from time to time, special exhibits.

For accommodations and tourist information visit the official Web site www.Washington.org or call a travel agent.

*If you have the time, two other major attractions en route from Philadelphia to Washington are:*

➤ *The Inner Harbor of Baltimore,* with lots of shops, restaurants, street and water attractions and the outstanding and very extensive Baltimore Aquarium. Call 800-Harbor-1 or visit www.Harborplace.com.

➤ *Annapolis, Maryland,* home of the Naval Academy and a charming waterfront town offering lots of history, museums, shops, and restaurants. The official Web site is www.ci.annapolis.md.us.

From here we will swing west to visit a few areas on the other side of our glorious country. My apologies to the city of Boston, the New England states, the areas south of Washington D. C. and everything else I have failed to mention between the East Coast and the Far West. I have no doubt my glaring omissions will be brought to my attention and most assuredly will be included in my next book or on my Web site. I welcome e-mails from any reader, travel supplier, or travel promoter of any destination. When you write, remember to tell me *why* your favorite destination or attraction will appeal to single adults traveling with children. My e-mail address is Brenda@SingleParentTravel.net.

## ARIZONA

I fell in love with Arizona the first time I visited, and although my kids and I have been there many times, each time we visit, we again fall prey to its charms. Many people, especially Easterners, think of Arizona as the Grand Canyon with desert all around it. Wrong, very wrong. Did you know the largest stand of Ponderosa Pine Forest in the world is in northern Arizona? Did you know you could go skiing in Arizona and not on artificial snow? Do I have your attention now?

Arizona can roughly be divided into two geological sections. The southern half, which is the desert floor; and the northern half, which, at a higher elevation, enjoys a more temperate spring-like climate. The dividing line is the Mogollon (pronounced *Muggy Own*) Rim, which runs through the middle of the state in an East-West direction. You can actually see parts of the rim and the geological upheaval from the road as you drive north or south through the state. Areas north of the rim, such as the Grand Canyon, are *on-season* in the summer and areas south of the rim, such as Scottsdale and the Valley of the Sun, are *off-season* in the summer.

Except for rush hour in Phoenix, driving through the state of Arizona is a joy. Roads are good and mostly uncrowded. In spite of the heat and intense desert sun, you can enjoy a summer vacation in Southern Arizona. You need to get an early morning start for outdoor attractions, and you must remember to always carry water with you and in the car. Drink water periodically, even if you are not thirsty, and wear lightweight loose clothing that covers your shoulders. Always wear a hat when out in the desert sun.

There is so much to see and do in Arizona that you cannot cover all major attractions in two weeks, so whether your vacation is one week, ten days, or two weeks, you will have to pick and choose. Here are some suggestions starting with Tucson and then proceeding north.

### Tucson

You can fly directly into Tucson, although many people elect to fly into Phoenix and then make the two-hour drive south to Tucson, as Phoenix usually offers more competitive airfares. Using Tucson as a base, you can visit numerous nearby attractions. Allow a stay of two or three nights or more, depending upon what you want to see. If you travel to Tucson in the summer, I suggest finding a resort hotel with a really nice pool, negotiating for a reasonable off-season rate, doing all sightseeing in the morning (get an early start!), and returning to the hotel at 2 or 3 p.m. for a refreshing swim. The sun is blinding if you swim earlier in the day, and you can easily stay in the pool until 6 p.m. or later without getting chilled. I also recommend buying a cheap cooler upon your arrival and filling it each morning with fresh water, fruit and picnic food. Tucson's official Web site is www.ci.tucson.az.us/.

The major attractions surrounding Tucson are:

➤ *Arizona-Sonora Museum*

This world-class outdoor museum is also a botanical garden and mini-zoo with more than two miles (3.5 kilometers) of self-guided trails to stroll. It borders Saguaro National Park, just west of Tucson. I recommend going early in the morning (it opens at 7:30 a.m.) and visiting it early in your trip so you can learn about the flora and fauna of the Sonoran Desert. It is great fun for everyone and very educational. Call 520-883-1380 or visit www.DesertMuseum.org.

➤ *The "New" Old Tucson Movie Studio*

Much of this Old West theme park and movie lot was destroyed in a 1995 fire, but it has been rebuilt, and you can still enjoy the old sound stages and sites where many John Wayne and western films were made. It is full of tourists and snacks are overpriced, but it is fun nonetheless. Located near the Arizona-Sonora Museum, it is possible to see both attractions in one day and still have time for an afternoon swim (if you get an early start). The Web site is www.desertusa.com/mag98/dec/stories/studio.html.

➤ *Saguaro National Park* (The "g" in Saguaro is pronounced like an "h")

Located both east and west of Tucson, both sites merit a visit so you can see both the old and the new growths of these magnificent sentinels of the Sonoran Desert. Visit www.nps.gov/sagu/.

➤ *Nogales*

Both the U.S. and the Mexican town share the same name. About a one hour and 15 minute drive south of Tucson, this typical border town offers lots of shopping for Mexican crafts. Leave your car on the U.S. side and walk over the border. Don't bother to change your money; all the stores accept U.S. dollars. Although border-crossing formalities are usually lax, in these towns there is always the chance you may be asked to show your proof of citizenship as well as written permission from your child's other parent allowing you to take your child out of the country, so be prepared with the appropriate documents. For information about shopping in Nogales, Mexico, click on www.azcentral.com/travel/destinations/mexico/nogshop.shtml.

➤ *Mission San Xavier*

En route to Nogales you can stop at Mission San Xavier, recognizable by that beautiful whitewashed façade often featured in advertisements of Tucson. It is located nine miles (14 kilometers) southeast of Tucson. For more information call 520-294-2624, or visit www.opus1.com/emol/tucson/SANXAVIER/SANXAVIER.HTML.

➤ *Tombstone*

Although it has changed through the years (the town's original dusty main street is now paved), it still has one of the funkiest cemeteries in the world. It is worth the trip just to read the tombstones and visit the graves of some of the most colorful figures in our Wild West history. Tombstone is about an hour and fifteen minutes southwest of Tucson. Be prepared for lots of tourists and stores with honky tonk wares. The Web site for "The Town Too Tough to Die" is www.americanwest.com/pages/tombston.htm.

➤ *Kitt Peak National Observatory*

If you have never visited an astronomical observatory, consider touring Kitt Peak, as it is one of the more accessible observatories. The road up the mountain is full of switchbacks, but it is an excellent paved road. Kitt Peak has the largest collection of optical telescopes in the world. Tours of the site are offered throughout the day. For further information call 520-318-8000 or click on www.noao.edu/kpno/.

*A note on shopping:* One of the best places to shop for quality Native American crafts and silver jewelry in the state of Arizona is the section of Tucson called "Old Tucson." This area offers an extensive selection of stores and crafts with reasonable rates. Some good buys can also be found on roadside stands throughout the state where the Native Americans sell directly to the public, but quality of workmanship isn't always reliable, so examine what you buy. Make sure the catches work properly and there aren't any sharp edges on the jewelry that could poke or pull your clothing.

## Phoenix, Scottsdale, and the Valley of the Sun

I don't recommend spending a lot of time in this area for single adults traveling with kids. Phoenix is a large city of more than one million people, the area tends to be pricey, and there are so many other areas in the state that offer many natural attractions that are unique to Arizona. Having said that, there are a few attractions in the Phoenix area I would recommend. Perhaps you can squeeze one or two into your itinerary on your way to or from another part of the state. The Scottsdale tourism Web site is www.ci.scottsdale.az.us/visitors/.

➢ *The Heard Museum of Anthropology and Primitive Art*

This is the premier museum of Phoenix and contains a vast and impressive kachina doll collection from the estate of former Senator Barry Goldwater. Visit www.heard.org/.

➢ *Boyce Thompson Arboretum*

Located 60 miles (97 kilometers) east of Phoenix near the town of Superior, this unusual place offers miles/kilometers of hiking trails through canyons and desert gardens. Allow at least two hours for the visit. Web site address is ag.arizona.edu/BTA/.

➢ *Out of Africa*

This wildlife park is unique in the world. The kids and I really enjoyed it and learned a lot about big cat behavior. It is not a zoo but a living area for big cats in a natural environment. The staff swims with the tigers, plays with the lions, and is even chased by a pack of wolves while bears dive in giant pools. There are no rehearsed shows; everything is spontaneous. The staff members are all ages, including retired gray-hairs. If you are fascinated with big cats like my kids and me, this is the place to go. There is a restaurant and gift shop on the premises. Allow about three hours for your visit, not including lunch. The wildlife park is located in Fountain Hills (Scottsdale), off the Beeline Highway, 87. Call 480-837-7779 or visit www.desertusa.com/mag00/oct/stories/out.html.

**Arcosanti**

About 90 miles (145 kilometers) north of Phoenix, right off I-17 is an interesting place to stop. Famed Italian architect Pablo Soleri has created an experimental architectural town in the middle of the desert. There is a small donation to enter the premises and tours are offered hourly. This is where artisans craft the famous Soleri wind-bells and sculptures, many of which grace the foyers of corporate headquarters around the world. There are little ones for sale as well. All are originals and make nice souvenirs. www.arcosanti.org/.

## Sedona

Sedona is a two-hour drive from Phoenix. I recommend those flying into Phoenix to either drive two hours south to Tucson or north to Sedona for your first overnight stay. Sedona is one of my favorite places in the world (my kids agree!) and one of the very few areas where I would consider living that is not near an ocean. The town is surrounded by glorious red rocks, soaked in mystical vibes, and gives off a peaceful, yet energetic feeling to those who visit. Restaurants and lodging vary from high quality expensive to plain and simple. There is always something going on in Sedona, such as a festival (cultural, musical, food), a psychic fair or an artisans' display. The perpetual spring-like climate makes it a year-round destination. As more people "discover" Sedona, real estate values will continue to go up, but it is a terrific place to visit. I recommend at least two full days to enjoy the area. Here are a few of the attractions:

➢ *Hiking* — There are many half-day hikes, but if your time is limited and you want drop-dead scenery on a short hike (less than an hour), be sure to hike up Bell Mountain (easy) or Cathedral Rock (a little harder). You will recognize Cathedral Rock as the poster child of Sedona. Many of the popular hikes are on vortices (plural for vortex). Don't be surprised to see a fellow hiker perched on a scenic rock in a state of meditation or contemplation.

➢ *Pink Jeep Tours* — Fun, but expensive on a single parent budget. If you can't afford it, just do the hikes. They are glorious.

➢ *Psychic Reading* — Fun to do and rates are reasonable, given all the competition.

➢ *Tlaquepaque* — This is a must-do shopping excursion for the whole family. Tlaquepaque is a recreated "perfect" Spanish village filled with one-of-a-kind shops. They are not cheap, but offer beautiful jewelry and artisan creations. There are lots of little restaurants too. Tlaquepaque is pronounced just the way it is spelled (tla kay PAH kay).

➢ *Slide Rock State Park* — Located just north of town, this park contains a natural (not man-made) water slide. The slippery moss-covered red rocks lead into pools of water. It is oodles of fun. Bring an old bathing suit or old shorts to wear over your bathing suit, as the rock surface may snag or tear new beachwear. Go early in the day; the number of visitors are sometimes limited.

➤ *Oak Creek Canyon* — refers to both the recreational area surrounding Sedona as well as the dramatically scenic drive leading north out of Sedona. Plan on doing that drive during the daylight to take in the scenery.

Tourist Web sites for Sedona are www.sedona.net/ and www.sedonavisitors guide.com/.

## Jerome

To the west of Sedona is an old mining town, which became a ghost town and later reemerged as a tourist center filled with artisan shops and historic buildings. The mile-high town sits on a steep hillside, and the drive up has sweeping views of the valley below. Visit www.azjerome.com/.

## Flagstaff

Not the prettiest of Arizona towns, Flagstaff is often used as a jumping off point for Sedona, the Grand Canyon, or other sights in the area. The main attraction in Flagstaff is the outstanding Museum of Northern Arizona, just outside of town, heading north on North Fort Valley Road. The outdoor exhibits of the various Indian pueblo periods are excellent. Click on www.musnaz.org/. There are a number of sites offering accommodation and tourist information on Flagstaff: flagstaff-arizona.com/, www.flagguide.com/ and www.flagstaff.az.gov/.

Following are three attractions we keep meaning to visit that are a short drive from Flagstaff. One of these days...

➤ *Sunset Crater National Monument* (north of Flagstaff). The attractions here are the dead volcanic cone, the colorful array of mineral formations, and the Lava Flow Nature Trail, which begins at the base of the crater and climbs 1,000 feet (300 meters) to the top. The summit offers a view of the Painted Desert and Humphrey's Peak.

➤ *Arizona Snow Bowl* — Just south of Sunset Crater this is the mountain where you snow ski in Arizona. The double-chair lift is open year-round.

➢ *Meteor Crater* — East of Flagstaff, this moon-like crater was featured in the movie "Starman" with Jeff Bridges. It has also been a training site for astronauts. For more details visit www.meteorcrater.com/.

## Grand Canyon National Park

If I have to describe the Grand Canyon in one word, awesome is the one I would select. In my following recommendations, first I will describe the sights at the South Rim, where 90% of the visitors stay. To sample the major sights of the Grand Canyon requires at least two days.

Try to book a hotel on or near the rim. To do so you will need to make reservations at least nine months in advance for summertime arrivals. El Tovar Lodge is the premier lodge in the area. If your budget cannot afford El Tovar, consider splurging for a dinner in its classy old world dining room (Advance reservations required). Failing that, at least visit the hotel.

The second best lodging choice at the Grand Canyon is the Bright Angel Lodge. This is a very historic building with old plumbing, but is a lot cheaper than the El Tovar and sits in a primo location. When we checked into our first floor room, my then 7-year-old son, always in motion, climbed out the window and returned to announce he had stood at the rim. Busy unpacking, I absentmindedly replied, "Yes, honey, we'll come look at the canyon." When I peeked out the window, I shrieked. We weren't near the rim. We were *at* the rim. Now *that's* a primo location! Bright Angel Lodge has a great Fred Harvey historical museum off the main lobby. Don't miss it.

For information and reservations on accommodations within the park, call 303-338-6000 or visit www.grandcanyonlodges.com/lodging.htm where you can make online reservations. Phone reservation hours are 7 a.m.– 6 p.m., Mountain Time, seven days a week. Hotel reservations may be made as far ahead as two years before scheduled arrival. You can also book mule rides and make dinner reservations on this site. Xanterra (formerly Amfac), the country's largest national and state park concessionaire, handles all reservations. For further information on the Grand Canyon and other national parks, check out their handy Web site www.xanterra.com. The new address for the official government Web site for Grand Canyon National Park is www.nps.gov/grca/.

Meal service in the grand old dining rooms of the historic lodges is slow but the atmosphere is great and the food is good, so plan accordingly. Do make advance reservations (See the Xanterra Web site address above). For breakfast or lunch, I recommend eating in one of the sterile cafeterias unless you have time to waste. Better yet, buy the ingredients for a picnic lunch and hit the trail.

Things to do at the Grand Canyon:

➢ *Sign up for a free ranger-guided tour.* You and your kids will learn all kinds of neat things. This is where I learned to bear hug a Ponderosa Pine Tree. Did you know it smells like butterscotch?

➢ *Hike down the Bright Angel Trail.* Even if you walk down for 10 or 15 minutes, you will have passed by thousands of years of geological history. Dropping down below the rim immediately changes your perspective on things. Keep in mind a hike of one hour down means a hike of two hours up. Take all the water you need on your hike, plus sunscreen and a hat. The temperature goes up as you walk down. There are no facilities on the trail.

To hike all the way to the Colorado River would require five to six hours down and ten hours up. People that do this stay overnight at Phantom Ranch, which is dormitory lodging at the bottom of the canyon. You must pre-reserve accommodations. Another way to make the trip is to take a Canyon Mule Ride. This is a very strenuous trip, with age and weight restrictions. You must pre-book this ride at least a year ahead. It is really not for families with young children as seven hours in the saddle is a long time for kids. What I do recommend is to linger around the rim early in the morning and listen to the cowboys give their lecture to the mule ride participants. It is both funny and serious and a whole different culture.

➢ *Visit the Yavapai Museum on the canyon rim,* which superbly explains the geology of the area. If time permits, take the East Rim Drive to the Tusayan Museum, which describes the life of the prehistoric Indians in this area 800 years ago.

➢ *Watch the sunset.* The changing of the colors of the canyon will amaze you. Have your camera ready with lots of film.

The North Rim of the Grand Canyon is more easily accessible if you are coming down from Utah. The only place to stay here is the delightful Grand Canyon Lodge. You must have advance reservations. The North Rim is higher and colder than the South Rim and is only open from May through October. We actually encountered a brief snowstorm on our way to the North Rim on a mid-July trip. The atmosphere is much quieter on this side of the canyon. For hotel and dinner reservations you can call Xanterra at 303-338-6000 or click on www.grandcanyonnorthrim.com/ for online reservations.

Other areas worth a visit in Arizona include:

➢ *Monument Valley Navajo Tribal Park*

Located about 125 miles (200 kilometers) northeast of the Grand Canyon, on the Arizona/Utah border, is one of the most remote and stunning places in the world. If it is at all possible to include an overnight stay at Monument Valley in your travel plans, do so. For details on this remarkable place, read the following section on Utah.

➢ *Four Corners Monument*

East of Monument Valley, this is the only place in the USA where four state borders meet — Utah, Arizona, Colorado, and New Mexico. The *de rigueur* photograph is to stand on the monument and pose as you touch all four states with your arms and legs. There's not much else to do here other than a few tourist shops. I wouldn't go out of your way to travel here, but it is a fun thing to do if you are sweeping down and around to another northeastern part of the state. The monument is part of the Navajo Nation and, as such, is subject to tribal laws and time zones. Visit www.navajonationparks.org/fourcorner.html

➢ *Canyon de Chelly*

Located in the remote northeast corner of Arizona, this beautiful red rock canyon area offers an opportunity to learn how the ancients lived, as well as an exciting jeep ride through the canyons with Navajo guides as your drivers. The name De Chelly is a Spanish corruption of the Navajo word "Tsegi," which means roughly "rock canyon." The Spanish pronunciation "day shay-yee" has gradually changed through English usage, and the name is now pronounced Canyon "d'shay." This is family fun for everyone. Allow a full day for the jeep ride and another half day to do the rim drive and some short hikes down to the canyon floor. There are half-day jeep tours, but I highly recommend the full day tour, which takes you out to the famous Spider Rock. It is worth the difference in price.

➢ Allow for a two-night stay in the area, either at the Thunderbird Lodge at the monument or in the nearby town of Chinle. Jeep tours may be booked through the Thunderbird Lodge. Their Web site is www.tbirdlodge.com/Tours.htm. For general information on the area, try the government Web site www.nps.gov/cach/. If you are having problems navigating the government site, other sites are:

www.navajoland.com/cdc/

www.desertusa.com/ind1/du_cdc_main.html.

*Heading south from Canyon de Chelly are two attractions worth a visit en route to the main road of I-40:*

➢ *Window Rock* — the Capital of the Navajo Nation. There are few tourist attractions here, other than the Tribal Museum and the nearby Natural Bridge, but it is interesting to see the construction of the buildings. The Web site is www.azohwy.com/w/windowro.htm.

➢ *Hubbell Trading Post* — This national historic site has preserved the trading post created by John Hubbell for his Navajo neighbors. You can still shop there today. Visit www.nps.gov/hutr/hubbell.htm.

➢ *Painted Desert and Petrified Forest* — These adjacent attractions may be covered in a full day if you get an early start. You can over-night in nearby Holbrook or further south in the towns of Snowflake or Show Low. The Painted Desert is as beautiful as it sounds and there are easy hikes you can take right off the main road. Bring plenty of water and sun protection with you. The Petrified Forest is interest-ing and very educational and offers many loop hikes. Make sure to see the short film at the Visitor's Center before venturing out into the park. When we hiked the Painted Desert I thought to myself, "Boy, this scenery looks familiar." That night, after checking into our motel, my son and I watched an old Western movie and we were delighted to see that the backdrop of the movie was the Painted Desert hike we had done earlier in the day. The government Web site is www.nps.gov/pefo/. Or try www.wmonline.com/attract/pforest/pforest.htm.

Just south of Show Low is the Lakeside/Pinetop recreational area, which straddles the Mogollon Rim. Along this rim are some beautiful easy hikes through the Ponderosa Pine area, one of which was a former pioneer trail. You are so completely surrounded by greenery you will find it hard to believe you are in Arizona. The trailheads are not well marked so you must ask directions of the locals. From here you head back to Phoe-nix via scenic State Highway 60. Just after the town of Miami is the

Boyce Thompson Arboretum, mentioned earlier under Phoenix. Plan to stop there.

We hope you are as captivated by Arizona as we are!

*Author's Note:* As this book went to press, the fires of June 2002 were raging around Show Low and the Pinetop Recreational area. Our hearts and condolences go out to the residents of that beautiful area.

## NATIONAL PARKS OF SOUTHERN UTAH

A combination of awesome scenery and unique history makes this area of the U.S. one of the most interesting and beautiful places to spend a vacation. Parts of Southern Utah were among the last regions to be settled by the white man and even today, the area still remains one of the most remote and "untouched" parts of the American West. Rates are reasonable in this region of the country. There are no big cities in Southern Utah, but there is some small town nightlife, especially in Moab. This part of Utah is a wasteland for interesting or fine dining. Consequently, unlike other destinations I recommended good restaurants where I was able to find them. Restaurant ownership changes, so forgive me if what was true a year or two ago no longer is. Readers are welcome to e-mail other restaurant suggestions to Brenda@SingleParentTravel.net for my Web site www.SingleParent Travel.net or for future book editions.

Places I recommend in Utah are (not necessarily in this order): Moab, Monument Valley, Salt Lake City, and the national parks and monuments of Arches, Canyonlands, Natural Bridges, Escalante, Capitol Reef, Bryce, and Zion.

### Getting There

The two closest major airports to Southern Utah are Salt Lake City and Las Vegas (Nevada). A third, further possibility is Colorado Springs. Salt Lake City is approximately a five-hour drive to the westernmost national parks (Zion, Bryce Canyon) and also five hours to the easternmost point (Arches, Canyonlands). Las Vegas is about 3 1/2 hours to the Zion/Bryce area and an eight-hour drive to Moab, the jumping off point for Arches and Canyon- lands. All roads to the national parks from these two airports are major high- ways, maintained year-round. Both drives are along scenic byways, so determining a flying destination is a question of preference, convenience and which entry city has the lowest airfare. Should you decide to fly into one city and out of another, be sure and check car rental one-way drop charges before making any flight reservations.

Starting from the eastern side of Utah and moving westward we begin with:

### Moab

Surrounded by gorgeous red rock canyons, this funky town is a mixture of modern and quaint and a haven for mountain bikers. With a population numbering more than 5,000, it is the largest town in Southeast Utah with a varied selection of restaurants and shops. Accommodations are mostly chain motels, such as Best Western, Days Inn, and Travelodge, all located on the main drag. There are no hotel or restaurant accommodations in Arches or Canyonlands, so Moab is where to stay or dine if you plan to visit these national parks. The town has a movie theater, the Slickrock Cinema, and the nightlife centers around the brewpubs serving tasty local microbrews. Depending upon the season, shops may close by early evening. Because of the unique environment, Moab draws a lot of international visitors, especially from Europe. For accommodations and activity information check out these two Web sites: www.moab-utah.com/ and www.moab.net/utahareaguides/moab/ or call 800-635-6622.

**Restaurants in Moab**

My favorite moderate-priced place for breakfast or supper is the *Slick Rock Cafe* at 5 N. Main St, located in an historic building and offering a varied eclectic menu. Their microbrews are great! There is also the *Jailhouse Cafe*, at 101 N Main, a pricier menu, but also good. You will need to pack a picnic lunch to visit the parks so head for the one supermarket in town which has a great selection of fruits, veggies, and sandwiches, all available in plastic picnic containers.

One (actually two) of the most enjoyable dinners I ever had has been at the *Grand Old Ranch House* Restaurant, located in an 1896 pioneer house at the north edge of town. The meal and service is elegant yet friendly, and the atmosphere absolutely enchanting. The wait staff wears formal attire, but you are welcome to wear your hiking/biking casual attire. The last time I dined there the place was filled with Europeans, all of whom were delighted with the meal and the ambiance (Never shy about asking travel-related questions, I queried them all!). There is a colorful history to the place, which the wait staff eagerly shares with you, and you are welcome to check out the cozy rooms filled with old photographs and newspaper clippings. The meal is on the pricey side but worth every dollar. A children's menu is provided and cocktails are served. The desserts are eye-popping confections created by one of the owners who travels to Europe each year to bring back new ideas for the restaurant's menu. This is a true gourmet oasis in the heart of no man's land. If one really great meal is in your budget, make this your splurge night. Advance reservations may be required in the summer months. Call 435-259-5753.

Another popular restaurant is *Mi Vida* located on a bluff overlooking Moab Valley. This was the home of former uranium king, Charlie Steen. I found the meal not up to par with the prices and the decor was what I would call "early waiting room." The drive up to the restaurant was the most exciting part of the evening. If you are going to splurge on your budget one night, I recommend you drive up to Mi Vida to enjoy the beautiful view and then turn right around and dine at the Grand Old Ranch House.

Check to see if restaurants are open depending on when you plan to travel, as many restaurants are seasonal.

## Arches National Park

One of the jewels in America's national park system, this is an easy park to hike and visit if you have young children or elderly people accompanying you. Most attractions are within easy reach of the main park road. It is also a park you can "do" in a day, if you get an early start. There are no concession facilities in the park, so take lots of water and bring a picnic lunch. There are picnic tables in the Devil's Garden area, or you can "tailgate" anywhere in the park. There are toilet facilities, called pit toilets, at the trailhead of all major hiking areas. There is usually plenty of toilet paper, but bring some tissue, just in case, especially during the busy summer season. There is no running water, so bring wipes, washcloths or anti-bacterial waterless hand sanitizer, especially for those kids' sticky little hands. The government Web site for Arches is www.nps.gov/arch/. An excellent private site is www.arches.national-park.com.

## Hiking

Inquire first at the visitor's center about ranger-guided walks to the *Fiery Furnace* the day you are there. If they are available, sign up for one and plan your hikes around this guided walk. You will want to visit *Balanced Rock* and the *Windows* section, an easy hike of an hour or more. *Sand Dune Arch* is a quick and easy walk and a cool, shady place to get out of the hot summer sun. There's also a short trail to *Skyline Arch. Devil's Garden* is a must, a stunningly beautiful one hour easy walk. (It is easy to shoot an entire roll of film on this walk alone). The most spectacular hike is the one to *Delicate Arch,* which is moderately strenuous and takes at least two hours round-trip. The hike culminates in a heart-stopping view of one of the most beautiful arches in the world, and so is aptly named.

The most difficult part of the hike is the wide-open slide rock incline early on in the hike; after that it gets easier. You can view this area from the trailhead or your car and decide if you can hike it. Slide rock can be slippery when wet, so get a good grip on those that need help, especially on the way down. The Wolfe Ranch, at the base of the hike, provides an interesting bit of history.

**Canyonlands National Park**

There are three districts of Canyonlands National Park. The entrance to Island in the Sky is ten miles (16 kilometers) north of Moab. The Needles district of the park is about an hour and a half south of Moab. The Maze District, south and west of Moab, has some of the wildest country in the U.S. and is visited by very few people. The government Web site is www.nps.gov/cany/. Two other sites are: www.travelwest.net/parks/canyonlands/ and www.canyonlands.national-park.com/, the latter site being more informative and less commercialized.

➤ *Island in the Sky*

This is the easiest area to hike, the most accessible, and offers the biggest bang for your buck if your time is limited. It is possible to squeeze in some short scenic hikes in a few hours. Like Arches, there are no dining facilities and even fewer toilet facilities, so plan accordingly. The "island" is actually a huge mesa with lookout points and short hikes all along the rim. Time and ability permitting, you can also do longer, steeper hikes from the rim down to the road below. Be sure and hike the easy short trail to *Mesa Arch,* one of the most photographed and photogenic arches in the world. Like a supermodel, the arch does not take a bad picture. *The Grand View Point* is a spectacular viewing point and the nearby picnic area makes a nice stopping place for lunch.

➤ *Newspaper Rock*

On the way to the Needles entrance you will pass by Newspaper Rock. The petroglyphs on this historical monument depict 2000 years of human history representing all the tribes that passed through Indian Creek Canyon during this span of time. It is the most extensive display of petroglyphs I have ever seen and particularly fascinating since so many time periods overlay one another. It will enhance your visit here if you do some pre-reading on petroglyphs or pick up a little book about it in one of the visitor centers. That way you can "read" some of the "newspapers." Visit www.desertusa.com/newut/du_newut_vvc.html.

➢ *Needles*

As you approach Needles the road becomes more rolling, sloping and scenic. There's little or no traffic in the off-season and you are easily lolled into complacency as you gaze at the scenery. Don't be surprised to suddenly see a big cow staring at you in the middle of the road as you come down over a hill. Much of this area is open grazing land so be prepared; otherwise your rental car will turn into mush, and you along with it. Two easy and very scenic hikes in Needles are *Pothole Point* and *Slickrock Trail*. Each takes about an hour.

Once you leave Needles and get back on the main road you are only two and a half hours from Monument Valley, on the Utah/Arizona border. Monument Valley is one of the "must-see" places in the Southwestern United States, so if you can, plan on heading south and spending at least one night there. It is possible to spend the night in Moab, hike Needles for a few hours and then head south for Monument Valley and squeeze in the sunset jeep tour that evening. It is a very tight squeeze, but if you are energetic, an early riser and can discipline yourself to leave Needles at a pre-arranged time, then you can do it. On a recent trip with my niece, we did it in October, right after daylight savings time changed, so our Monument Valley sunset tour finished up in the dark but we made it. During the long summer days you should be OK.

## Bluff

This town, located on Route 191, just before you veer off for Route 163 to take you to Monument Valley, makes a worthwhile stop. There is the Bluff City Historic Loop to visit back street pioneer houses but it is hard to find the signs. There is also a very interesting cemetery atop a small hill overlooking the town, which is worth the detour — a great view and interesting inscriptions. The Twin Rocks Trading Post sells high-quality Indian crafts, much of it produced by the local Navajos. The adjoining cafe offers an inexpensive tasty lunch. Their specialty is Navajo tacos, of course! The town, population 300, maintains a Web site, which includes information on local festivals and activities at www.BluffUtah.org.

## Monument Valley Tribal Park

This totally awesome place, which has been the backdrop for so many movies from John Wayne's "Stagecoach" to more recent flicks such as one or more of the "Back to the Future" and "Raiders" series, must be seen on a Navajo guided jeep tour, either at sunset or sunrise. After three visits to this place over a 13-year period, I can safely say it remains as beautiful and pristine as the first time I saw it. The Navajos have done an excellent job of keeping it accessible to tourism without over-commercialization. Although the people of the Navajo Nation are full-fledged American citizens, this is Navajo Tribal Land, and, as such, the Navajos operate the land under their own laws and police force. For example *Navajo Tribal Land does not adhere to daylight savings time* so when it is 4 p.m. in Utah or Arizona on a summer afternoon, it is 5 p.m. in Navajo Land. Unaware of this fact on our first trip to Arizona, we almost missed our sunset jeep tour. An informative Web site, which includes some history of the Navajo tribe, is navajo_nation.tripod.com/gbook.html. Another Web site is www.americansouthwest.net/utah/monument_valley/.

**Places to Stay**

Hands down, the best place to stay is *Goulding's Lodge,* built into a butte, right in the heart of Monument Valley. You will need to book accommodations many months ahead, especially in the high summer season. Thirteen years ago Goulding's was just a one level motel unit with about 20 rooms. It has gradually grown to be a delightful mini resort lodge, complete with a small indoor pool, a lovely and extensive gift shop featuring Navajo crafts, a two-level museum building housing interesting artifacts from the art of movie making at Monument Valley, and a very pleasant restaurant with a lovely view of the monuments and an accommodating Navajo staff. Rates vary according to season. If you are not lucky enough to secure accommodations here, at least visit the museum, historical sites, and gift shop. Everything is built into the butte, so the property is multi-level and will require walking up and down steps to get to where you are going. There are no elevators, but you can drive right up to your room. You can make hotel reservations online via www.gouldings.com/ or call 435-727-3231.

If you cannot get a room at Goulding's or have a tight budget, there are some accommodations in Mexican Hat, Utah, population 50, north of Monument Valley. A good place is the *San Juan Inn & Trading Post,* perched on a dramatic location above the San Juan River. Click on www.utohwy.com/s/sanjuain.htm or call 435-683-2220. You can tube down the river in the summer months. South of Monument Valley is a *Holiday Inn* in the town of Kayenta. You can book online at

www.sixcontinentshotels.com/holiday-inn?_franchisee=KAYAR or call
Holiday Inn reservations at 800 465-4329.

## Navajo Guided Jeep Tours

You absolutely have to take the jeep tour in order to properly experience
Monument Valley. Driving by on the main road just isn't the same. That
would be like trying to experience snow by looking at a distant snow-
capped mountain peak. Goulding's offers the standard two- to three- hour
jeep tour of Monument Valley, which you can pre-reserve. You should
reconfirm this tour time at least twice before you arrive, as it changes
without notice. Another possibility is for you to drive to the Tribal Park
and sign up for one of the tours. There are many booths offering tours,
and they run about US$5 to US$10 cheaper than Goulding's. I can't
vouch for the quality of tour guides at the tribal park, but we struck gold
on our last trip with Gilbert Whitehorse, a young, handsome, energetic,
and entertaining Navajo. We were enthralled when he sang a Navajo
chant for us and he was very sensitive to the needs of photographers as
well. I recommend you take the three-hour rather than the two-hour tour
and that you do it at sunrise or sunset for better lighting, even if you are
not a photographer.

Before the entrance to the tribal park, and again at John Ford's Point, there
will be several stalls of local Navajo jewelry and pottery for sale. The quality is usually good to excellent and the prices are the lowest you will find
anywhere. Bring cash and lots of small bills. Some of the more expensive
booths may accept credit cards, but don't count on it. It's a great place to
pick up inexpensive gifts. Also at John Ford's Point you will find some
Navajos in their native dress, often on horseback, who will gladly pose for
you for a tip of US$1 or US$2.

No matter which direction you are heading, *remember to fill up with gas at
Goulding's before you leave* Monument Valley.

## Moki Dugway

Shortly after leaving Mexican Hat, as you head up Route 261, you will
come upon a large mesa facing you. Believe it or not, the road goes straight
up this mesa on a series of hairpin turns, which you can't see from a distance. In fact you can't even see the road close up. This stretch of road is so
infamous it even has a name — the *Moki Dugway.* This is a three-mile dirt
road up the side of the mesa, so check out road conditions that morning if

there has been recent rain. It is an interesting experience and for most people, myself included, a white-knuckle drive. For pictures of the road, click on www.so-utah.com/souteast/powerdrv/mokidgwy/homepage.html.

## Natural Bridges National Monument

It is a five-hour drive from Monument Valley to Capitol Reef National Park, and Natural Bridges is a perfect midway point to break up the trip and do some hiking. This entire drive is incredibly beautiful and by the end of it, you may undergo what I call "scenic stress" or scenic overload. You finally reach the point where you can no longer stop and get out of the car to take a picture. You say to yourself "Enough already!" and then you go around a bend of the road and another irresistible dramatic panorama unfolds before your eyes.

Natural Bridges has a scenic loop drive, and I recommend you hike at least one of the trails down to the three natural bridges. *Sipapu* is a steep trail and fairly strenuous. You will have to climb some steps and a ladder. The last few feet (1 meter) of the trail are over a rather steep and smooth rock area with only some strategically placed railings for support. A hiker coming up with camera equipment said the view under the bridge was not worth the effort of getting down to the very bottom. We took his sage advice and chickened out just short of the bottom. Another trail, which we didn't have time to hike, takes you down to *Kachina Bridge*. We did take the easy stroll down to the base of *Owachomo Bridge,* which I recommend. If you have the time, you could hike down Sipapu, and stroll along the riverbank and then come up the Owachomo Trail or vice versa. This is a moderately difficult hike of five to six hours. The government Web site for Natural Bridges is www.americansouthwest.net/utah/natural_bridges/national_monument.html. Another site is www.nps.gov/nabr/.

## Capitol Reef National Park

Most people say their first glimpse of Capitol Reef National Park is dream-like. See if you agree. Probably the least known and least populated of America's national parks, Capitol Reef is remote even today. It was the last area of the U.S. to be "discovered" by the white man and even as late as World War II it was accessible only by wagon. The name Capitol Reef derives from two things. "Capitol" refers to some of the rock formations, which look like our capitol dome. "Reef" refers to the Waterfold Fold, a 1,100 mile-long geological upheaval that runs north to south in Southern Utah. It was a formidable barrier to the early explorers and pioneers. Used to nautical terms, they called it a reef, since it was blocking their passage. You will need at least a full day to cover the highlights of the park and a second full day to visit the remote areas on a tour. The government Web site is www.nps.gov/care/. Another site is www.infowest.com/Utah/colorcountry/Nationalparks/Capitolreef/capitol.html.

## Places to Stay in Capitol Reef

There are no hotel accommodations or concessionary facilities in the park, but there are several chain and independently run motels a few miles/kilometers away. The *Best Western Capitol Reef* is near to the park. You can call Best Western at 800-528-1234 or book on their Web site www.bwdiscoverthewest.com/Utah/CapitolReef/dining.htm. In the town of Torrey, about ten miles west of the park, is the *Wonderland Inn.* For reservations call 877-854-0184 or visit www.capitolreefwonderland.com. Also in Torrey is the *Days Inn.* You can call 800-325-2525 or book online at www.utohwy.com/t/tordayin.htm. A new property, *Hidden Falls Resort,* was just being built when I last visited the area. The reservation number for Hidden Falls is 888-232-4082 or you can book online at www.holidayinncapitolreef.com/. They offer Internet specials. A Web site for booking several properties in Torrey is www.travelwest.net/parks/capitolreef/. Regarding the chain hotels, I recommend price comparison shopping on major travel sites, such as Expedia.com, as discussed in Part I of this book. You can also book through a travel agent. Check out the Appendix for agencies that specialize in Single Parent Travel.

## Dining

Like most of southern Utah, this area is a wasteland for fine dining. A pleasant exception is the *Cafe Diablo* at the western end of Torrey, which offers a varied tasty menu specializing in Southwestern cuisine. It is closed during the off-season, so call ahead at 435-425-3070. Their Web site is www.cafediablo.net. The same advice applies to other restaurants in nearby towns. It is best to call ahead as some close without notice. The motel restaurants are open year-round.

## Historical Sites/Scenic Drives

The visitor's center is located in the heart of what once was a Mormon pioneer village. The town is named *Fruita* after the numerous groves of fruit trees, which still exist today. Park rangers tend them, and during summer and fall you can pick your own fruit and pay for what you pick (unless you eat it on the spot). As you leave the visitor center parking lot, turn right and drive through parts of the old village, stopping at the blacksmith's shop and one of the former pioneer homes. From there continue on to the *Scenic Drive* which is about 20 miles (32 kilometers) round trip. Allow an hour for the ride, which will include some picture taking. The road is paved but narrow, and is fine for all rental cars. Sometimes the gullies flood due to recent rains and then the road is closed. The reef cliffs are visible throughout the drive, so drive it in the early morning or the late afternoon for best lighting effects.

After this drive, go back to the visitor's center, turn left on the main road and you will soon come to a pretty tree-lined area known for its *petroglyph markings*. Take a few minutes to do the short walk and examine the glyphs. After that is the not-to-be-missed *one room schoolhouse*. Push the button at the side of the building to hear one of the former schoolteachers talk about her experiences as a young woman in this rough and remote town. Outside of Fruita, the Behunin Cabin is worth a stop. So is the side road to *The Goosenecks Overlook,* between Torrey and Fruita.

If you really want to get into the remote areas, I highly recommend taking a day tour to *Cathedral Valley*. Only five percent of park visitors see this remarkable area. This rugged 60 mile loop drive in the northern park of the park will require four wheel drive and most of the day to complete the trip. Particularly striking are the stone monoliths such as the Temples of the Sun and Moon and the Walls of Jericho. I walked around behind this area where the stone formations surround you as they soar upwards, and within a few minutes was surrounded by silence so complete it was eerie. Not even the sound of a bird or the wind was there to break the "heaviness" of the silence. Later in the drive you go through an area that looks like a lunar landscape.

Another full day trip is to the rugged, remote southern area of the park called the *Burr Trail,* which crosses over Burr Road. The drive to the top of Waterpocket Fold offers fantastic views both enroute and at the top. Once again you will need four-wheel drive. To do either or both of these full day trips I recommend the services of *Hondoo Tours*. Their Web site is www.hondoo.com where you can book online or call 800-332-2696. You can join one of their daily vehicle tours or create your own tour.

On two different trips I had Dale King, a retired rancher, as my guide. He was not only knowledgeable but also delightful. His family history in the area goes back several generations when the area was first settled by

Mormons. My favorite story is the helicopter rescue of his grandfather when he was herding cattle in a very remote area. Be sure to ask him about that if he is your guide. Hondoo can set you up for any size group and a homemade picnic lunch is included with the tour. There is something special about an extensive picnic lunch being served in a fabulously scenic remote area with great company to boot. I call it good living.

## Hiking

There are over a dozen different day hikes, some a few hours and some all day. *Grand Wash, Capitol Gorge, Sunset Point and Goosenecks* are easy. The rest are more difficult. Grand Wash is a very scenic one-hour walk in a gravel riverbed surrounded by soaring rock faces. In the Narrows area, midway through the walk, the light comes in only from straight above. If you walk all the way it will take two hours round trip, unless you can pre-arrange someone to pick you up at the other end. If your time is limited and no one can meet you at the other end, I recommend at least hiking midway, and then going through the Narrows before turning back to retrace your steps. This trail closes down when heavy rains threaten.

The trail to *Hickman Bridge* is moderately strenuous, very scenic, and will take about an hour to the top. The trail is self-guiding with numbers marking important points.

## Escalante Grand Staircase National Monument

Appointed a national monument by former President Clinton, this enormous area encompasses 1.7 million acres of pristine wilderness. At present there is no formal visitor's center and it is primitive, with no marked trails, but you can call the Escalante Interagency Visitor's Center for further information. The number is 435-826-5499. They are open daily from 7:30 a.m. to 5:30 p.m., Mountain Time. An informative Web site on the area is www.desertusa.com/escalante/. For a virtual reality tour of Escalante, click on www.pbproductions.com/escalante/. We did not hike, but instead stopped to take pictures enroute from Capitol Reef to Bryce.

## Bryce Canyon National Park

The drive from Capitol Reef takes about three hours. The road is incredibly scenic and subject to changing road conditions. Check ahead if you are doing this during the winter. We saw snow in the higher elevations even in October. The drive takes you through the remote and beautiful *Escalante* area, where you can stop and stretch your legs while taking some glorious photos.

Bryce Canyon is gorgeous any time of the year. Having hiked it both in late fall and mid summer I can't say I have a preference. The late afternoon summer sun makes the rocks glow a little more pink, but the winter snow dusting on top of the hoodoos makes Bryce Canyon look like a beautiful frosted pink pastry. The sun is intense in the summer but the shoulder seasons (spring and fall) can be quite chilly due to the high elevation, so dress warmly when hiking at those times and be prepared to layer down or up as needed. There is often some snow in the higher elevations from October onward. The government Web site for Bryce is: www.nps.gov/brca/. Another excellent informative site is www.bryce.canyon.national-park.com/.

### Hiking

To see Bryce Canyon you *have* to hike it. The main outstanding trail is the four hour *Navajo Trail* which goes down into the gorge and up again onto the rim. Be sure to take the side loop trail to *Queens Garden*. Young children can easily negotiate the trail. There are no treacherous parts and once you reach the bottom it is an easy walk along the canyon floor. If you are out of shape you will huff and puff on the way back up, but there are plenty of places to stop and rest and the scenery is non-stop all the way. *This is a must-do hike.* Take lots of film and water with you.

### Places to Stay at Bryce Canyon

There is only one lodge inside the park — the Bryce Canyon Lodge. Listed in the National Historic Register of Hotels, it is beautifully restored, is comfy, cozy, and the center of action. There are cabins as well as the main lodge. The food is great. Plan on eating at least one meal here even if you are staying outside the park. Dinner reservations are required and you should call two to three months ahead for peak summer period. Phone 435-834-5361. Dining attire is casual. Check out the ranger evening activities during the summer. The lodge closes from late fall to early spring. To make hotel reservations you must contact Xanterra at 303-338-6000 or book online at www.Xanterra.com/properties/bryce.htm.

If the lodge is closed, not available, or not within your budget, a good second choice would be Ruby's Inn, located right outside the park and open year round. This lively place is the starting point for many tours. For reservations call 800-468-8660 or book online at their Web site www.rubysinn.com/. If rates at Ruby's are still outside your budget, then consider staying at one of the chain motels in the town of Cedar City, which is about an hour away from Bryce and Zion. Lodging information can be found on: www.travelwest.net/cities/cedarcity/lodging.html.

## Zion National Park

Zion is a leisurely one and half-hour drive from Bryce, about three hours from Las Vegas, or five hours from Salt Lake City, depending on how fast you drive. The scenic drive into Zion will knock your socks off. Weather is generally warmer here than in Bryce. To cover the major hikes of this park, you should plan on spending two full days here.

## Hiking

There are dozens of hikes in Zion, but there are three I recommend for everyone. *Emerald Pools* is a two-hour easy hike with great photo opportunities. *Weeping Rock* is an easy trail to a series of springs above an overhang. The glistening drops of water that fall over the rock overhang give the trail its name. Then there is *Riverside Walk,* one of the loveliest and most popular walks in the park. It is two miles (3.2 kilometers) round trip, but allow one to two hours for the hike.

At the end of Riverside Walk is one of the most dramatic and unusual hikes you will ever experience. It is called *the Narrows.* There is no trail, just the river to walk through, with sheer cliffs rising on either side. The water can be cold and, depending on the season, the water level may rise to your waist or higher, although at the beginning of the trail it is no higher than your knees. There is little direct sunlight in the Narrows. The rocks on the riverbed are hard on your feet so it is best to hike with sneakers. Plan on keeping dry shoes in your car to change into, or at least dry socks. To hike the length of the trail would take twelve hours, but if you can, plan on at least a half hour or one hour hike into the river. Watch out for hypothermia and flash floods. If the skies are at all threatening, turn back *immediately.* As recently as a few years ago, a group of hikers, in excellent shape and traveling with a guide, were swept away to their deaths by a flash flood. Having said that, it still is a pretty nifty hike and a very spooky place. The Native Americans considered it haunted at night and never entered the area after dark.

For some of the best views of Zion Canyon, try the *West Rim Trail* up to *Scout Lookout*. On the way you will hike up through *Walter's Wiggles,* a series of narrow switchbacks that will have you huffing and puffing. It is considered a strenuous hike but it is not so bad if you take your time. Allow several hours for the hike.

### Places to Stay at Zion

The only place to stay in the park is the *Zion Lodge,* which like Bryce Lodge, is comfy, cozy and the center of activities. The lodge is historic, centrally located and worth the money you pay, which varies with the season. There are cabins in addition to the main lodge and the restaurant has very good food and excellent views. Reservations are required for dinner. Call two-three months ahead during the busy summer season: 435-772-3213. Casual attire is the norm. To reserve a room you must contact Xanterra. You can call 303-338-6000 or book online at www.Xanterra.com/properties/zion.htm. Short or long horseback rides can be arranged in the lodge lobby. Experienced riders as well as greenhorns will find their riding needs met at very reasonable prices.

If Zion Lodge is not available or is beyond your budget, there are a number of places to stay in the appealing town of *Springdale,* south of Zion, just outside the park boundaries. The town has interesting shops, an IMAX theater, and a few small restaurants. On our last trip there we purchased some one-of-a-kind wind chimes created by a local artisan. Reservation information for some B&Bs is as follows:

➢ *Zion House B&B* — phone 800-775-7404 or book online at their Web site www.zionhouse.com/

➢ *Zion Canyon B & B* — phone 435-772-9466 or book online at www.zioncanyonbandb.com/

➢ *Harvest House B&B* — phone 435-772-3880 or book online at www.harvesthouse.net/

There is also a *Best Western Zion Park Inn.* For reservations call 800-934-7275 or book online at their Web site www.bwdiscoverthewest.com/Utah/ZionPark/zionpark.htm. You can rate shop on the major travel Web sites such as Expedia.com or contact one of the travel agents listed in the Appendix.

North and west of Zion National Park is the back county area of the *Kolob*. It has a five-mile scenic drive and a small visitor's center. If you have time you can check it out. Because of the higher elevation, it can be cold in the off-season. We did the scenic drive and nearly hit a deer that leaped out of a wooded area. Although beautiful to see, I found the main scenic drive in Zion National Park much more compelling.

### Points of Entry and Departure for Southern Utah

As a single adult traveling alone with a child or children the focus of your trip will naturally be on seeing the Great Outdoors of southern Utah. However, you should consider spending a morning or an evening at your major city entry point to enjoy its unique attractions. It will add a little zest to your trip and your kids will talk about the experience for years to come.

### Las Vegas

Little can be said about this glitzy neon city that hasn't already filled volumes of tour brochures and Web sites. If you are planning to fly in and out of this city, I suggest arranging your itinerary to spend at least one full evening to enjoy the sights with your kids. Las Vegas is not one of my favorite vacation destinations, but it is a wacky and wild place and fun for a day. One way to experience Las Vegas nightlife is to arrange for show tickets in advance, budget permitting. Two sites that offer online show ticket reservations are: www.lasvegashost.com/lvhshows.htm and www.ads-tickets.com/las_vegas.htm. If you are considering seeing one of the top billed shows such as the perennial favorite, Siegfried and Roy, you should make show reservations many months in advance.

Another, much cheaper, way to enjoy the nightlife is to stroll down the strip and take in all the "free" shows along the way. Where else but in Las Vegas can you experience hi-tech overhead animation, an erupting volcano, and a looping roller coaster ride over Manhattan all in one evening (There is a charge for the roller coaster ride.) For a great overhead view of all the glitter and lights of the strip, walk up onto the bridge that leads to the Excalibur Hotel. If you will be in Las Vegas during the day, take the tour of Hoover Dam, located just outside the city.

For Las Vegas hotel listings and reservations, go to www.LasVegasHotels.com. Las Vegas hotel rates are competitive, so shop around. Try the major travel sites such as www.Travelocity.com or www.HotelDiscounts.com or contact one of the travel agents in our Appendix. Hotel rates are most expensive for those properties located on the strip. For cheaper rates, check out properties off the strip or those located in the downtown area (the original Las Vegas). The downtown area is the one you usually see in all the movie chase scenes.

## Salt Lake City

Surrounded by glorious mountains, Salt Lake City is a clean and attractive city, not nearly as exciting as Las Vegas, but worth a visit for its unique attractions. This is the founding city and world headquarters of The Church of Jesus Christ of Latter-day Saints, whose followers are commonly known as Mormons. Practicing Mormons do not drink, smoke, or use drugs. Out-of-staters sometimes mistakenly think that the entire state of Utah is dry, but that is not the case. The laws governing the sale and serving of alcohol are somewhat different here than in other states, but you can get a drink if you are so inclined.

The outstanding must-see attraction of the city is *Temple Square*. First visit the *Tabernacle*, where the famous Mormon Tabernacle Choir performs, and where you will get the "pin-drop" acoustical demonstration. If you are planning to fly home on a Sunday, book an afternoon flight so you will have time to enjoy the Sunday morning live radio performance of the *Morman Tabernacle Choir*. It is thrilling to hear and beautiful to watch. The audience is filled with people from all over the world. There is no admission charge. For information about the history of the choir and radio broadcast times click on www.lds.org/basicbeliefs/placestovisit/1101.html. Plan on being in your seat by 9:15 a.m. if you plan to be present at the radio broadcast.

After visiting the Tabernacle, time permitting, you can take the tour of the other buildings and learn about the history of this religion. You will be greeted by smiling young multi-lingual missionaries as you leave the Tabernacle. On Sunday morning it is an impressive sight as the missionaries line up outside the front entrance sporting placards with the languages they speak. Once you agree to take the tour, be aware that these smiling folk are on a mission. They will persistently attempt to convert you. Some people find this intrusive and annoying. I found it to be an interesting cultural experience. For information on the Mormons, click on www.mormons.org/.

If genealogy is one of your interests, be sure to visit the *Family History Museum,* right near Temple Square, which houses the largest collection of genealogical material in the world. Your visit will be more meaningful and efficient if you read their Web site first, at: www.genealogy.org/~uvpafug/fhlslc.html. The site also contains information for hotels located near Temple Square.

Salt Lake City has many hotels and motels in various price ranges, some located within a block of Temple Square. To book try calling a travel agent or check out the major travel Web sites, such as Orbitz.com for listings and rates.

Enjoy your stay in scenic Utah!

## THE OREGON AND NORTHERN CALIFORNIA COAST

I agonized whether to make this last area in Group #1 the California Coast or the aforementioned title. There is so much to do and see in California, all of it wonderful, and it is such a single-parent-family-friendly destination. In the end, I decided to focus on Oregon. There were two reasons:

1.  The attractions of the California Coast are so well known to everyone.

2.  As stated at the beginning of this destinations chapter, I want my readers to start thinking "out of the box," and Oregon is a less familiar destination.

My apologies to all my California friends and travel suppliers who reside south of San Francisco, many of whom subscribe to my e-mail newsletter and are regular visitors to my Web site, www.SingleParentTravel.net. You can e-mail your "raspberries" to my Web site or directly to me at Brenda@SingleParentTravel.net. (For our readers in the UK and other countries, "raspberries" is an American euphemism for expressing one's displeasure). Given sufficient response, we will add a California section to my Web site and include this destination in a future edition of my book.

Oregon is a land of incredible beauty. The coast, with its famous backdrop of monoliths, is both brooding and mystical at the same time. Inland are the majestic snow-capped peaks, which frame the city of Portland and all throughout the state are trees that have to be seen to be believed. In one of the opening episodes of the former, quirky TV series called "Twin Peaks," the main character, an FBI agent, newly arrived in Oregon, exclaims to the local sheriff, (and I paraphrase) "The trees! The trees! I have never seen such trees! What kind of trees are they?" The local sheriff nonchalantly replies, "Evergreens." There is nothing nonchalant about Oregon evergreens, fondly called "Oregon toothpicks" by the locals. These are majestic creations of nature that look nothing like any other trees you have seen. The enormous size, scope, and the deep rich green color, set them apart from their more ordinary cousins. My first glimpse of a stand of Oregon evergreens was after a bend in the road, enroute from Portland to the coast. Shrouded in mist, they dwarfed the cars driving by. I was left breathless at the sight. Years later, I still think about that moment.

We will begin our foray into Oregon with the beautiful city of Portland and then head directly west to the coast continuing south to San Francisco.

## Portland

If you are flying into Portland from out-of-state and your vacation time is limited, you may choose to pick up your rental car and head straight for the coast. However, if you have a day or two to devote to visiting Oregon's major city, you will find the visit worthwhile. For accommodation information and rates, I recommend speaking to a travel agent (try one in the Appendix) or price shopping the major travel Web sites, such as www.Travelocity.com. To plan your activities in Portland, I recommend viewing this excellent Visitor's Center Web site www.pova.com/. Here are some of the family fun activities everyone will enjoy in Portland:

➢ *Pioneer Square*

Start your visit here, at one of the most successful and active public squares in America. For information on the square and all its activities, visit www.pioneersquare.citysearch.com/. A major attraction of the square is the "Weather Machine." Three weather symbols, accompanied by musical fanfare, mist, and flashing lights, announce the weather forecast at noon each day.

➢ If you prefer not to drive through town, consider riding the new *Portland Streetcar System,* which allows you free transportation in the "Fareless Square District." This district is a 4.8-mile loop linking the downtown Cultural District, the Pearl District, the Nob Hill neighborhood and Portland State University. For more information check out the Web site www.pova.com/visitor/index.html

➢ *CM2 — Children's Museum 2nd Generation*

Designed for children from six months to 13 years, this "hands-on" museum offers lots of opportunity for expression and creativity. The address is 4015 S. W. Canyon Road. For operating hours and exhibit information visit www.pdxchildrensmuseum.org or call 503-223-6500.

➢ *Oregon History Center*

A landmark in the heart of Portland's Cultural District, this lively museum portrays Oregon's rich cultural history with colorful exhibits and spectacular eight-story trompe l'oeil murals. The address is 1200 S. W. Park Avenue. For information on the exhibits and hours of operation call 503-222-1741 or visit www.ohs.org.

➢ *Willamette Jetboat Excursions*

Located behind OMSI, this two-hour excursion is a nice outdoor complement to the science museum visit. The ride takes you by the waterfront and up to Willamette Falls. The jetboats run from late April to mid-October. Advance reservations are recommended. For rates and information, call 888-JETBOAT (888-538-2628) or locally 503-231-1532 or visit www.jetboatpdx.com.

➤ *Oregon Museum of Science and Industry (OMSI)*

Imagine a place where you can journey to the outer reaches of the galaxy, feel the power of an earthquake, climb aboard a real submarine, uncover a fossil, enter the world of virtual reality, or travel the globe in a five-story domed theater. With more than 200 hands-on exhibits, there is something for everyone. The Riverside Café on the premises has a lovely view of the city. The museum is located on the waterfront, at 1945 S.E. Water Avenue and is open year-round, but hours may vary. For more information call 503-797-4000 or visit www.omsi.edu.

➤ *Portland Saturday Market*

The market, also open on Sundays, is the nation's largest open-air crafts market. Stroll down row upon row of local handcrafted items and homemade foods. Featured items are sold by the people who made them, so you can talk directly to the artists and learn about their creative styles and products. Rain or shine, the market is open Saturday (10 a.m.–5 p.m.) and Sunday (11 a.m.–4:30 p.m.) from the first weekend in March to December 24. The market is located in the heart of Portland's historic Old Town under the west end of the Burnside Bridge. For more information call 503-222-6072 or visit www.portlandsaturdaymarket.com.

*From Portland we travel northwest for two hours to the coast. Turning south on scenic Highway 101, our first stop is ...*

**Cannon Beach**

A Mecca for artists, photographers, and writers, this seaside town is known for beachcombing, tide pools, and Haystack Rock, the world's third largest monolith. (First is Ayers Rock in Australia and second is Stone Mountain, Georgia). Cannon Beach maintains a terrific Web site with lots of information on activities, (the site lists 101 nifty things to do!) dining and accommodations at www.cannonbeach.org/, or you can call the Chamber of Commerce at 503-436-2623.

## Tillamook

This coastal town, where cows outnumber the human population by a ratio of six to one, is about thirty-five miles (56 kilometers) south of Cannon Beach. There are several worthy attractions in the area:

*Tillamook Creamery* — This must-see attraction is located two miles (3.2 kilometers) north of town right on Highway 101. There is a cheese museum, a self-guided tour through the creamery to see how cheese is made, and a gift shop and café where you can sample or ship to your friends the tasty Tillamook cheeses. Locally made ice cream and fudge are also available. Tillamook cheeses are often served on U.S. domestic airline flights and it always gives me a pleasant little memory jolt to see the packet on my plate. (Marcel Proust wrote about these triggered memories in his epistle, "Remembrances of Things Past." Proust was required reading for French majors like me). The creamery is open daily but hours vary by season. For more information call 503-815-1300 or visit www.tillamookchamber.org/.

*Tillamook County Pioneer Museum* — Housed in a restored courthouse, this small museum is a very interesting place. There are wonderful old photographs and many, many artifacts showing how life was lived by both the pioneering white man and the original Native American settlers in this area. There is also a children's room displaying toys and musical instruments. The museum is located in town at 2106 Second Street. For more information call 503-842-4553 or visit www.oregoncoast.com/Pionrmus.htm. There is no admission fee, but donations are welcome.

*Capes Scenic Loop* — Time permitting you can drive the 38-mile loop west of town. For a full description of the things you will see on the loop drive, click on www.tillamookchamber.org/ and click on "Attractions." This Web site also has information on the other attractions in the Tillamook area.

## Lincoln City

About another 40 or so miles (64 kilometers) down the coast from Tillamook, this charming resort town is famous for:

➢ Locally designed kites

➢ No sales tax shopping sprees

> Recreational and cultural activities year-round

> The shortest river in the world, the D River

> More hotel and motel rooms than any other community between Seattle and San Francisco

In addition there is beach combing, tide pooling, hiking and biking (bike rentals and bike trails are available) and bird, seal and whale watching. The list goes on and on. Check out their very informative Web site, which has everything from activities to accommodations, including a kid's section: www.oregoncoast.org/index.html. You may also call for information at 800-452-2151. Another informative Web site is www.lcchamber.com/.

## Depoe Bay

About 10 or 12 miles (16 to 19 kilometers) south of Lincoln City, the town of Depoe Bay is known for its unique tidal attractions, spouting horn, and churning waters of Devil's Punchbowl State Park. Geyser-like sprays arch over Highway 101, which make for great photo opportunities. Be prepared to get wet. For more info visit www.ohwy.com/or/d/depoebay.htm.

## Newport

The coastal town of Newport, about 10 miles (16 kilometers) south of Depoe Bay, offers a glorious harbor, shops, canneries, galleries, numerous restaurants, and a selection of accommodations ranging from B&Bs to moderately priced motels to elegant inns. The Chamber of Commerce Web site explains it all at www.newportchamber.org/visit/ or call 800-COAST-44.

## Oregon Coast Aquarium

Considered one of the top 10 aquariums in the U.S., this is the primary Newport attraction, enjoyable and educational for the whole family. Visitors get up and close and personal with sharks, sea lions, and sea otters. The stunning jellyfish exhibit mesmerized me. The aquarium is located on 2820 S.E. Ferry Slip Road. Allow two hours for your visit. For hours of operation and information on the exhibits, click on www.aquarium.org/ or call 541-867-3474. For our European friends, the Web site translates into five continental languages.

## Oregon Coast History Center

To learn a little history about all the peoples who settled Oregon's Central Coast, pay a visit to the log cabin museum and 1890's boarding house. The history center is at 545 S.W. 9th Street. For further information visit the Web site at www.newportnet.com/coasthistory/ or call 541-265-7509. Admission is free.

## Sylvia Beach Hotel

There are many interesting inns and B&Bs in Newport, but I feel compelled to mention this one because it is so unique. The inn sits atop a 45-foot bluff overlooking the ocean. Popular with artists, writers, and book-lovers of all ages, the hotel has no phones, TVs or radios in the guest rooms. There are lots of books however, both in the guest rooms as well as in the comfortable reading room. Each guest room is themed for a writer, such as Agatha Cristie or Edgar Allen Poe. We chose Dr. Seuss. The room was filled with well-worn copies of all his books. For information and reservations call 888-795-8422 or locally 541-265-5428 or visit their Web site www.sylviabeachhotel.com/. The address is 267 NW Cliff Street.

## Yachats

Yachats (pronounced YAH-hots) is derived from the Chinook Indian word, Yahuts, meaning dark waters at the foot of the mountain. Nestled between the lush forested mountains of the Coast Range and the lapping waves of the Pacific Ocean, Yachats is a quiet tiny town, less bustling than some of the larger coastal resort towns. The Chamber of Commerce maintains a Web site at www.casco.net/~yachat/. There are several major attractions just south of Yachats listed as follows:

## Cape Perpetua

This is the highest point on the Oregon Coast and a great place for photos. The 800-foot headland offers a panoramic view of the ocean. Hiking trails for all levels and abilities lead off in various directions from the

Interpretive Center. For details check out the Web site www.newportnet.com/capeperpetua/.

## Haceta Head Lighthouse

This is the most photographed lighthouse in the world.

## Sea Lion Caves

Located one mile south of Haceta, this is a must-see attraction. Visitors descend an elevator 200 feet (60 m) to access a 1,500-foot (460 m)-long cavern, which leads to the outdoor viewing area. Here, within the confines of the largest sea cave in the world, you can view hundreds of sea lions in their natural habitat. The roar of the waves combined with the roar of the sea lions as they jockey for position on the rocks is a memorable experience. You can call 541-547-3111 or visit their Web site at www.sealioncaves.com/. Or try this one: www.ohwy.com/or/s/sealionc.htm.

## Florence

Just south of the Sea Lion Caves is the town of Florence and *Sandland Adventures,* where you can take a dune buggy ride (guided or self driven) to the top of South Jetty Dunes. The dunes rise hundreds of feet (90 m or so) from the shore. The tours are operated with special permission from the U.S. Forest Service. Sandland Adventures also offers bumper boats, go-carts and miniature golf. The park is located about a mile south of the Florence Bridge. For information call 541-997-8087 or check the following Web sites for information on Florence and Sandland Adventures:

www.florenceoregon.net/

www.florencechamber.com/

## Reedsport

Reedsport is a coastal playground in the heart of the Oregon Dunes. It attracts photographers, artists, crabbers, clam diggers, fishermen, wildlife watchers, beachcombers and of course, dune buggies. There are a number of attractions in the immediate area:

➢ *The "Hero,"* the world-famous ship that explored the Antarctic. Visitors can tour this 300-ton vessel and its intriguing hull, which was designed to withstand the coldest of conditions. It is now moored next to the Umpqua Discovery Center.

➢ *Dean Creek Elk Viewing Area,* which is home to a large herd of magnificent Roosevelt Elk. The best viewing times are early morning or at dusk. Located on Highway 38, east of Reedsport.

➢ *Umqua Discovery Center* is a fascinating hands-on center that includes a working weather station and interpretive displays of the area's dunes and landscape. The local phone number is 271-4816.

➢ *Umpqua River Lighthouse,* built in 1893, is one of the few lighthouses that still uses the original lenses. Its beam can be seen 20 miles (32 kilometers) out to sea. There's also a whale-watching platform.

Information on these attractions and the town of Reedsport can be found at www.pacific101.com/oregon/Reedsport/reedsport.htm.

## Coos Bay

Coos Bay is one of the largest ports for forest products. Local attractions include a guided tour of the Myrtlewood Log Factory and the casino newly built in 1996. For further information visit the Web site of the Visitor's Center: www.oregoncitylink.com/coosbay/attract.htm or call 800-824-8486. Local number is 541-269-0215.

## Bandon

This is the storm-watching capital of the world. The beaches are strewn with semi-precious stones such as agates and jasper. The Oldtown Harbor District has craft shops, cafés, and galleries. A must-see attraction is the *West Coast Game Park* with a walk-through safari. Visitors can walk among and feed and pet 450 creatures including bears, cougars, leopards, lions, and tiger cubs. Allow at least one hour for your visit. This is not a zoo but is a preserve with breeding grounds where the animals are studied. Bandon's informational Web site has everything you need to know about attractions, dining, and accommodations at www.bandon.com. The game park is located on Highway 101 about seven miles (11 kilometers) south of town. For operating hours and further information click on www.gameparksafari.com/index.html or call 541-347-3106.

## Gold Beach

Seated at the mouth of the mighty Rogue River, this area abounds in multi-cultural history. Gold Beach has been inhabited and explored by several Native American cultures, Spanish explorers, European fur trappers, pioneers, loggers, ranchers, and miners. The informative Web site has everything you need to know about Gold Beach, including a kid's section at www.goldbeach.org.

## Tu Tu' Tun Lodge

This is such a special place that I wanted to mention it. This magnificent property sits seven miles (11 kilometers) up the north side of the Rogue River, overlooking the river. It is pricey but worth every penny if you want to consider a splurge. The setting is magnificent, the rooms beautifully appointed and the gourmet cuisine is prepared with fresh local ingredients. Boat trips run up the Rogue River on a daily basis. Everyone gathers before dinner on the outdoor deck or before a massive stone fireplace. Although the majority of guests are couples, they come from all backgrounds, and single parent families will not feel out of place. The gracious and charming family that owns and operates the lodge also arranges the placing of guests at dinner. Check out the Web site and decide if it is within your budget at www.karenbrown.com/california/tututunlodge.html, or call 800-864-6357. There usually is a two night minimum stay.

## Brookings

The 30 or so miles (48 kilometers) between Gold Beach and Brookings offer some of the most outstanding vistas along the Oregon coast. Thanks to the mild climate, flowers bloom year round in Brookings; in fact 90% of the country's Easter lilies are grown locally. East of Brookings is a one mile nature trail in Loeb State Park. The phone number for the Chamber of Commerce is 800-535-9469 or 541-469-3181. I couldn't find a comprehensive Web site, but this one has some general tourist information: www.oregoncitylink.com/brookings/.

## Crossing into California...

Since the focus of this itinerary is on the Oregon Coast, we will only cover the major highlights of the drive from Oregon to San Francisco.

## Crescent City

There are several points of interest in and around this town, including Ocean World Aquarium, which includes a reef exhibit and tidewater touch pools. The major nearby attraction is Redwood National Park. For more information visit www.caohwy.com/c/crescent.htm. You can book accommodations online or call 800-343-8300.

## Redwood National Park

If time is limited you can plan to spend about three hours in Redwood National Park and visit some of the major attractions. Among the must-sees are:

➢ Tall Trees — several walking and driving trails veer off from here.

➢ Trees of Mystery Park — a forest of redwoods containing a number of oddly formed trees.

➢ Trail of Tall Tales — contains chainsaw-carved redwood sculptures that depict the legend of Paul Bunyan and other loggers.

For more information check out these two informative Web sites: www.nps.gov/redw/ and www.redwood.national-park.com/.

## Eureka

Eureka is a nice stop to break up the trip south. The town is a lumbering city with many Victorian dwellings. For information on attractions, dining, and lodging, check out www.onroute.com/destinations/california/ eureka.html.

From Eureka, you can veer west to Ferndale and Capetown and drive the *"Lost Coast of California."* This is a secondary road, so allow plenty to time for this detour. Once you reach *Shelter Cove* you can drive east to Gerberville. You can also do Shelter Cove as a side trip from Garberville. The main attraction here is the spectacular view of the ocean along with several miles/kilometers of tidal beach.

## Garberville

About five hours north of San Francisco, in the heart of redwood country, Garberville is a likely overnight stop on your way south. For information on surrounding attractions and accommodations, check out these two Web sites: www.caohwy.com/g/garbervi.htm and www.garberville.org/.

## Mendocino

Famed for its artist's colony, the Mendocino area offers lots of B&Bs should you decide to overnight in the town. For information on the Mendocino coast click on www.mendocinocoast.com/.

## Bodega Bay

About 65 miles (105 kilometers) north of San Francisco you will drive through a pretty little town made famous as the setting in Alfred Hitchcock's movie thriller "The Birds." The schoolhouse still remains, as well as several other buildings and docks used in the film. For more information on the film visit www.norcalmovies.com/TheBirds/. For general information on the town, click on www.bodegabay.com/vistor_info/overviewmap.html.

## San Francisco

The approach to San Francisco and the Golden Gate Bridge from the north is mind-bogglingly beautiful. If the light is just right, you will come around the final bend and be visually confronted with a vast expanse of sailboats speeding across the sparkling deep blue San Francisco Bay. The enchanting hilly city forms the backdrop and the magnificent world-famous red bridge draws your eye immediately into the picture. Sometimes the view is obscured by the thick fog, which appears like magic and can disappear just as quickly. There is a special viewing and photo-taking area, just off to the left at the north end of the bridge, but you cannot turn into it if you are heading south.

*If you have only one day in San Francisco, I suggest doing the following:*

➤ *Take a cable car ride.*

Be prepared for one-hour waiting lines at the tourist areas, such as Fisherman's Wharf. Lines are shorter early in the morning. This is a uniquely San Francisco experience and a thrill ride as well, especially as you speed down the steep hills (Cable cars have the right of way).

> *Visit Alcatraz Island and take the award-winning self-guided audio tour.*

Not only will this excursion take you out into the bay for a stunning view of the city, but also you will learn all about the colorful and fascinating history of this rock island. Allow time to visit the gift shop where former prison guards will chat with you about their experiences. For information and the history of "The Rock," check out the official Web site at www.nps.gov/alcatraz/. Tour tickets often sell out a day or two ahead during busy seasons, such as summer. It is possible to buy tickets from local tour operators on the spot, but to be on the safe side, I recommend pre-ordering tickets online at www.blueandgoldfleet.com/ or calling 415-705-5555.

> *Stroll around Fisherman's Wharf.*

Grab a snack of fresh seafood or sour dough bread sandwiches as you stroll and enjoy the fabulous view and endless activity of tourists and locals alike. Your kids will enjoy the seal wharf, which is an official tourist attraction. So many seals began gathering around one of the wharfs that the city built a sightseeing boardwalk so tourists can come and watch the seals sun themselves. There are several piers containing dozens of shops on the Wharf not to mention all the seafood restaurants. Fisherman's Wharf is a huge, crowded, tourist area, pricey but still fun.

*If you have more than one day in the city, some family fun activities are:*

> *Coit Tower* — Climbing up the steps of the residential area leading to the tower is a neat experience. We were convinced the postman who delivered mail on that route was probably the most aerobically fit person in the city.

> *Lombard Street* — This is the most crooked street in the world and has been featured in numerous films and TV chase scenes.

> *Chinatown* — A great place for reasonably priced shopping and dining in the evening.

> *Muir Woods* — Located just a few miles/kilometers north of the Golden Gate Bridge, this national monument is a wonderful half-day excursion. There are excellent hikes among the tall trees as well as ranger-guided walks. A short distance away is the charming town of *Sausilito* with lots of shops and good restaurants.

For information on the city and to order a Visitor's Guide online, click on www.sfvisitor.org.

We hope you enjoy the Oregon Coast and your visit to "Everybody's Favorite City."

## GROUP #2 - GOING TO THE NEXT STEP

### RIVIERA MAYA

The Riviera Maya, located 40 minutes south of Cancun, Mexico, is a 50-mile stretch of beautiful coastline anchored by the rapidly growing and delightful town of *Playa del Carmen*. It is an ideal place for a single parent family vacation, no matter what the ages of your children. Hotel and meal prices are very reasonable. In addition to beautiful beaches, there is a fabulous selection of activities, ranging from visits to ancient Mayan ruins to snorkeling in sacred rivers. The tourists who come here are a mixed bag of singles, couples, and families of various ages and nationalities. The Riviera Maya is not overrun with American tourists, as is Cancun. Until recently, the area was a vacation mainstay for Europeans and for middle class Mexican families. Americans began to discover it a few years ago.

### Playa del Carmen

I recommend staying in or near the town of Playa del Carmen. It's the center of action and has a great pedestrian street, called Quinta Avenida (5th Avenue) that is filled with restaurants and shops that come alive at night. The strolling nighttime crowd is an eclectic mixture of singles, families, and couples, mostly Mexicans, Europeans and Americans. It is a safe place and great for teens. Mothers and daughters and longhaired sons: get your hair braided the first night. Everyone can go native with a henna tattoo. The beaches in and around Playa are mostly public and all have access to food and drink and rented beach chairs. The surf is ideal for little ones. Playa del Carmen is undergoing explosive growth. I visited the town twice within nine months and was astounded by the changes and expansion in that short amount of time.

### Hotels

On my last visit, in early 2001, most of the hotels were geared toward European tastes. Europeans tend to insist on good value for their money, eschewing high-priced hotels with lots of fancy amenities in the rooms. This may change as more Americans descend upon this resort town, but currently you can find neat, clean, pleasant rooms for as little as US$40 or US$50 a night, located one short block from the beach. There are many new properties being built on the periphery of town, that offer spacious well-appointed villas with tiled floors and native materials. Currently these places run around US$100 a night if rented for a week or more. Although the Riviera Maya has a few chain hotels (mostly European), Playa del Carmen specializes in unique small hotels with 50 rooms or less. Many can be reserved online. For information on hotels, check www.playadelcarmen.com/. Another good Web site for hotel, activity and restaurant information is www.cancunsouth.com/cit_playa_main.html. New Web sites emerge continually as new properties are being built, so do an Internet search for "Playa del Carmen hotels" or "Riviera Maya hotels" to view the latest information.

There are a few all-inclusive properties along the Riviera Maya. All-inclusive usually means the hotel rate includes accommodations, meals and most or all sports activities offered by the hotel. One such resort is *Caracol, a Splash property,* located just outside of Playa del Carmen. Occasionally the hotel offers a single parent special rate. You can call them at 877-92-SPLASH or visit their Web site at www.splashresorts.com. There are pros and cons to all-inclusive properties. The advantage is that you save money on your total costs. The disadvantage is that you lose dining flexibility as your meals will be confined to the hotel's restaurants.

## Restaurants

There are many excellent restaurants in Playa del Carmen representing cuisines from all over Europe and North and South America. I hesitate to recommend my favorites as the restaurant scene changes with alacrity, but one in particular stands out which I hope will remain a permanent fixture in Playa:

*Yaxche Maya Cuisine Restaurant* offers a fantastic fusion cuisine of Maya, Yucatecan and European influences. Although the restaurant is upscale, the prices are reasonable. Like all restaurants in Playa, casual dress is the norm. You can eat under a roof or under the stars, and the menu selection is varied enough to please even fussy kids. I have dined there three times and each time the meal was excellent. The restaurant maintains an informative Web site containing a history of Mayan cuisine, Mayan recipes, and a coupon offering 10% off your meal. www.mayacuisine.com/. Tell the manager you read about Yaxche in *The Single Parent Travel Handbook.* Yaxche Maya is located on 8$^{th}$ Street, a half block off Playa's famous Quinta Avenida (5$^{th}$ Avenue).

## Tour Packages

Many tour operators offer all-inclusive packages to Playa del Carmen that include airfare, hotel, and transfers and, in some cases, meals and water sports. Call your travel agent (or find one in our Appendix) or check the travel section of your Sunday newspaper for advertisements. Compare these prices to booking everything individually by yourself and then determine which travel arrangement is best for you. Some of the best all-inclusive packages are offered by Apple Vacations, with departures from more than a dozen major cities throughout the U.S. They have a Web site, www.applevacations.com, but it does not include rates and the travel agent information is not regularly updated (Apple Vacations can only be booked through a travel agent). However, the Web site has photos and information on the hotels. Look under Cancun to find the Riviera Maya. An interesting looking site claims to offer discounts on all the major tour operators to this area. I have not tried it, but you welcome to do so at discounttravelpackages.com/playa_del_Carmen.htm.

## Activities and Attractions

If you are planning an active vacation, one in which you will be doing two or more excursions, I highly recommend you rent a car. The roads are in good condition with well-marked signage. Parking is free in the town of Playa, although you may have to park a few blocks from your hotel if it does not offer a private parking area. Some primary attractions along the Riviera Maya are:

## X-Caret

This is an eco-archaeological park and a "must-see" attraction. The park is located just south of the town of Playa. If you are not renting a car, you can sign up for a day's excursion, which includes round-trip bus transportation. Plan on spending the entire day and evening here, and try to arrive when it opens if you hope to fit in all the attractions, along with some "lazy time." Admission fee includes all activities except the dolphin swim. Some of the park's attractions are:

➤ *Underground River* — This is a fabulous 30-minute snorkel down a gentle sacred Mayan River. The first few minutes are quite dark and might be scary for little children. If they have never snorkeled before, I recommend you acquaint them with snorkeling beforehand. (Snorkel equipment is available for rent at a nominal fee).

➤ *Mayan ruins* — scattered throughout the park.

➤ *Natural history educational exhibits* — including bats, butterflies, sea turtles, and manatees.

➤ *Great beach and small bay areas* — plus snorkel areas, restaurants, hammocks, and scenic walkways.

➤ *Dolphin swim* — (extra charge) — must be pre-reserved.

➤ *Excellent evening show* — including a demonstration of "pelota," the ancient Mayan ball game, precursor to today's soccer, and a full outdoor stage show, complete with folklore dances. The show moves from an amphitheater to the pelota ball court and then through the walkways around the river.

*Do not apply any sunscreen before coming to X-Caret.* You can exchange your sunscreen when you arrive or buy the park's non-water-polluting version.

### Xel-Ha National Park (pronounced Shell HA)

This is another "must do." The park centers on a wide, crystal clear sacred Mayan River with multiple easy entry areas, perfect for small children. This park offers some of the best snorkeling I have ever experienced. There are many other activities plus numerous hammock grottos. Restaurants abound along with snorkel and dive gear rental booths. Once again, use only the non-polluting sunscreens.

### Tulum

Many people choose to combine a visit to Xel-Ha with a visit to the nearby Mayan ruins of Tulum. Tulum is about 45 minutes south of the town of Playa. Do Tulum first and try to get there before 10 a.m., which is when all the cruise excursion passengers arrive.

### Chichen-Itza

This is one of the major Mayan cities and is located about a two and a half hour drive west of Playa del Carmen. Be prepared for a hotter, drier climate. Sign up for one of the ranger-guided two-hour tours of the city upon your arrival. This is a long day and might be taxing for a small child, but it is a fabulous educational experience and is fun to climb to the top of the temples.

**Cenotes** (pronounced "Say NO Teys")

These are underground caverns that abound throughout the Riviera Maya. For a dollar or two admission fee you can swim surrounded by stalactites and stalagmites. Take hold of small children as you approach the water as the surface may be moss-covered and slippery.

**Cozumel Island**

You can hop the ferry from the dock at Playa del Carmen. Cozumel offers great jewelry shopping. It is also famous for snorkeling, but personally I found the snorkeling to be much better at Xel-Ha.

**Isla Mujeres** (pronounced EES la moo HER ays)

This small island, north of Cancun, has an underwater national park, which is quite interesting. However the area is very quiet and does not offer as many activities as Xel-Ha.

*Author's Note:* Mexican law requires that a single adult traveling alone with children must carry a letter stating that he or she has permission from the other parent (or the parents) to take the child out of the country. If you, as the parent, have sole custody of the child, then you must show proof of that fact. You may not be asked to show these documents but you *must* be prepared to do so. *See our documents section for more detail.*

For general information on the Riviera Maya, click on www.rivieramaya.com.

¡Buen Viaje! (Have a great trip!)

## COSTA RICA

Bordered by Nicaragua, Panama, the Pacific Ocean and the Caribbean Sea, Costa Rica is the most developed country in Central America for adventure tourism and is known throughout the world for its bio-diversity and its incredible variety of wildlife. About 30% of the country is protected land, many of the hotels and tour programs are geared toward eco-tourism, and the certified wildlife guides in Costa Rica are among the best trained in Latin America. Costa Rica is also a very peaceful and democratic land and has been so for many years. There are no armed forces and democratic elections have been conducted since the 19th century. Costa Ricans enjoy one of the highest standards of health care in Latin America, as well as an excellent educational program, with a literacy rate of over 90%, and, like all Central American countries, the people are warm and friendly and eager to show you their beautiful country. It is the perfect single parent family destination — exciting, fun-filled, educational, and safe. Everyone I have interviewed who has been to Costa Rica had a good time and is eager to return to this beautiful, unique country.

There are a couple of colloquialisms you should know before you enter Costa Rica. The first is the phrase "Pura Vida" (*POO rah VEE dah*) which literally translates as "Pure Life" but means "Way to Go!" or Awesome!" To the Costa Ricans it is a joyful way of expressing approval. The second is the word "Tico," which is the nickname for Costa Ricans. The word is used frequently throughout the country and is not considered derogatory.

There are three ways to plan your vacation in Costa Rica:

1. *Buy a pre-paid package that includes hotel, transfers, and sightseeing.* There are many packages available. Some include a beach vacation only; others are a combination of beach and sightseeing throughout the country. The one you choose will be a personal decision based on your preferences. If you are uneasy about renting a car and traveling on your own in a foreign country, then this is the best arrangement for you.

2. *Consider a combination trip.* Perhaps you could buy a three or four night sightseeing package and rent a car and drive from San Jose to the coastal beach destinations. This gives you freedom of choice for part of your trip, along with the thrill of exploring on your own.

3. *Travel on your own throughout the country by rental car.* This free-wheeling option is certainly the most exciting, but I do not recommend it if you have small children and are planning to drive up to remote mountain

areas. Some of the mountain roads are not paved, driving conditions can be dicey, and you will need to pay full attention to driving and not to your kids. This was the way we traveled to Costa Rica on our first trip, but my daughter had just turned 21 and was a skillful mountain driver. We had a blast the entire trip but I would not recommend it for the faint-of-heart.

To help you in your itinerary planning and decision-making process, here are some highlights of the major tourist areas:

**San José and Surrounding Areas**

Besides the capital city of San Jose, this area includes the picturesque mountain towns of Barva, Alajuela, Sarchí, and Zarcero, plus the national parks of Poas Volcano, Braulio Carrillo, Irazu Volcano, and the Rain Forest Aerial Tram.

*San Jose*

This sprawling low-rise metropolitan area has close to one million residents and serves as the hub of Costa Rica. The international airport of San Jose is small but quite modern. As you leave the airport building you will find the taxi stands out front. There is an official, price-controlled cab rate for a ride into downtown. If you are renting a car, you may have to look for your car rental company outside the airport building. In cases where the car rental company location is off-site, the car rental agent will come looking for you. The crowd can get very thick right outside the airport building and it may be difficult for the rental agent to find you immediately upon your arrival. Usually within 10 minutes of arrival everybody gets connected. As of late 1999 the main highway into town was being rebuilt, consequently the ride to downtown may take anywhere from 25 to 45 minutes.

At first glance San Jose does not appear to be your typical Central American city. It has no colonial districts and the North American fast food chain restaurants proliferate the capital. With closer observation you begin to uncover the city's Costa Rican character. There are a number of very good restaurants, many of which serve typical "tico" (Costa Rican) food. The climate, like much of Costa Rica, is often spring-like. One word of caution: San Jose is known for petty theft, so carry your valuables in a safe place and keep your car doors locked and your car windows rolled up when you are stopped for a traffic light. On our first trip to Costa Rica, we rented a jeep and as we waited for a traffic light to change in the middle of the city, a man ripped my sunglasses right off my face. After that I kept the window up when driving through San Jose.

The center of town is laid out in a grid system with avenidas (avenues) running north and south and *calles* (streets) running east and west. Calle (*pronounced CAY yay*) Central is the dividing point. Avenidas south of Calle Central are even-numbered; those north are odd-numbered. In similar fashion, calles west of Calle Central are even-numbered; those east are odd-numbered. Directions are given using this system as well as using local landmarks.

Most travelers use San Jose as a base to explore other regions throughout the country. I recommend spending minimum time in the city. If your itinerary does allow for some sightseeing time in San Jose, there are many excellent museums in the city. The three prominent ones are:

➤ *Museo de Jade* (*Moo SAY oh dey HAH Dey*) — This is the most famous museum in Costa Rica and contains the world's largest collection of American jade. It is located on the 11th floor of the Instituto Nacional de Seguros on Avenida 7 between Calles 9 and 11. It is open 9 a.m. to 3 p.m. Monday to Friday. There is a nominal admission charge.

➤ *Museo Nacional* — The exhibit is a mixture of archeology, colonial and natural history, and art. Located on Calle 17, between Avenidas Central and 2, it is open daily except Monday. Hours are from 8:30 a.m. to 4:30 p.m. except for Sundays when it opens at 9 a.m. There is a small admission fee.

➤ *Museo de Oro Precolombino* — As the name implies, the museum displays pre-Columbian art, especially gold. It is open Tuesday to Saturday 10 a.m. to 4:30 p.m. and is located on Calle 5, between Avenidas Central and 2. Admission is US$5. Security is tight; you will be required to leave your bags at the door.

For information on current events and tourism in the city, check out the local "Tico Times" at www.ticotimes.net/.

*Outside of San Jose*

Heading northwest from San Jose there are a series of delightful small towns around San Jose and in the mountains. The highlands of Costa Rica are one of the greenest places on earth, especially during or after the rainy season. Bring plenty of film on your drive. One such day trip would be Barva and Poás Volcano. Another day trip could be Sarchí and Zarcero and possibly Alajuela. It is best to head to the furthermost point first, such as Poás or Zarcero, and then sightsee on the way back. This gives you a better gauge on your time and you are less likely to find yourself driving down the mountains after dark, which you *don't* want to do (and we did, un-planned of course!). Decision points on mountain roads are not always marked, rendering maps useless. Ask directions if you are not sure, but be prepared for one of only two responses: "Por aquí" (this way) or "Por allí" (that way). On our first trip to Costa Rica we ended up in Poás when we meant to go to Zarcero. But at least we knew which turnoff to take on the next day's excursion.

### Barva

Just a few miles/kilometers outside of San Jose, this entire town is consi-dered to be a national historic monument. It is pleasant to spend an hour or two strolling and enjoying the colonial buildings. Coffee plantation tours are available right outside of town.

### Alajuela

About 10 miles (16 kilometers) outside of San Jose, this small town is famous for being the birthplace of Juan Santamaría, the national hero of Costa Rica. Back in 1856, an audacious American named William Walker marched through Nicaragua intending to conquer all of Central America, make the entire region a slave territory, and use the labor to build a canal across the isthmus. Costa Rica had no army at the time, but a small militia was gathered and forced Walker into a wood fort. Juan Santamaría, a teen-age drummer in the militia, volunteered to torch the fort. Walker was forced to flee Costa Rica, but Santamaría died in the fire. A museum and park in his birthplace commemorate the young national hero.

### Parque Nacional Volcán Poás

The park is about 20 miles (32 kilometers) north of Alajuela and offers a ranger station, visitor center, and snack bar. Poás is an active volcano and you are able to peer down into its crater, assuming volcanic steam clouds do not obscure the view. Nearby are short nature trails. There is interesting flora to observe as well as numerous species of birds, especially humming-birds. The park is open daily 8 a.m. to 4 p.m. Admission is about US$6. For images of the park, go to volcano.und.nodak.edu/vwdocs/volc_images/north_america/costa_rica/new_poas.html.

For an overall view of Poás and other national parks of Costa Rica, visit www.centralamerica.com/cr/parks/.

## *Sarchí*

A little over halfway between San Jose and Zarcero, this little town is the major craft center of Costa Rica. The drive up is lovely; it is interesting to observe the artisans at work; and it is a favorite place for shoppers. There is no pressure to buy and the prices are the best you will find anywhere. Here you can watch the famous wooden oxen carts (*carretas*) being carved and painted in bright colors. You can buy ox carts of any size and color from miniature souvenir carts to larger ones used as indoor tables, bars, and sideboards. The larger ones can be taken apart for transport. Also available for transport are the beautifully carved wooden and leather rock-ing chairs. The vendors will box any of these items for you and they can be checked with your luggage when you fly home. Costa Rica is famous for its carvings using the local natural woods. You will find beautiful wooden jewelry here as well as the unusual wooden carving boards, an-other popular gift item. If you plan on buying any bulky items, you can store them at your San Jose hotel until the end of your trip, or plan your itinerary so that you shop in Sarchí on the last day. For further informa-tion on the town and its crafts, click on www.worldheadquarters.com/cr/destinations/sarchi/.

## *Zarcero*

This mountain town, located about 15 miles (24 kilometers) north of Sarchí, is famous for its cheeses, peach preserves and its huge garden of beautifully sculpted shrubs depicting birds and animals. The town sits at over 6,000 feet (1,800 meters) so bring a sweater, as it can be cool unless it is sunny.

Heading northeast and east of San Jose are several other attractions:

## *Parque Nacional Braulio Carrillo*

Thanks to its various life zones, this park contains a tremendous array of plant and bird life. You can hop out of your car for a brief stop as you travel through each altitudinal zone or linger over a longer hike. One possibility is to hike Barva Volcano which takes about five hours round trip. The fabled elusive quetzal, Central America's "flagship" bird, resides here. Our Costa Rican friends tell us that once you have viewed a quetzal, you will fall in love with its beauty. Its feathers shimmer and change color as they catch the reflection of light.

### Rain Forest Aerial Tram

This unique tram is one of only two such attractions in all of Central America. The tram is located on the San Jose-Limón Road, on the right, just as you exit Braulio Carrillo National Park. Each of the trams takes five passengers and a naturalist guide, and glides silently through the rain forest canopy on a 90-minute roundtrip ride. The ride includes a pre-briefing and use of trails before and after the ride. The cost is expensive but worth it — about US$50 per person with discounts available for students and children. For further information visit www.rainforesttram.com/.

### Parque Nacional Volcán Irazú

Located east of San Jose, Irazú Volcano is the highest active volcano in Costa Rica. A paved road takes you to the summit at 11,300 feet (3,440 m), where you will find a small information center. Bring food, water, sunscreen, and lots of warm clothing. There is a great view at the top though it is often clouded over. Admission fee is about US$6.00.

## Tortuguero and the Caribbean Coast

### Puerto Limón

Puerto Limón, usually called simply Limón, is the capital of Limón province. This Caribbean port town does not offer much for the tourist. Travelers who go here are usually just passing through. The weather here is warmer and much more steamy than the spring climate of San Jose.

### Tortuguero

Tortuguero National Park, the major tourist attraction of Costa Rica's Caribbean coast, is one of the world's primary nesting sites for large sea turtles.

Nesting season is July through October and sometimes into early November, which is the best, and busiest, time to come. Even if you come during the "non-nesting" season you will still have an enjoyable time and learn a great deal about the local wildlife, including the sea turtles. Tortuguero is not a place where you come on your own. All bus and boat transfers are set up as part of a package that includes lodging, meals and sightseeing with a certified guide, who is well versed in the local wildlife. Most packages are set up for a two-night stay in Tortuguero, which is the ideal amount of time. Tour prices vary depending on your accommodations and the number of transfers included. All lodges are comfortable and include private bath and hot water.

The first day of your Tortuguero excursion consists of a bus ride for several hours during which you will cross over the Continental Divide and drive through the heart of acres of lovely banana plantations. Costa Rica is the world's second largest producer of bananas next to Ecuador. Your guide will explain some interesting facts about bananas and plantation life as you pass by. Stops are made to observe unusual wildlife. Our guide spotted a sloth in clear view at the top of a tree and we were fortunate enough to observe him move several times in the course of a few minutes — a rare occurrence for a sloth! Later you will board a covered motor launch to cruise down a waterway that is replete with all kinds of wildlife, both on land and in the air. You'll be able to spot caimans (small alligators), Costa Rican water buffalo, egrets, herons, terns, sandpipers, turkey vultures, monkeys, snakes, and more.

Throughout your stay at Tortuguero you will have numerous opportunities for excursions — hiking, boating, museum visits and wildlife excursions. Some are standard inclusions in your package and some are available at additional cost. Take advantage of everything you can. Each excursion offers an opportunity to discover something new. Be prepared for rain and bugs and all kinds of weather from hot and humid to chilly and wet. Although the hotel provides boots and heavy long rain coats, sometimes there are torrential downpours in the preserve when it rains so hard the water seeps into your clothes through openings in your coat, and you will drenched down to your underwear by the time you finish your hike. You only need bring a small suitcase or duffel to Tortuguero; check the rest of your luggage at your San Jose hotel. Make sure your suitcase is covered with a plastic bag and that you have brought at least two additional changes of clothing plus raingear, mosquito repellent, sunscreen, a sweater, a bathing suit, plastic bags for wet clothing, and a brimmed hat or baseball cap. Don't count on the hotel's laundry service. Clothes dryers in Central America are often inefficient and very slow. One more helpful hint — when you return from a rainy excursion, don't dawdle. Jump right into the shower before everyone uses up the hot water.

If all this sounds a bit dreary, remember that you are in the heart of a rain forest and to experience its exciting wildlife you may have to endure a little discomfort. Some of the exciting wildlife you will see on your hikes is brightly colored poisonous tree frogs, whose skin coating was used to make poisonous darts. If your guide is skillful enough he will place one on his hand for you to see up close — shades of the Discovery Channel! You will also have the opportunity to meet insect-eating bats hanging upside down under the tree leaves, and you may even get to enter a vampire bat cave. Boat rides down the narrow inlets will reveal howler monkeys swinging in the trees. Tortuguero National Park is comprised of 60,000 acres of land and water and if some of it looks vaguely familiar to you, you are correct. "George of the Jungle," as well as several James Bond movies were filmed here.

If you are fortunate enough to be here during turtle-nesting season you will be taken to the beach for a night walk to watch the turtles lay eggs or see the babies hatch and head out to sea. You need to wear dark clothing, no heavy perfume, and move quietly. The sea turtles have no ears (due to their need to dive deeply) but they see and smell very well. It takes a sea turtle two and a half hours to lay all her eggs and once the process is started, it cannot be stopped. If disturbed in any way by unusual sights or smells, the turtle immediately heads out to sea, dropping her eggs as she goes, leaving them as easy targets for predators.

When baby turtles hatch, they imprint their birthplace on their brain and return as mature females to hatch their eggs at exactly the same spot on the beach. At the local museum you can "adopt" an endangered sea turtle for US$25. You will receive an official Certificate of Adoption with the turtle's picture and tag number and you get to choose the name. Sea turtles come ashore to nest every two to four years and you will be notified when your turtle is spotted. This is a terrific topic for a school paper. Extra credit!

For information on the turtles, check out the following Web sites at www.cccturtle.org/tortnp.htm and photo2.si.edu/turtles/turtletop.html.

**Pacific Coast**

*Guanacaste*

This northwest region of Costa Rica continues to develop and is becoming one of the most popular areas for vacationers. Guanacaste hotels are mostly focused on simple outdoor pleasures such as beaches, wildlife excursions, and nature walks. There is little, if any, tennis, golf, or discotheques and no casinos. It is a peaceful area, popular with families and couples. In the center of it all is the town of Liberia, which serves as the capital of Guanacaste Province and contains the local airport. Hotels located near the airport are inexpensive, close to the national parks and about forty minutes from the beaches. Hotels located on or near the beaches offer more resort facilities and are more expensive.

There are numerous beaches running down the northwest Pacific coast. A few notable ones are:

➢ Playa Hermosa — offers a fine beach, good swimming, deep-sea fishing and water sports.

➢ Playa del Coco — has good swimming and some snorkeling.

➢ Playa Flamingo — is a big fishing area.

➢ Playa Tamarindo and Playa Junquillal — known for surfing and deep-sea fishing.

➢ Golf of Papagayo — located up north, it has some good diving sites.

Surrounding the town of Liberia are several national parks and preserves, all of which contain a huge variety of wildlife:

*Parque Nacional Santa Rosa*

Located north of Liberia, it is one of the oldest and largest national parks in Costa Rica. Originally created to mark an historic military battle involving William Walker, it has also become an important biological site. Wildlife is best viewed during the dry season, but the wet season is the best time to see turtles nesting, especially the months of September and October.

*Parque Nacional Guanacaste*

Adjoining Santa Rosa National Park, Guanacaste National Park was established in 1989 in order to create a "mega-park," thus giving the animals a range of habitat from coastal areas to the highlands.

*Parque Nacional Rincón*

Just south of Guanacaste National Park, this park contains several active volcanoes as well as fumaroles, steam vents, and boiling mud pools. The park contains four life zones due to the changing elevation.

*Parque Nacional Palo Verde*

Located south of Liberia, this park is a paradise for bird-watchers. Its various habitats attract many different species, both residential and migratory. You can view herons, storks, waterfowl, spoonbills, egrets, scarlet macaws, toucans, parrots, and currasows, to name just a few.

*Parque Nacional Barro Honda*

Plans are underway to join this park and surrounding preserves with Palo Verde National Park to create another "mega-park."

For more information on Guanacaste visit www.guanacaste.co.cr.

*Jacó Beach*

Located on the Pacific Coast, a pleasant two hour drive southwest of San Jose, this beach area is the closest one to the capital city and very popular with locals. It may be difficult to get rooms on weekends and holidays unless you reserve ahead. This whole area is popular with surfers because of the consistent waves.

It is also possible to swim, but there are strong rip tides, so you must exercise caution. A rip often appears as a muddy streak leading out from shore. If you get caught in one, don't fight it. Swim parallel to the shore and when you are free of the rip tide, swim ashore. For the movie buffs among you, the European version of the movie, "Christopher Columbus," starring Gérard Depardieu, was filmed on Jacó Beach.

Just north of Jacó is *Playa Herradura,* a quiet black sand beach lined with palm trees. South of Jacó is *Playa Hermosa,* another well-known surfer's beach. An annual surfing contest is held here in August.

## Quepos

The pleasant coastal drive from Jacó to Quepos is about 40 miles (64 kilometers) on a paved road. There are numerous beaches along the way where you can swim or surf but be careful of rip tides. Quepos is a sports fishing center and is also popular because it is the closest town to Manuel Antonio National Park. If you stop here for lunch and eat outdoors, don't be surprised if you spot a monkey or a sloth or any number of birds. There is lots of wildlife around this area.

## Manuel Antonio National Park

Although the smallest national park in Costa Rica, it is also one of the most popular with both locals and foreigners. The park contains three beautiful beaches, as pretty as you would find anywhere in the world. Wildlife is abundant and omnipresent. Bring everything you need into the park — water, food, film, sunscreen, bug repellent — nothing is sold there — but pack lightly as you will do a lot of walking. Bring plastic bags to remove your trash. Arrive early as the park limits its visitors to lessen the impact on wildlife and the environment. Park hours are 7 a.m. to 5 p.m. daily except Monday, when the park is closed. Admission is about US$6.

Cars are not allowed in the park, and getting there on foot is a bit of an adventure. First you need to wade an estuary, which can be almost waist-high during high tide. This creates lots of giggles and great photo opportunities. Then you must hike for about 45 minutes to get to the beaches. It is all well worth it, as the scenery and wildlife is nothing short of incredible. There are three main beaches in the park conveniently labeled — First, Second, and Third Beaches. There is also a Fourth Beach, excellent for snorkeling, but you need to arrange a ranger escort to visit the Fourth Beach. First Beach is more exposed and subject to strong rip tides. Keep on walking to the Second or Third Beach, both of which are more sheltered and safer for swimming. Third Beach, one of the most popular, is often referred to as Manual Antonio Beach. The sun can get hot and it is tempting to park your beach towel under the shade of the nearby trees. Don't! The monkeys love to urinate on the unwitting tourists and you may find yourself getting a shower you didn't expect. Speaking of monkeys, they present more of a theft problem than humans. You cannot leave any item unattended on your beach towel without the risk of it being stolen. If there are only two of you, one must swim while the other watches the gear, unless you make arrangements with your neighboring beach buddies to watch your gear.

Wildlife is everywhere in Manuel Antonio National Park. You will see lots of monkeys, especially the white-faced monkeys. My son was so entranced with them that he borrowed my camera, went to the end of the beach, broke open several coconuts and waited patiently while they scurried down the tree branches to feed. Thirty-eight pictures later he returned quite satisfied, having taken some remarkable shots of his new friends. Other commonly sighted animals are sloths, armadillos, coatimundis, raccoons, and peccaries. In addition there is a variety of lizards, iguanas, and snakes, plus more than 350 species of birds. Besides the beaches, you can also observe wildlife on a few nearby trails.

For information on Quepos and Manuel Antonio National Park check out www.biesanz.com/quepos.htm.

## Monteverde Area

*Monteverde — The Community*

Monteverde is one of the major tourist attractions in Costa Rica and also one of the most interesting. Its location is directly west of Palo Verde National Park and northwest of San Jose. Getting there is part of the adventure. The best approach is to come in from San Jose, but even that road can be difficult, especially in the rainy season. If you plan to drive to Monteverde on your own you absolutely must have a four-wheel drive vehicle. Once you leave the main highway the roads to Monteverde are steep dirt roads, often with lots of potholes. Specialty vehicle rentals are expensive, but in this case, necessary. The other choice is to buy a package for one or more nights and let someone else do the driving. It takes several hours to drive to Monteverde from San Jose so you should plan on staying at least one night. Two nights would be ideal.

The name Monteverde refers to two different things: the Quaker community of Monteverde as well as the adjacent cloud preserve. The history of the community is interesting and bears repeating. Back in the early 1950s some Quakers from the state of Alabama were jailed for refusing to register for the draft in the U.S., and decided to move to a more peaceful country whose military policy coincided with their Pacifist beliefs. Costa Rica, having no army, fit the bill. There were 44 original settlers from 11 different families. Some flew to San Jose while others drove from Alabama, a three-month journey. Eventually they settled in the Monteverde area where land was cheap and plentiful. They supported themselves through dairy farming and cheese production. Today their modern factory supplies cheese to all of

Costa Rica. The Quakers, respectful of the land and its fragility, have been instrumental in keeping Monteverde and the surrounding area in its pristine state.

There are several art galleries and craft centers to visit in Monteverde as well as the cheese factory, called La Lechería. The Hummingbird Gallery is a must-see. Being completely surrounded by buzzing hummingbirds is one of Monteverde's fun experiences. They sound like little jet planes as they skim by your ears. You can also arrange for horseback riding and guided wildlife walks. Because of the Quaker heritage English is widely understood in this area. There are several lodges in the Monteverde area, as well as in the nearby town of Santa Elena. Most sell out during the busy winter and summer season. You can reserve these properties on a room only basis as well as on a package basis. We recommend you reserve ahead.

## Monteverde — The Cloud Forest Preserve

This privately owned and operated cloud preserve is the major attraction of Monteverde. You can hike it on your own — there are several trails — or you can hire a guide for a half-day or more. Guides run about US$15 for a half day and we recommend going with a guide. The cloud forest is a very misty place and it is hard to see wildlife. The guide can point out things you would ordinarily miss on your own. Other special tours may be offered or can be arranged upon request, such as night tours of the preserve or birding tours. More than 400 species of birds have been recorded at Monteverde, including the resplendent quetzal. There is a limit to the number of people who can enter the preserve at one time. Plan to arrive as soon as possible after the opening time of 8 a.m. Admission is about US$8. The preserve can be wet and muddy, so bring raingear and boots.

An excellent Web site for information on the Monteverde area and its attractions is www.monteverdeinfo.com.

### Volcán Arenal National Park

Located a few miles/kilometers west of the town of Fortuna, this national park contains one of the most active volcanoes in Central America, the Arenal Volcano. There are only a few visitors' services at the park; the main attraction is viewing the smoldering or fiery volcano, especially at night. If the volcano is active, you will be able to see the eruptions from outside the park. Day Tours are available to see the volcano and often include other activities available in the surrounding area. This is an all day trip from Monteverde.

For information on the country of Costa Rica call the tourist bureau at 800-343-6332 or visit their official tourism Web site at www.tourism-costarica.com/. We hope you enjoy your adventure in Costa Rica!

# HAWAII

Hawaii has often been called one of the world's favorite vacation spots. There is no doubt that this is one of those rare places on Earth that truly offers something for everyone, including the single parent family. Depending on your interest you can enjoy exciting nightlife or complete isolation, warm tropical relaxing beaches or high altitude volcanic mountains with exciting hiking terrain, ultra plush expensive hotels or very inexpensive laid-back lodging one step above a grass shack, and almost every type of sport imaginable, including skiing! Californians often have special fares from their state, making Hawaii a doubly tempting destination for west coasters.

To experience the culture and beauty of Hawaii doesn't mean you have to spend large sums of money on accommodations, but you certainly can, if that is your choice. And that is one of the reasons why Hawaii is such a great vacation destination for single parent families. There are all kinds of choices. Once a traveler has decided to visit Hawaii the very first question he or she asks is "What island(s) should I visit?" and the second question is "How long should I stay there?" The answers to both questions depend on your personal tastes and interests. There are no wrong choices in Hawaii; some islands are better suited to your preferences than others. All are wonderful.

There are four major tourist islands in Hawaii — Oahu, Maui, Kauai, and Hawaii, often called the Big Island. In addition there are several other less visited islands: Molokai and Lanai, whose tourism levels are increasing annually, and Niihau and Kahoolawe, both essentially inaccessible. In this section we will discuss the four major islands, as they are most appropriate for single adults traveling with children.

Keep in mind that by law *all* Hawaiian beaches are public. So you need not feel like a poor cousin if you stay in a three star hotel and visit the beach at a nearby five star hotel. You won't have access to all of their deluxe facilities, but at least part of the beach will be set aside for public use.

## Oahu — "The Gathering Place"

Nearly one million people populate this beautiful island, the vast majority of which live in and around the capital city of Honolulu. There was a time where visitors vacationed only on Oahu and some never left the beautiful area of Waikiki, the resort section of Honolulu. Today that is no longer true.

Many visitors bypass Oahu entirely, heading straight for one or more of the outer islands so they can experience the "real" Hawaii. The "real" Hawaii can be experienced on Oahu as well. If you are looking for nightlife and are interested in museums and history, this island offers the best selection for those activities, along with beautiful secluded beaches and hikes on the outskirts of Honolulu. There are so many varied things to do on the island it would be impossible to see it all in a week. If you are spending a few days in Honolulu, we recommend renting a car for at least a day or two to explore the areas outside of the capital city.

Starting with Honolulu, here are a few of the major attractions.

➢ *Pearl Harbor*

A "must-see" attraction. One can't help be moved by the Arizona Memorial which played such as pivotal role in one of the most defining moments in the history of the United States. We recommend getting there as close to 9 a.m. as possible to avoid the crowds. This is a wonderful place to wear your newly acquired lei and leave it over the memorial in honor of those young men who died during that fateful day in December. For more information visit www.nps.gov/usar/ or members.aol.com/azmemph/usarlink.htm.

➢ *Diamond Head*

You need to be in fairly good shape to make this hike. It is best to do it early in the morning before the sun gets too hot. Bring plenty of water, sunscreen, and a hat. The view from the top is terrific. From Diamond Head you can continue on for a pleasant drive counter clockwise around the island. For background information on Diamond Head, visit this Web site at volcano.und.nodak.edu/vwdocs/volc_images/north_america/hawaii/diahead.html.

➢ *Iolani Palace*

America's only royal residence is open during limited hours and may be entered only with a guided tour. I recommend making reservations at least a day or two in advance. For tour times and ticket reservations call 808-522-0832 or visit http://alaike.lcc.hawaii.edu/openstudio/iolani/. For a brief history of the palace click on http://alaike.lcc.hawaii.edu/openstudio/Iolani/PALACE1.HTM.

➢ *Bishop Museum*

Located on the grounds of the University of Hawaii, this group of stone buildings houses a superb collection of relics and historical information on Hawaii and Polynesia in general. Get an early start, as there is a lot to see. For further information call 808-847-3511 or visit www.bishopmuseum.org.

➢ *Punchbowl Cemetery*

Located in the crater of an extinct volcano, this National Cemetery of the Pacific honors 25,000 men and women who fought in various wars starting with the Spanish-American War up to present day. Click on www.interment.net/data/us/hi/oahu/natmem/.

If you choose to stay in Honolulu for a few days, you should get outside of Waikiki and either do a half-day excursion or drive part or all the way around the island for a day. I highly recommend a half-day excursion to *Nuuanu Pali Lookout.* From there you have an easy hike down a paved path with stunning scenery. You will recognize the view from the movie "Pearl Harbor. Legend has it that this is the place where Kamehameha the Great pursued his enemies to their death over the cliff, thus uniting all the Hawaiian Islands in 1795. For photos, directions, and information click on www.hawaiiweb.com/html/pali_lookout.html. If you do decide to circle the island, you can do the *Dole Pineapple Maze* (world's largest maze) and swim at the beach at the infamous *Banzai Pipeline* (calm in summer). For information on the pineapple plantation maze, call 808-621-8408 or visit www.hawaiiweb.com/html/dole_pineapple_plantation.html.

Unless you plan to spend your entire time on the beach, I would rent a car. It's quicker and easier to get around, especially with active teen-agers. Many people will tell you not to rent in Honolulu but it was better for us since we are on the move a lot and liked the flexibility of stopping at various beaches for quick swims along the way. On the outer islands you will definitely need a car. Rent the smallest one you can that is comfortable. Jeeps are great fun, but do cost more.

To save money on a Honolulu hotel, pick a moderately priced hotel a block or two off the beach. Outrigger has some good ones. Any of the other chains will do too, such as Best Western or Holiday Inn. Ask about family specials. On the outer islands, most places are beachfront or very close to the water.

Obviously Honolulu will have the largest number of single people. Next in line, but not a close second, would be the Lahaina area of Maui.

**Maui — "The Valley Isle"**

There is plenty of tourist action in the town of Lahaina, where teen-agers and college age kids can do the "Lahaina Strut." Here are the really adventurous fun things to do on the island:

➢ Do the snorkel excursion at *Molokini Crater.* For photos visit the Web site at http://205.166.249.77/molokini.html.

➢ *Iao Needle Valley State Park* is a beautiful hiking area with easy trails. Click on www.ibackroads.com/SHORT_TRIPS/hawaii/maui/iao_valley_sp.html.

➢ *Hike down Haleakala.* This is the world's largest dormant volcano. The scenery here is awesome, with clouds rolling in and out of a moon-like landscape. I would rank it one of the ten best three-hour hikes I have ever done. Lots of biking tour operators sell you a trip that takes you to the top to see the dawn and then you bike down the mountain road. This costs US$50 or more per person. Instead we drove to the top, then hiked down inside the crater (for free) and took the Sliding Sands Trail. Be aware that hiking one hour down means hiking two hours up. Bring a light jacket. It is cool up there. The trail starts at 10,000 feet (3,000 meters) and drops down to 9,000 (2,700 meters) or more, depending on how far you choose to hike. The official government Web site is www.nps.gov/hale/. An excellent informative site is www.haleakala.national-park.com.

➢ *Dine at Haliimaile General Store.* Located on the slopes of Haleakala Crater, this country-style gourmet restaurant is in the middle of one thousand acres of pineapple fields and once served as the general store for plantation workers. We last dined there in 1999 and had a wonderful meal. Prices were on the high side but worth it.

➢ *Drive the Hana Road.* This will take a full day. There are 55 bridges and numerous waterfalls along the way. Bring plenty of film and be prepared to stop frequently. Ninety-nine percent of the tourists go as far as the Seven Sacred Pools and turn back. For a real adventure, continue onward on the dirt road, and eventually you will circle back to your hotel. Start early, as it is a long day. Grab lunch at one of the cheap roadside stands with lots of fresh picked fruits. The Seven Sacred Pools is a name created by tourists. These pools are not and never were sacred to the Polynesians. For more information on this fantastic 50-mile strip of road, click on www.mauigateway.com/~diving/hana.html.

## Kauai — "The Garden Isle"

This is my son's favorite island, the smallest, the most lush, and the most laid-back. When the movie setting calls for "paradise," this is where the moviemakers come. Numerous films and TV shows have been shot here. Among them: "South Pacific," the remake of "King Kong," and "Fantasy Island," ("De plane! De plane!").

You will definitely want to do the following:

➤ *Drive up to Waimea Canyon,* the Grand Canyon of the Pacific. For more information click on www.kauai-hawaii.com/west/waimea_c.html.

➤ *Hike the Na Pali Coast.* The scenery is nothing short of drop-dead. The Awaawapuhi Trail, a three-hour fairly strenuous hike, offers fabulous views high above the Na Pali Coast and takes you to the wettest spot on earth. There are short easy family hikes as well. You can also sign up for a zodiac and kayak excursions to this remote and beautiful coast, accessible only by water or foot. Kayaking excursions are strenuous and can take all day, so check it out first. For photos and information on the Na Pali Coast make sure to view the following Web sites www.state.hi.us/dlnr/dsp/NaPali/na_pali.htm & www.kauai-hawaii.com/north/napali_c.html.

➤ *Eat a snow cone.* They are served all over the islands, but Kauai reigns supreme with this delicious treat. Forget what you know about snow cones on the boardwalks of the east coast. Kauai snow cones are prepared lovingly and artfully, with more than a dozen flavors in one. Get the super special and get the sweet beans. (Vanilla is a sweet bean.) Sounds awful but they are sweet and delicious and provide a textual contrast to the shaved ice. Eating a monster snow cone in Kauai is a social event. Relax outside with the locals while you imbibe and ingest.

➤ *Visit the Fern Grotto.* Even though this is considered a major attraction of Kauai and a popular place for weddings, we passed it by in favor of a longer hike along the Na Pali coast. I welcome reader feedback on this attraction. For information click on www.kauai-hawaii.com/lihue/fern_grotto.html.

## Hawaii — "The Big Island"

This is my favorite island, although I love them all. Be aware that the Big Island is not famous for its sandy beaches, since most beaches are lava rock.

If sandy beaches are your thing, you should select one of the other islands. If you choose to stay here, I recommend you split your stay between the east and west coast. (It takes 10 hours to drive all around the island and about four hours to drive from east coast to west coast, using the northern road). I would spend a couple of nights at the Volcano House in Volcano National Park. It perches right on the rim of an active volcano (active in that it steams, but not erupts). There are lots of interesting easy trails to hike, such as Devastation Trail. Request the cheapest room available at the Volcano House. It may not have a view (ours had no windows), but the restaurant has a full frontal view of the volcano so who cares? You can make hotel reservations online at www.volcanovillage.com/V_house.htm or call 808-967-7321.

You can fly into Hilo (east side) and out of Kona (west side) but you may have to pay a rental car drop fee. Check around with the car companies. After that I would spend several nights at a resort hotel on the west side of the island. Hotels tend to be very deluxe and pricey here, but there are more moderately priced ones close to the town of Kailua Kona, which is a lively growing town with lots of shops and moderately priced restaurants.

*Things to do:*

➤ The black lava is everywhere and actually blocks the road, called *Chain of Craters Road,* into the park. You must go the long way around to get into Volcano National Park. It is interesting to drive up the road until you can go no further just to see how the lava flow destroyed and blocked the road. (Note of caution: Do not remove any lava rocks from the island or you will suffer from the curse of Madame Pele, the Polynesian Goddess of Fire. The Polynesians take this very seriously).

➤ Currently there are no lava flows around the park, but if you sign up for a *helicopter ride,* you might be able to fly over active lava, and one of the volcanoes may still be active. It's expensive, but worth it. Bargain for a "family rate."

➤ Take the excursion down *Waipio Valley.* What a great little adventure! Every 10 years or so, a tsunami comes roaring into this area and sucks away everything in the lush valley below the cliffs. For a view of the valley, click on www.waipio.com/. Unless you have nerves of steel and reinforced brakes on your rental car, I urge you to sign up for a local guided tour, rather than drive down into the valley yourself.

➤ Visit *Lava Tree State Monument* — scenic interesting walk around trees that have been "lavafied." For information on the park visit www.wildernet.com/pages/area.cfm?areaID=HISPLT&CU_ID=1.

➤ Drive to *Parker Ranch,* the largest ranch in the U.S. This is a pretty drive and Parker Ranch is a great place to get a hearty reasonably priced ranch breakfast. Bring a sweater if you start out early morning, as the ranch is at a higher altitude. Check out their informative Web site for tours and a history of the paniolos (Hawaiian cowboys): www.parkerranch.com/.

➤ Drive to the *southernmost point in the U.S.* This is a very windy area with a windswept landscape that is quite different from the rest of the island. Make sure to bring sunglasses to protect your eyes and a hair band if you wear long hair.

➤ Visit the *green sand beach.* There are lots of easily accessible black sand beaches on the island, but the green sand beach is hard to get to. It is an adventure. You will need a jeep and you *must* know how to drive in deep sand without getting stuck. There is not likely to be anyone around to help you. The green sand beach is not far from the southernmost point in the U.S. Ask for directions when you get there. There are no signs.

*Some final recommendations for your visit to the Hawaiian Islands:*

➤ Should you decide to do two or more islands, check into special rate booklets with Hawaiian and Aloha Air. Sometimes you can buy a booklet of six or eight inter-island flight tickets for a special price, which everyone in your party can use. You may need to pre-purchase them outside of Hawaii and you should make advance reservations. There may be other offers as well, such as one week unlimited inter-island travel. Aloha Air may be reached at 800-367-5250 or visit their Web site at www.alohaairlines.com/. Hawaiian Air may be reached at 800-367-5320 or visit www.hawaiianair.com/.

➤ If your family enjoys hiking, I recommend pre-purchasing *Hawaii's Best Hiking Trails,* by Robert Smith. It is published by Hawaiian Outdoors Adventures. I bought my copy at Borders, but other bookstores may carry it as well, including www.amazon.com.

➤ For recommendations on good food at moderate prices you should purchase a copy of *Cheap Eats in Hawaii* by Sandra Gustafson. The book is now out of print, but you might be able to locate used copies on www.amazon.com. The recommended restaurants cover a wide range of prices. The book was our source for the unique Haliimaile General Store.

➤ A great source for moderately priced gifts for friends and family back home are the ABC stores located on all of the islands. Here you will find all the usual tourist stuff — T-shirts, tank tops, beach towels, Kona coffee, and macadamia nuts. My son bought a five-year supply of tank tops during our last visit thanks to some great sale prices. ABC stores are not in high rent districts, so you will have to seek them out in the smaller shopping malls or side streets.

➤ Contact the tourist boards of the islands you plan to visit and order all the material they offer. It's free, informative, and the booklets often include discount coupons for meals and attractions. The official general Web site for the Hawaiian Islands, which includes vacation planning information for each of the islands, is: www.gohawaii.com/. You can call toll free at 800-GOHAWAII or call locally at 808-923-1811. Contact information for the individual islands is as follows:

Oahu Visitor's Bureau
(Maui/Molokai/Lanai)
www.visit-oahu.com
Phone: 808-524-0722

Kauai Visitor's Bureau
www.kauaivisitorsbureau.com
Phone: 808-245-3971

Maui Visitor's Bureau
www.visitmaui.com
Phone: 808-244-3530

Big Island Visitor's Bureau
www.bigisland.org
(Hilo) Phone: 808-961-5797
(West Hawaii) Phone: 808-886-1655

We know you will enjoy your stay in heavenly Hawaii. We hope this information has helped you in your decision-making process. If you have further questions on Hawaii you are welcome to e-mail me directly at Brenda@SingleParentTravel.net.

Aloha and Mahalo!

# ALASKA

There is a look and feel to Alaska unmatched by any other place in the world. First there is the vastness — the enormous space of the place. Distances are deceiving. What appears to be an easy five-mile hike in actuality is a 50-mile expanse. And then there is the silence, the blanket of quiet that envelopes you for miles around, only to be pierced suddenly by the screech of an eagle echoing through the sky. Once you experience Alaska the word "grandeur" takes on a whole new meaning.

When people commonly think of Alaska, they envision groups of gray-haired couples, dressed in Lands End sportswear viewing the coastline of the Inland Passage from the comfy deck of a cruise ship. There is another side to Alaska tourism — the vast interior — long ago discovered and frequently enjoyed by the Alaskans themselves. As a single adult traveling with children, you can enjoy the excitement of the Last Frontier on a moderate budget. The state offers everything for a memorable single parent family vacation — boundless nature, cultural variety, funky towns, and a rollicking pioneer style nightlife that welcomes and appeals to every age and family group. You don't have to spend big bucks to enjoy Alaska. This section will tell you how to plan an exciting trip through the Alaskan interior.

## Planning your flight reservations

Your point-of-entry city will be Anchorage. For U.S. citizens living on the West Coast, you may be able to find some bargain airfare sales into Anchorage. For Midwesterners and East Coasters, airfare specials into Anchorage are far and few between. Cash in your frequent flyer bonus points if you have enough for one or two tickets. Remember to make flight reservations many months in advance, nine months at minimum.

## Planning your hotel reservations

Compared to other parts of the country, hotels in Alaska are priced very high for what you receive in amenities. The season is short and the hotel owners must recoup their expenses over a five-month period. Sometimes there are reduced prices in the shoulder seasons (May and September). If your children finish school before June or start after the first few days of September, this is something to consider. Bear in mind the weather may be cold, depending on where you travel. I heartily recommend staying at B&B's and guest houses whenever possible. Alaskans are hard-working people and look to earn their living in a variety of ways, one of which includes renting rooms in their homes. It's a great way to meet the locals.

We sampled six B&B's on our last trip. All were neat, clean and comfy, and all were quite different and with one exception, the owners were an absolute delight. The prices generally run about half that of a first class hotel and you get a full breakfast to boot! Many B&Bs include a VCR in your room and local video rentals are quite cheap in Alaska, as it is a popular pastime. For information on B&B, contact the Alaskan Tourist Bureau and get a copy of the *Milepost Magazine,* which is an invaluable guide to trip planning.

The official tourism Web site is www.travelalaska.com/homepage.html, or call for information to 907-465-2010. To order "Milepost" Magazine, click on www.themilepost.com or call 800-726-4707. Canadians should call 800-663-5714. For overseas orders call +[1] 706-823-3558. Just like flight reservations, hotel reservations should be made at least nine months in advance for the summer season.

## Planning your rental car reservations

All major rental car companies operate out of Anchorage Airport — Budget, National, plus local companies advertised in *Milepost Magazine.* Shop around on Web sites or by phone to determine the best price for you. Check into the insurance policies. Most of the companies refuse to cover you if you choose to drive on certain interior roads. The night we flew into Anchorage was late and we were dog tired, so I never noticed the signs stating which roads were not covered under the insurance. When I dropped off the car two weeks later I read the sign and was amused to see that we had driven on five of the six "banned" or "excluded" highways.

One reason these roads are excluded from insurance coverage is that so much construction takes place on Alaskan highways during the summer to repair winter damage. The construction sites often have lots of loose gravel around which can cause damage to your windshield or headlights. There are protective "grills" you can rent from a local garage to protect your rental car. Inquire at the time you rent your car. RVs abound in Alaska. If your kids are old enough to help out with all the chores that an RV requires, you may wish to consider renting one. RV rentals sell out quickly for the summer season. Book at least nine months ahead for best selection.

## Planning your sightseeing

Two of the most scenic and exciting places to visit in Alaska's interior are the Kenai Peninsula, south of Anchorage, and Denali National Park, north of Anchorage. If your vacation time is 10 days or more, you can cover both areas at a leisurely pace. We'll start with Anchorage, loop down to the Kenai Peninsula, then up to Denali and Fairbanks, and then head east circling around back to Anchorage through Valdez.

### Anchorage

If you are pressed for vacation time, head straight out to the glorious scenic areas of Kenai or the interior but if you can spare a day in Anchorage, here are some highlights:

➤ Start with a visit to the *Anchorage Tourism Bureau* at 524 W. 4th Avenue. They will provide maps, helpful information and tidal timetables for Turnagain Arm.

➤ Plan your day around a visit to *Beluga Point at Turnagain Arm*, just south of Anchorage. If the tide is rolling in you will witness eight-foot waves bringing in the second highest tidal surge in North America (30 feet/9 meters!).

➤ Do a *walking tour* of the downtown area. The tourism bureau will help you plan it.

➤ *Check out the shops* in town. Many feature native crafts and carvings. The T-shirt selection in Alaska is phenomenal. The shirts are often high quality with beautiful renditions of the native wild animals such as wolves and bears. Apone T-shirts maintains one or two shops in town. They have a great selection. Ask to be placed on their catalogue mailing list. Whatever you see that you like in Anchorage, buy it. Prices will be higher elsewhere.

➤ Visit the *Alaska Experience Theater and the adjoining Earthquake Exhibit*. You will learn about the 1964 earthquake (8.6 on the Richter Scale) that leveled Anchorage and also get to experience what an earthquake feels like.

The contact information for the Anchorage Visitors Bureau is phone: 907-278-5559, e-mail: info@anchorage.net, Web site www.anchorage.net. For B&B accommodation information click on www.bedandbreakfastnetwork.com.

## Portage Glacier

This is a must-see stop on the way to Kenai. Here you can stand nose-to-nose with an iceberg. The visitor's center has an ice cave and also provides a viewing area of the icebergs. There are two short easy trails to hike — the Moraine Loop and the Byron Glacier Trail. Dress warmly. It is cold, I mean really cold. If the wind picks up it will feel like winter as you approach the icebergs.

## Kenai Peninsula

The drive from Anchorage to Homer takes about a half day and is gloriously scenic. It is an easy drive with ample places to pull over and enjoy the view or take pictures. You can break up the trip with a brief stop in the town of *Kenai,* the second oldest settlement in Alaska, founded by Russian fur traders. Check out the Holy Assumption Russian Orthodox Church built in 1896. For general information on the Kenai Peninsula, visit www.kenaipeninsula.org/ or call 907-283-3850.

## Homer

It's hard to describe Homer without using superlatives. It has been called the "Acapulco of Alaska" due to its mild climate, and also the Halibut Capital of the World, many of which tip the scales at more than 200 pounds. Set on a promontory overlooking Kachemak Bay and the magnificent Kenai Mountains, the scenery alone is enough to mandate a visit to the town. In addition you have marvelous fishing, kayaking, hiking, wildlife, photo opportunities, and artist colonies. Homer is a feast for the senses. While in Homer be sure to take a scenic drive up and over the town for some unsurpassed views of the bay and the mountains. Head out of town on the Sterling Road, then turn right onto West Hill Road, then onto Skyline Drive. Also check out East End and East Hill Road to see the expensive homes, each with a million dollar view.

## Homer Spit

This four-mile-long finger of flat land hosts fishing docks, canneries, tourist boardwalks, public camping and the famous Salty Dawg Saloon. Dating back to 1897, this saloon is a local landmark. Drop in for a beer and some local color. Allow time for beachcombing at the far end of Homer Spit. Sit back on a rock and enjoy the magnificent view and soon you will see whales and otters and other sea creatures coming to feed and play. If you enjoy the sweet taste of fresh-caught Alaskan salmon and halibut, stop by at one of the local seafood distributors. Get on their mailing list and have them ship some home to you. The salmon steaks or filets arrive in individual vacuum packs and make great gifts for friends and family. For a complete list, visit www.xyz.net/~artntype/other.htm#INFO. We used to order from Katch Seafoods, but the owners retired. They recommend a place in Soldotna called Alaska Seafood Direct. You can call them toll free at 800-656-6070, or visit their Web site at www.seafooddirect.com and place your order via e-mail.

For further information on the town of Homer, visit the official Web site homeralaska.org/ or call 907-235-7740. A free brochure about Homer may be ordered online or by phone. There are many excellent B&Bs and tourist homes in the Homer area. We stayed at the Seekins B&B and found it to be quite satisfactory. Phone number: 907-235-8996. For other listings check out www.bedandbreakfastnetwork.com/cgi-bin/frames.cgi?ak&search.

## Seldovia

This small fishing village, a short ferry ride from Homer, was originally settled by the Russians and is on the same latitude as Oslo, Norway. We spent the day here on the fourth of July enjoying an old-fashioned picnic celebration. There is a wonderful easy hiking trail, maintained by the local middle school students, that winds through the lush forest and along the shoreline.

## Halibut Cove

This small village, also a ferry ride away from Homer, is known for its scenic setting, galleries and bird sanctuary. We did not have time to visit it during our stay in Homer, but were told by other tourists that it was an enjoyable excursion. I welcome reader feedback on this attraction.

## Seward

Located about 125 miles (201 kilometers) south of Anchorage, this historic and scenic community bills itself as "The Gateway to the Kenai Fjords." Depending on your vacation schedule, you may choose to spend a night or two here or perhaps plan a day's visit to the area on the way

back north from Homer. For information call the Chamber of Commerce
at 907-224-8051 or visit their informative Web site www.seward.net/
chamber/.

## Denali National Park

Denali. The Great One. Even the name is full of grandeur. I have hiked 90
percent of the major national parks in the United States and nothing comes
close to Denali. It is in a category all by itself: the largest (six million acres),
and the wildest and the most pristine park in the United States national park
system. Originally called McKinley National Park, it was renamed in 1980
when it reverted back to its original Native American name. Many people
come to the park to see Denali Mountain (or Mt. McKinley). Topping over
20,000 feet (6,100 meters) it is the highest peak in North America. Often
shrouded in fog, the mountain creates its own wild weather and is visible
only a third of the time. If Denali Mountain appears in its glory during your
stay, consider it a bonus.

*Denali is not like other national parks.*

➤ Visitors can only enter the park via a shuttle bus. Advance reservations
are essential. Two-thirds of the seats are released for sale many months
in advance. One-third of the seats are offered for sale two days in
advance. Don't expect to arrive and find seats available that day, especially during peak season. You will be disappointed. For bus shuttle
information visit www.nps.gov/dena/home.html

➤ There are no trails in Denali National Park. You simply signal the bus
driver where you would like to get off and you hike wherever your
heart pleases in this vast land. You can always orient yourself from the
road or a river. The park rangers do "trail sweeps" at the end of the day,
which is a contradiction in terms since there are no trails, but we were
told there are certain popular hiking areas. If you are going far from
the road, make sure you know how to use a topo map and compass and
take it — and be aware that being closer to magnetic north will change
the declination on your compass! When you finish your hike you
thumb a ride back on the first available shuttle bus. Don't worry if the
first one or two buses are full; you won't be left behind to sleep with
the bears.

➤ Distances are deceiving. As stated earlier, what appears to be five miles
(8 kilometers) away, is probably 50.

> There are no concessionary services in the park. Nothing. Absolutely nothing. Bring everything you need — food, drink, sunscreen, layered clothing, toilet paper, and bags to carry your trash out of the park.

*Keep in mind the following when hiking Denali:*

> The Alaskans are very protective of the pristine environment of their state and especially their national parks. Don't even think about littering or leaving trash behind. Our bus driver was a petite, colorful and crusty school bus driver who, in typical Alaskan pioneer fashion, left her husband and kids home for the summer while she went up to Denali to drive her shuttle bus. Her expertise was Alaskan flora, which she graciously explained to all the passengers. Whenever a passenger disembarked to go hiking, she disembarked as well and firmly lectured each person about staying clear of animals and keeping the park clean. "This is my state and my bus," she would say, "and I'll know if you disobeyed the rules and come after you." It was amusing to watch some tall Texans or Germans nod meekly in agreement.

> There is a saying in Alaska: "If you don't like the weather, wait 10 minutes and it will change." This is quite true. You will need to layer when you hike the park — rain jacket, sweatshirt, T-shirt, hat. We hiked Denali in mid-July. It was sunny, cloudy, drizzly, cool, and warm — all in one day. The day before it had snowed.

> This is not Yellowstone National Park. The animals are not sensitized to human visitors. Keep well clear of all wild animals and keep your food sealed in plastic bags so odors do not travel. Don't even think about approaching or feeding an animal.

> Most importantly, if you want to experience Denali, *you have to get out of the bus.* I know this sounds obvious but I have spoken to so many people who sat in the bus for the 10-hour round-trip ride and then complained that they didn't see much wildlife. Even tour programs recommend staying in the bus. Think about it. What wild animal is going to deliberately approach a large moving vehicle carrying 30 or so humans? You have to get out on their terrain. During our all day hike we saw elk, Dall sheep, a wild wolf, moose, foxes and critters I didn't even recognize.

*Miscellaneous Information about the park:*

> Denali National Park is about a five-hour drive north of Anchorage.

> When you arrive, head over to the Denali Park Hotel and sign up for any ranger guided walks and lectures featured during your stay.

➤ There are many comfortable and pricey hotels near the park entrance, plus a number of B&Bs in the nearby town of Healy.

➤ Plan on having dinner at the Denali Park Hotel. The food is great and the prices are fairly reasonable by Alaskan standards.

➤ The official government Web site is www.nps.gov/dena/. Another useful site with lots of information is www.denali.national-park.com/. You can also call 800-622-7275 for park information.

## Nenana

Originally a gathering place for various tribes of Athabascan Indians, this historic full-service town of about 500 residents is still culturally diverse with a notable Native American population. Now famous for the Nenana Ice Classic, the town is a convenient and enjoyable stop on the drive from Denali to Fairbanks.

The Nenana Ice Classic — Alaska's Coolest Lottery — is a must-do attraction in the town. Each year in mid-winter, the locals place a large tri-pod on the frozen Nenana River attached to a trip wire and clock. A guard post is set up nearby to ward off any potential lottery cheaters who might consider tripping the wire prematurely. Bets are then taken to determine the exact date and minute in the spring that the ice will break on the river. The 2001 lottery paid off more than US$300,000. One of the winners was from Japan. Each ticket costs US$2. For information on the town and the Ice Classic, check out theses two Web sites. You can request lottery tickets online atwww.mtaonline.net/~ncc/Nenana/Nenana_Alaskax.html and www.ptial-aska.net/~tripod/.

## *Fairbanks*

Located in the heart of Alaska's interior, Fairbanks is the state's second largest city. Some of the city's attractions are:

➤ *Alaskaland* — an enjoyable and educational historic theme park focus-ing on Alaska's colorful history. One of the park attractions is a recreated gold mining town where everyone has a chance to pan for gold. There is also a train and steamboat ride, a salmon bake and craft exhibitions. There is no one official Web site for Alaskaland. Each of the following three sites offers different information:

www.ptialaska.net/~rcoghill/alaskaland.html

www.akpub.com/akttt/akilometersrd.html

www.fairnet.org/fbks/Pictorial/pictor05.html

➢ *Pioneer Air Museum* — displays the rollicking history of aviation in this pioneer state. For further information click on www.ptialaska.net/-akttt/ aviat.html or call 907-452-2969.

➢ *University of Alaska Museum* — houses an excellent collection of cultural and natural science exhibits pertaining to Alaska, such as wildlife, gold, and permafrost exhibits, along with a display of Russian and Native American artifacts. The museum maintains an excellent Web site www.uaf.edu/museum/.

➢ For evening entertainment check out the *Howling Dog Saloon*, a local hangout known as the northernmost "rock and roll" bar in the world.

For comprehensive information on the town of Fairbanks, accommodations, and restaurants, click on www.aktourguide.com/Fairbanks.html and www.ExploreFairbanks.com.

*There are several interesting attractions in the vicinity of Fairbanks.*

## North Pole

Although very touristy, it is a fun place to visit, and your children will enjoy mailing cards to their friends postmarked "North Pole." There is a visitor's center and, of course, many Christmas shops. Throughout December the local post office is swamped with mail for Santa Claus, receiving more than 10,000 a season to the jolly old elf, all of which are answered by students from the North Pole Middle School. For more information check out this Web site www.ptialaska.net/~rcoghill/north.pole.html.

## Ester

This former boomtown has a few buildings left from its mining days. One of them is the refurbished bunkhouse of the Cripple Creek Hotel. The kids and I stayed here one night as an alternative to Fairbanks. The bunkhouse prices are very cheap. Accommodations are clean but Spartan. There was one drawback: most rooms share a bathroom with an adjoining unit. That is OK until the people in the other room forget to unlock the bathroom doors when they finish. Then you have a problem. For rates and online booking click on www.akohwy.com/c/cripcrre.htm.

## Malamute Saloon

Part of the Cripple Creek complex, this historic building is host to the Robert Service musical extravaganza, held nightly in the summer. You will be treated to dancing, singing, and renditions of Robert Service poems, complete with sawdust on the floor and beer on the table. Las Vegas it is not. Alaska it is. Show times vary during the week. Call 907-479-2500. Sometimes shows sell out so arrive early or purchase tickets ahead of time.

## Coldfoot

*The Drive — Dalton Highway*

If you have the time on your vacation and want to do something out-of-the-ordinary, consider driving the Dalton Highway north from Fairbanks to stay overnight in the town of Coldfoot, which is about 50 miles (80 kilometers) north of the Arctic Circle. There you can experience 24-hour daylight in the summer. I do not recommend this for single adults traveling with young children. Although scenic, it is a long five-hour drive north from Fairbanks and it would be hard to keep the children entertained for the entire trip. This is a truck haul route, not designed for tourists, and there are very few stops along the way.

Most of the time the road parallels the Alaska Pipeline. There are a few places to stop and read the signs and learn a little about the pipeline. For example, there are large mechanical devices called "pigs," so named for their potbellied shape, which are sent down the pipeline to scour it. The "imaginary" Arctic Circle has a marker and a tourist platform where you can "toast" crossing the line. Some tourists do it with a photo, others with a bottle of champagne. There is a full service rest stop about midway along the drive.

When we drove the road in 1993 it was still a "shoulder-less" dirt road and flat tires and punctures were common. Fortunately we had our flat as we pulled into Coldfoot. No one was around, so my daughter jumped out of the car and proceeded to jack up the tire. Within seconds, no less than three men emerged out of nowhere and proceeded to change the tire. "I *know* how to do this, " protested my daughter, but to no avail. Pretty young ladies are in short supply in the remote regions of Alaska, and these gents were intent upon jousting each other to perform a service in return for a smile.

*The Town of Coldfoot*

Coldfoot, so named for some early settlers who got "cold feet'" and left, is known for its extreme temperatures which have ranged as low as 82 degrees below zero Fahrenheit (27.8°C) in the winter to as high as 90 degrees (32.2°C) in the summer. Coldfoot contains the northernmost truck stop in the world, a few accommodations and some very independent and resourceful residents. The nearest supermarket is a five-hour drive away. For some information on what it is like to live there, check out the Web site a local resident maintains at: msnhomepages.talkcity.com/resortrd/bushbride/. For information on the town itself and available accommodations, visit these Web sites:

www.sourdoughfuel.com/coldfoot.html

www.akohwy.com/c/coldfoot.htm

www.ilovealaska.com/Alaska/Coldfoot/

**Driving North to Prudhoe Bay**

For those folks with oodles of vacation time, you can do as the Alaskans say and "Don't stop 'til you get to the top." Continue your drive north the next day until you reach Prudhoe Bay, terminus for the Alaska pipeline, on the north coast of Alaska. Prudhoe Bay, population 49, is strictly devoted to oil production, but they do get a handful of tourists. We chose not to go this far, but were told there is quite a bit of wildlife viewing from the road this far up. For information on the town and its accommodations, check out www.prudhoebay.com/. For photos and an interesting log of the drive north, visit this site http://web.hulteen.com/eric/deadhorse.html.

**Tok**

For those that have ten days or more vacation time, you may wish to consider heading south from Fairbanks for several hours on the famed Alaska Highway and overnighting at a town called Tok. Here you can stay at a unique B&B called the Stage Stop, which accommodates both horses and people. The place is very homey and the owner used to raise Arabian horses in California. For information and online reservations click on www.akpub.com/akbbrv/stage.html or call 907-883-5338. In Alaska you can call toll free at 800-478-5369. Tok is a sled dog breeding and training center and many local activities center around this. For more information on the town click on www.tokalaskainfo.com/.

## Valdez

From Tok it is a beautiful four or five-hour drive to the port town of Valdez made world famous by the 1989 oil spill. With a population of 4,400, this is a big town by Alaskan standards and there are lots of places to stay and plenty of things to do.

➢ Spend a little time climbing up above the town and watching the super tankers ease into port.

➢ Visit the pipeline terminal.

➢ Take an alpine tour. Valdez is known as Alaska's "Little Switzerland."

➢ Catch a salmon or a halibut. Valdez is a premier fishing destination offering many charter boat excursions.

➢ Check out Prince William Sound and the Columbia Glacier - "must-see" attraction.

For information on all these attractions along with accommodations, visit www.valdezalaska.org/.

To learn more about Columbia Glacier, click on www.valdezalaska.com/ columbiaglacier.html.

Several tour operators visit the glacier. We used Stan Stephan's Charters and were satisfied. If you take this excursion, dress very warmly. Even on a sunny summer day, it feels like midwinter when glaciers surround you.

## Palmer

The scenic drive from Valdez to Anchorage takes about five hours. Palmer, the salad alley of Alaska, is a convenient midway stop. When people think of things to eat in Alaska they think of salmon and halibut, but not usually lettuce. Fresh fruits and vegetables abound in Alaska in the summer, much of it grown in Palmer. The lettuces grow to an enormous size in a short amount of time due to the long days. Fresh caught seafood and fresh picked salad ingredients are dining room staples during the Alaskan summer — quite a different atmosphere from our trip out to the American West a few years prior where ubiquitous roadside signs proclaimed "Real men eat beef."

For general information on Alaska and to order an Alaska Planner brochure, visit www.dced.state.ak.us/tourism/ or call 907-929-2200 Extension 201. Enjoy your Alaska adventure!

## GROUP #3 - TRIPS OF A LIFETIME

### EGYPT

To visit Egypt is to be forever changed about how you view history and human accomplishments throughout the ages. In the egocentric, technological world we live in, we assume that we have built the greatest civilization ever, created by some of the greatest minds ever to live on this planet. A week in Egypt will dispel that belief forever. Egypt is living, captivating history. The architecture of the pyramids, the temples, and the tombs will enthrall you. The stories they tell will entrance you. The Nile will beguile you. Couple all this with the warm hospitality and diverse cultures of the Egyptian people, and you and your children will be drawn into the irresistible web that is the charm of ancient and modern Egypt.

Egypt is a Mecca for tourists from around the globe and deservedly so. The country offers something for everyone's taste and budget. Besides antiquities, there are beaches, bazaars, some of the best diving in the world and those exquisite desert evenings. The tourism infrastructure has been in place since time immortal. The earliest tourists on record were the ancient Egyptians themselves, who traveled down the Nile to visit the glorious pyramids built by their predecessors, later to be followed by the ancient Greeks and Romans. Any place you want is visit or explore is easily and safely accessible. Egypt is one of the few countries in the world that maintains a staff of tourist police in addition to a regular police force. These officers are ready to help you with tourist-related issues, such as giving directions or resolving a dispute with a cab driver over a fare. As a single adult traveling with children you will be comfortable, safe and absolutely awed by what you see.

There are three ways to visit Egypt:

➢ On tour

➢ On your own

➢ A combination of the two

All of the above are safe, viable options. Some pros and cons on each:


**On Tour**

The advantage is that you have no planning and booking worries. One reservation does it all. There may be a savings on the airfare, which will probably be a tour-based or group airfare. Individual excursion airfares to Cairo tend to be high as there is little airline competition on that route, especially since TWA was gobbled up. On a fully escorted tour the guide is with you at all times, leaving little, if any free time to mingle with the locals, linger where you want, or seep in the flavor of the place at your own pace. Start your tour search by consulting your local travel agent and the Internet. Keep in mind travel agents and tour operators tend to sell you upscale, pricey hotels, which may negate your airfare savings. Understandably, travel agents also tend to sell fully escorted tours rather than book semi-independent trips with lots of separate, time-consuming reservations. Call one of the travel agents listed in the Appendix of this book. They specialize in serving single parent families.

## On Your Own

The advantage here is that you have complete flexibility. You can pre-book as little or as much as you want and tailor-make your itinerary to your specifications. You can also seize any individual hotel savings opportunities that are revealed in your research. The drawback is that you will have to shop carefully and thoroughly for the best transatlantic airfare. You also will need to hire local guides wherever you go. Unless you are an Egyptologist, don't even *think* about visiting the temples or the tombs without one. Their services are essential.

## Combination

If you want some independence and yet want the security of having a tour for the core elements of your trip, this may be your best solution. Consider buying a "tour package" and then add some independent elements to it. We pre-purchased a Nile cruise package, including transfers, local air flights, and an Abu Simbel extension before we left the States. Then we independently booked our Cairo hotel and an extra night in Luxor. While in Cairo and during the extra day in Luxor, we arranged for local guides where needed. We were obliged to buy an independent transatlantic excursion airfare as we flew first to Damascus, Syria and then returned home from Cairo. This semi-independent arrangement worked out very well for us.

To get started on your planning and research here are a few Web sites to visit:

➢ ww3.interoz.com/hotels/toursearch22.ihtml. From here you can do a mass mailing to all the Egyptian tour operators. What have you got to lose?

➢ www.touregypt.net/aetbi/members.htm This one provides a listing of various tour operators.

➢ www.epinions.com/trvl-Tour_Operators-All-7400085-Egypt. This is a listing of U.S.-based tour operators, so they probably will all be rather pricey.

After perusing the above sites and looking at a few brochures to get some idea of what you want to do, I then highly recommend you call MISR Travel. This is an Egyptian-based tour operator with an office in New York City. The consultants in New York are extremely knowledgeable and helpful. This is the company we used when planning our trip to Egypt. MISR can plan whatever you want — independent, package tour, combinations. They are aware of all the Nile cruise schedules, and can walk you through the logistics of planning an independent or semi-independent trip. Their toll free number in New York is 800-223-4978. Check out their jazzy Web site at www.egypt-vacation.com/. I am sure there are other tour operators that are just as good, but this one I know to be from personal experience.

Spend time perusing the official Web site for the Egyptian Tourist Authority at www.touregypt.net/. This is a very informative Web site on just about everything you need to know about travel to Egypt, and it has an excellent Web page for children.

**Visas**

If you are a U.S. citizen, you are required to obtain a tourist visa in order to enter Egypt. The cost currently runs around US$20 per person. With the application form you must submit a valid passport. If your passport is due to expire within six months, you will need to get a new one before applying for the visa. Photos will be required as well. Your local AAA office provides passport and visa photos at reasonable cost to their members. *Reread my information on "Documents" before sending the application.*

If you are purchasing an escorted tour, the tour operator will attend to your visa and will fax or send you the application forms and instructions. If you are traveling independently you must make these arrangements on your own. The addresses and phone numbers for U.S.-based Egyptian consulates are:

Egyptian Embassy
2310 Decatur Place NW
Washington D.C. 20008
Phone: (202) 895-5400
Fax: (202) 244-4319

Egyptian Consulate — New York
1110 2nd Avenue
New York, NY 10022
Phone: (212) 759-7120/1/2
Fax: (212) 308-7643
Web site: www.egyptandus.net

Egyptian Consulate — Chicago
500 North Michigan Avenue
Chicago, IL 60611
Phone: (312) 828-9162
Fax: (312) 828-9167

Egyptian Consulate — Houston
2000 West Loop South
Houston, TX 77027
Phone: (713) 961-4915/6, 961-4407
Fax: (713) 961-3868

Egyptian Consulate — San Francisco
3001 Pacific Avenue
San Francisco, CA 94115
Phone: (415) 346-9700 or (415) 346-9702
Fax: (415) 346-9480

For worldwide locations of Egyptian consulates, click on ceg.uiuc.edu/~hagag/embassies.html. Hours of operation can vary with each consulate location. Most are open from 9 a.m. to 2 p.m. Monday through Friday. Consulates may be closed for both Egyptian and U.S. holidays. Verify all information and operating hours before sending in documents or visiting in person.

**What to See in Egypt**

It is impossible to see all the highlights of Egypt in a 10-day or two week vacation. This section will concentrate on the three core areas most U.S. tourists prefer to see: Cairo, Luxor, and the Nile Cruise. If you have an extended vacation or prefer to concentrate on specialty interests, there is the marvelous city of Alexandria, plus the beautiful beaches and diving areas off the coasts of Egypt. For more information peruse the Web sites mentioned earlier in this chapter.

**Cairo**

How can one describe a bustling city of fifteen million people that mixes ancient history and modern day sophistication all at one time? The tempo is infectious. Just *being* in Cairo is an adventure. You will need at least three full days to cover the major sightseeing highlights. If you are traveling in summer like we did, you must plan your day around the heat of the desert sun. Get an early start in the morning, have a leisurely lunch, perhaps a swim in the pool, and then continue your sightseeing late in the afternoon. Shopping can be done in the evenings. All shops stay open late in the evening when the temperatures drop to a pleasant dry 80 degrees. The major sightseeing attractions are:

**The Pyramids of Giza**

In spite of its being one of the most fabled and awesome sights in the world, you are never prepared for the immensity of the pyramids until you stand facing them and look up. Giza is right on the outskirts of Cairo, so it is a cheap cab ride. From there you can approach the pyramids by car, by camel or on foot. We chose to walk so I could stop and take pictures from many angles. If you do that, expect to be besieged by the camel drivers wanting to be in your photo lens and of course receive a tip. It got so annoying I finally had to tip them just to stand out of the way, so I could take photos of the pyramids standing serenely alone. One camel driver was so persistent I begrudgingly took a few extra shots of him and his camel in front of the Pyramid of Cheops. His smile was so engaging and his camel so colorfully adorned that this turned out to be everyone's favorite photo of the pyramids. All of my friends said, "This is what I think of when I think of Egypt." So much for serenity.

You can buy tickets to go inside all three pyramids. There are no treasures inside, but you will be able to walk up and down some of the secret passageways. Be sure to go in at least one of them.

*Special Hint: Before you leave for Egypt, purchase a small battery-operated rubber fan for each member of your family and carry it with you whenever you visit temples, tombs and pyramids. Bring a set of extra batteries as well. We found our rubber fans in a local hardware store. Trust me, they are essential.*

## The Great Sphinx

Even though it is only a short walk from the pyramids, one close look will tell you that the Great Sphinx belongs to another era. The surrounding dry earth also reveals extensive water seepage, evidence that this desert area was once a fertile land. The Sphinx is very photogenic; take lots of pictures. It's also a great place to meet people from all over the world. You take their picture, they take yours. Pretty soon a conversation ensues and voilà, you have new friends.

## Egyptian Antiquities Museum

Two million people visit this museum each year and the extent of its treasures is mind-boggling. To avoid museum overload, allow for a two–to three-hour visit and carefully select what you will see. The two "must-sees" are the Hall of the Royal Mummies and the treasures of King Tut's tomb. When we visited the museum in 1996 it was not air-conditioned, except for the mummy hall, so bring your rubber fans. The Hall of the Royal Mummies contains 11 mummies encased in individual climate-controlled glass coffins. Among them is the legendary Ramses III whose face, even in death, portrays a man of power and dignity who believed himself to be a semi-deity. For more information on the museum, check out the aforementioned Tour Egypt Web site. The exact Web page is at www.touregypt.net/egyptmuseum/egyptian_museum.htm.

## Christian Cairo

Sometimes referred to as "Old Cairo," this area of the city contains the following notable attractions.

> *The Coptic Museum* — offering a history of Christian Egypt.

> *The Hanging Church* (al-Muallaka) — which lies suspended across the Roman towers.

> *St. Sergius* (Abu Serga) — the oldest of Cairo's Coptic churches, built where the Holy Family lived while Joseph worked at the fortress.

## Islamic Cairo

Except for the Khan al-Khalili, rarely do casual tourists visit this area, so you will have the places to yourself, a rare treat in bustling Cairo:

> *Mosque of Ahmad Ibn Tulum* —- the oldest and most moving in the world.

> *Gayer-Andersen Museum* — an interesting restored 16th century Cairene house, adjoining the above mosque. Learn about the secluded life that women lived at that time.

> *Madrasa of Sultan Hassan* — a 14th century complex containing one of the world's largest mosques with an architectural slight of hand.

All of the above attractions are within walking distance of one another and are easily seen on your own.

## Khan al Khalili

Commonly called "The Khan," this shoppers' paradise is a labyrinth of bazaars, tiny restaurants, and winding streets. Plan on spending lots of time here to get the feel, smell, and taste of Cairo, and of course to obtain some great buys!

## Saqqara

Located about 15 miles (25 kilometers) south of Cairo, this complex has served as a burial ground for kings and nobility. The two most famous attractions are the Step Pyramid of Discovery Channel fame and Djoser's Funerary Complex, both designed by Imhotep. The Step Pyramid is note-worthy as the world's first pyramid. Imhotep is one of the world's great minds ever to walk this planet. He was a noted physician, architect and scribe, to name just a few of his talents. The excavation goes on constantly in this area, with new discoveries every week. The best way to get there is by cab; negotiate a price with the driver. Bring everything you need — water, sunscreen, etc as there are little or no concessionary services.

*Author's Note:* While service can change at hotels, I must mention what I consider to be one of the best city hotels in the world — *The Cairo Marriott.* The site of the hotel is a 12-acre former sultan's palace on Gizera Island in the Nile River. Set away from the hustle bustle of Cairo, it is like a resort hotel in the heart of the city. The hotel was built around the palace, which is still used today for special events. On the grounds you will find a large pool, numerous shops and restaurants, most of them outdoors. Our favorite was called "Egyptian Nights." Every evening two sweet-tempered women would bake fresh Egyptian bread in a hearth oven right under your nose. We had to be careful not to burn our fingers from the hot steam when we broke open the rolls. Adjoining the restaurant was an open walkway where we enjoyed the passing parade of Europeans, North Americans, Middle East-erners and Africans, as they strolled back and forth between the restaurants and shops. Desert nights at the Marriott were enchanting; the weather was perfect and the people watching unparalled. If you cannot afford to stay at the Marriott, at least have dinner there and spend some time enjoying the passing parade.

## The Nile Cruise

There are several companies running Nile cruises; Sheraton and Sonesta are two of them. You can inquire directly with either hotel company or visit their Web sites, but if you are traveling independently, it is best to book the cruise as a tour package through a local tour operator. Be sure to include with it transfers, local Egyptian Air flight and an optional excursion to Abu Simbel. For more information on the Nile Cruises check out the sites below, but remember to look around at other Web sites to shop for best prices, such as www.cruise.com or www.orbitz.com, or check with your travel agent.

www.egyptontheweb.com/SheratonCruises/sheraton.html

www.sonesta.com/page.asp?pageid=4744

Nile cruises are four days and three nights in length, and begin in Aswan and end in Luxor or vice versa. These are sightseeing cruises designed around visits to the fabulous antiquities, therefore do not expect Las Vegas type entertainment or large sumptuous midnight buffets. The passenger list will be varied, with all ages and nationalities and a mixed group of families, couples and singles. Expect to make some interesting new friends by the end of the cruise. The cruise price includes all meals and entertainment, as well as daily services of an onboard antiquities guide. We lucked out with our guide, one of the best we ever had. A history professor at the University of Cairo, his command of English was as superior as his knowledge of Egyptian antiquities. From the start he informed us that we would, like it or not, learn about Egyptian history before the cruise was over. And learn we did! We were frequently asked to act out scenes from Egyptian mythology; no one was spared. As silly as we felt doing this, we noticed that, by the end of the day, what we remembered most were the lessons that we role-played.

## Abu Simbel

Offered as an optional excursion to the Nile cruise, this attraction is a *must-see.* This complex of temples was threatened with submersion when plans for building the Aswan Dam were finalized in the 1960s. With the help of an international team of archeologists and engineers and funding from UNESCO, the temples and the monuments were moved, block by block, to a new site overlooking the Nile River. The Sun Temple of Ramesses II is impressive in its enormity. When taking the short flight from Aswan, try to get seats on the port (left) side of the plane for the best view. For photos of the site, take a look at homepage.powerup.com.au/~ancient/abus.htm.

## Luxor

The Nile Cruise begins or ends in this city and allows you a half-day visit to Luxor. This enchanting and historical city deserves at least one extra day, so if you are traveling independently, plan on at least one extra night's stay. There are three major attractions in the city:

➤ *Luxor Temple* — Famous for its Avenue of the Sphinxes, this beautiful temple, actually a huge complex, could be seen on your own, but is much more appreciated if you hire a local guide to take you through.

➤ *The Temple of Karnak* — Built over several generations of pharaohs, this magnificent complex contains Egypt's most famous hypostyle hall, a mighty forest of pillars. It should be visited during the day and again at night. Sign up for one of the Sound and Light Shows, most of which is a walk through, making history come alive. The temple has a very different look at night.

➤ *The Luxor Museum* — One of the few air-conditioned buildings in Luxor, other than the first class hotels, this museum is a pleasant respite from the hot noonday summer sun.

Luxor is a delightful town with a broad selection of hotels, restaurants, and shops. The tourists come from all over the world and the locals are happy to extend their warm Egyptian hospitality to anyone who visits. Be prepared to sit and chat over tea or a cold drink as you make a purchase and a new friend. The ubiquitous cafés come alive at night as the locals and the tourists enjoy the splendid desert nights. We had a delightful overnight stay in Luxor at the Hotel Mövenpick Jolie Ville Hotel on Crocodile Island. The best feature of the hotel was a sprawling pool with sloping edges so you can lean back, soak in the water, and stay cool in the hot afternoon sun. The summer desert heat is energy draining, so we weren't in the mood to swim laps after our morning sightseeing excursions. The hotel is about two miles (3.2 kilometers) outside of town, but there is a free shuttle service into town. For more information on the hotel, check out this Web site at www.pride-holidays.com/luxor_hotel_3.htm.

For general information on Luxor, click on www.memphis.edu/egypt/luxortm.htm.

I came across this funky site about Karnak Temple that kids (big and little) will enjoy. It includes games from Ancient Egypt: www.eyelid.co.uk/karnak1.htm.

## The Valley of the Dead

Across the river from the lush oasis of Luxor is a very barren landscape, but one that draws thousands of tourists every day. Buried beneath the sands of the Sahara are the tombs of some of the most famous and powerful people in history — the pharaohs of Ancient Egypt. You can visit the tombs independently or as part of a tour group, but if you go on your own, you should hire a guide for the day or a half-day. If you are traveling in the summer a half-day is all you will be able to handle in the desert heat. You should also plan to meet your guide *before* dawn in Luxor so that you are back in town by 11 a.m. at the latest. Upon your return you will want to cool down quickly, so drop into the Luxor Museum for a visit. It is fully air-conditioned. Follow that with lunch and a long languid dip in the pool and you have a perfect day! When making arrangements with the guide, negotiate for the best price and have your guide pre-purchase all entry tickets you will need, including permission to use your camera at each of the sites. There are no ticket booths at the sites. Dress to protect yourself *thoroughly* from the sun, including head, neck, and arms, and bring an ample supply of water.

There are dozens of tombs to visit. It takes about an hour for each one, including travel time to and from, so do your research and plan accordingly. Some of the most popular tombs are:

## Valley of the Kings

- ➢ Tomb of Thutmose III — A good example of early-style tombs, it contains a star-studded ceiling and wall painting of 741 deities. Unfortunately this tomb was closed during our visit.
- ➢ Tomb of Amenhotep II — Famous architect, doctor, and builder of pyramids.
- ➢ Tomb of Tutankhamun — Our beloved King Tut.
- ➢ Tomb of Ramsses III — Offers scenes of daily life unique in a tomb.

## Tomb of the Nobles

- ➢ Tomb of Sennefer — This was difficult to find, but worth the search. Hidden beneath a little village, this delightful tomb has engaging scenes of family life and a sloping ceiling painted to represent a grape arbor. The kids and I felt like we were visiting someone's home.

## Valley of the Queens

- ➢ Tomb of Queen Nefartari — This tomb has stunningly beautiful wall scenes but limited visitation. You may need to book a visitation in advance. It was closed during our visit.
- ➢ Temple of Hatshepsut — This impressive above ground temple was built to honor one of the few, and the most famous, of Ancient Egypt's female pharaohs.

For photos and information on the Valley of the Dead, visit homepage. powerup.com.au/~ancient/luxor.htm.

May your visit to Egypt be as thrilling as the sites you visit. Inshallah (God willing).

## THE GALÁPAGOS ISLANDS

People frequently ask me "What's your favorite place in the world?" That's a tough question to answer as I have so many favorites. I love every place that I visit. Each is special. But if there were one place in the world that I could visit over and over again for its uniqueness, and never grow tired of, it would be the Galápagos Islands.

Made famous by Charles Darwin's *Origin of the Species,* the Galápagos Islands are a group of volcanic islands located roughly 500 miles (805 kilometers) due west of the Ecuadorian mainland. The islands, which belong to Ecuador, are all part of the Galápagos National Park System. Most of the islands can only be visited in the company of a certified naturalist guide. To minimize the impact on wildlife and their habitat, the annual number of visitors to these islands is strictly limited. What makes the Galápagos so unique? Perhaps I can explain it this way: When you go to the zoo, you watch the animals in a man-made habitat. When you go on safari in Kenya you watch the animals in their natural habitat. When you travel to the Galápagos Islands, you *become part of the animal life in their own habitat.* It is a visceral experience, one that you will never forget and yearn to do again and again (At this point I should mention that the animals of the Galápagos Islands, unlike those of Kenya, are not man-eating).

During our visit to the Galápagos my kids and I frolicked in the water with seals, had snorting contests with the iguanas, stood by a family of sea lions while the parents had an argument, and mingled with the male blue-footed boobies while they courted their potential mates. Blue-footed boobies are birds, about the size of large ducks, with long rounded beaks and brightly colored blue webbed feet. They look like something created by the Disney imagineers forced to use up an over-shipment of unmatched bright blue paint. The courtship ritual consists of the male lifting up one webbed foot perpendicular to the ground and gracefully and softly placing it down and then repeating the process over and over from foot to foot. This lasts about 45 minutes. When the female is ready, he mounts her and mates with her. This lasts about 45 seconds. After the boobies were finished with their mating, a male member of our group remarked, "Wow, that was a real 'Wham Bang Thank You Ma'am.' " A female member of our group hastily replied, "Yes, but think of the foreplay!" We all laughed.

Getting to the Galápagos Islands is an expensive and complicated project. You must fly into Quito, the capital city of Ecuador, or Guayaquil, the large coastal city. Although Quito is a slightly higher airfare to the Galápagos, I recommend you spend your overnight stay in Quito. From Quito or Guayaquil it is a one-hour morning flight to the Galápagos Islands. At the airport you are met by your naturalist guide, who will accompany you during your transfer by bus and boat to your Galápagos cruise ship. Bear in mind these are not luxury Caribbean cruise ships, but are small comfortable ships, clean and neat, with ample deck and cabin space. There is no programmed entertainment, nightly dancing to a band, or midnight buffets. You will rise early, tour an island, perhaps do some snorkeling, return to the ship for lunch, and enjoy a brief rest as the ship makes its way to the next island for your afternoon visit, perhaps sailing by a former pirate's cove along the way. After dinner everyone attends the one-hour lecture by the naturalist guides explaining the next day's activities. This might be followed by a board game, some friendly conversation in the lounge or at the bar and then off to bed.

### Let's Talk About the Water

A major concern of first-time travelers to Latin America is whether they will get sick from the food or the water. Not to worry. Ecuador has a major tourism infrastructure in place. The Galápagos Islands is a huge tourism cash cow for the government. There are well-enforced sanitary regulations in place to ensure that the permanent denizens of the Galápagos stay well and healthy as well as the visiting tourists. The shower and bath water on board the cruise ships is double purified. The drinking water is triple-purified. Both are safe to drink. Food is prepared only with the triple-purified water. Chef-prepared meals are served buffet style. Although not gourmet, they are delicious, easy on the stomach, and appealing to the eye. There is a varied selection of local foods, so even the picky eater will find something pleasing to his or her palate. Foods are seasoned with local herbs, rather than heavy spices, with emphasis on healthy foods, rather than greasy fried stuff. At the end of three days the kids and I remarked on how well and full of energy we all felt, which is not always the case when we travel to foreign countries, given the change of diet. Part of it was no doubt due to the cuisine and, of course, the pristine air of the mid-Pacific Ocean.

### Planning Your Trip

There are many types of small sail craft authorized to sail around the Galápagos Islands. People who have explored the Galápagos in this manner find it to be a great adventure. The drawback is that you need a three or four week vacation to cover an adequate sampling of islands. As single parents or single working adults, most of us have only one or two weeks of vacation time. With that in mind, here is what I suggest:

The cruise ships of the Galápagos operate with three itineraries:

8 day, 7-night cruise

5 day, 4-night cruise

4 day, 3-night cruise.

I highly recommend taking the eight-day cruise if you can. Although you do not visit all the islands on an eight-day cruise, you will visit a full sample of what the Galápagos has to offer. Each island is very different in terms of animal life, topography, and activities. If your vacation time permits, add on a couple of days in Quito, more if you can. This will allow you to see some of the sights within an hour or two of Quito. We chose the five-day cruise because we wanted time in Quito and had also planned to spend five days in a remote tourist camp in the Ecuadorian Amazon. The five-day cruise was all we could squeeze in within the confines of a two-week vacation.

I also recommend buying a package tour for the Galápagos. Shop around for the best buys. You can purchase one that includes airfare from the U.S., plus transfers and the cruise. If you like to travel independently, ask the tour operator or your travel agent if you can book an extra couple of days in Quito and then explore on your own. Also inquire as to the cost of the tour-basing airfare that is included in your tour package. Then shop around the Web sites to see if you can do better. If you can, then book the air on your own and just buy the land package (cruise, transfers, and possible hotel extension). Don't be afraid to negotiate a discount on the cruise price if you are booking directly with the cruise line. Often the cruises sell out months in advance but there are off-peak weeks. We sailed on the Isabela II, a deluxe large yacht custom built for cruising the Galapagos. The ship held 20 cabins, but it was only half full when we sailed in early July, usually a busy month. We found out later that the sailing was light because that was the final week of the World Cup soccer matches, and Europeans and Latin Americans tend to stay close to home during that week to follow the games. That cruise departure was ripe for bargaining a good rate.

The main tour operator in Ecuador is Metropolitan Touring. They own and maintain most of the cruise ships as well as renting them out to other tour operators. We had booked our trip to Ecuador with their U.S.-based representative, Adventure Associates, a very informative and helpful agency. It appears Adventure Associates is no longer in business under that name. The Web site for Metropolitan Touring is www.metropolitan-touring.com/, but the site offers only general facts about the country and no information on a U.S.-based representative. I e-mailed them for more information and was advised that Adventure Associates is setting up a new Web site with an undetermined completion date. Check with one of the travel agencies listed in the Appendix.

An excellent Web site for information and facts on the cruise ships is www.ecuadortoursonline.com/. Keep in mind you want to select a ship and an itinerary that will cover as many islands as possible during your cruise. This is the most fun for the whole family. Gather up brochures and information from the Web sites, tour operators, and bookstores, and then start researching.

*Important Facts for Traveling to the Galapagos*

➢ This is not a beach vacation. Touring the Galapagos is an active, adventurous trip. Children and adults of any age can enjoy it, but there is a lot of walking and occasional clambering over lava rocks. If your children are pre-school age, wait until they are older.

➢ Pack lots of protective clothing for the sun. Cover your head and shoulders and wear lots of sunscreen. Remember you are on the Equator. The sun's rays do not get any more direct than this.

➢ Pack twice as much sunscreen and three times as much film as you think you will need and you should have just enough. I say this not in jest, but from my own personal experience and that of my friends'. These items are very expensive and often unavailable in the Galápagos Islands.

➢ Check the documentation section for instructions on determining what you will need as a single parent family in addition to valid passports.

➢ Admission to Galápagos National Park is frightfully expensive, about US$80 for adults, half that for children under 12. Students age 26 and under, pay a reduced rate of US$40 if they have a student ID from their university or hold an International Student ID card. Rules are about to change on this so check with your travel supplier. Just remember to bring along some form of student ID for the older children. You can order a student ID card online at www.counciltravel.com/idcards/default.asp or call 800-2-COUNCIL. If you travel overseas, it is a good idea to have one of these IDs for older children anyway. Student discounts are available in many museums and theaters when you flash the card.

➢ Expect the unexpected and revel in it. We played water games with the seals (They always won). Stare into their eyes and see the mischievous delight. My son and I encountered a shark during a surface dive, but he was well fed and went on his way. As we sped to the surface, I nearly collided with a Galápagos penguin that was furiously paddlewheeling his way in my direction. Unlike other countries where you expend energy seeking out the animals, in the Galápagos, you expend energy staying out of their way!

➢ There are rules to follow while visiting these special islands. You are never allowed to reach out and touch the animals or disturb them in any way. However, if you lie or sit still like a rock, as my son often did, they will approach you, sniff you, and often treat you like a rock by climbing over you, which is perfectly OK. There are even "vampire finches" that swoop down and suck a drop or two of your blood if you have an open cut (We didn't get to that island). Of course you never ever litter or feed the animals and, where indicated, you follow the indicated path to lessen the impact on the vegetation. Brief your children on these rules and make sure they respect them.

➢ The iguanas look ferocious, but they are not. Go nose-to-nose with one of them and have a snorting contest like we did. The spray from their nostrils is seawater and quite harmless. Great photo opportunity!

➢ Plan your trip as far ahead as possible, nine months to a year is ideal. This gives you a full choice of accommodations and also plenty of time to budget for the trip.

Lastly and most importantly, don't get discouraged if your trip plans fall through. A trip of a lifetime doesn't always leave the drawing board on the first try. For five years the kids and I talked about going to the Galápagos and twice our trip plans defaulted. Then one year everything came together — the money, the vacation time, and the scheduling, and we were off on an adventure of a lifetime!

## Extending Your Stay In Ecuador

There is so much diversity in this delightful country that you could easily spend two weeks on the mainland and not see all the highlights. However, if you can extend your Galápagos vacation by two or three days here is what I recommend:

## Quito

*Base yourself in Quito for two or three nights*

This two mile high capital city is the second highest world capital. (The highest is La Paz, Bolivia.) Quito enjoys a year round spring-like climate similar to May in New England. This charming colonial city is also a major vortex (energy center) and a World Heritage Site. Ecuadorian food is varied and not highly spiced, and there is a multitude of atmospheric moderately priced restaurants, many of which are located in former Spanish colonial homes. And the shopping — aaahh the shopping. Vendors are everywhere, on the street corners, on the church steps, all selling the beautiful woven goods of Ecuador — soft woolen Alpaca sweaters, jackets, ponchos, and wall hangings. The prices were so reasonable that the kids and I each bought dozens of items for ourselves and for friends and family. Having run out of room in our suitcases, our Ecuadorian friends provided us with a sturdy box and tape which we quickly filled with additional sweaters and woven goods to bring home on the plane. Those beautiful sweaters and jackets are still keeping us warm.

*Sightseeing Highlights in Quito*

➤ La Ronda — a well-preserved, narrow cobblestone street in colonial Quito, full of old, balconied houses, many of which are open to visitors. This is a "must."

➤ The churches of Companía de Jésus and Iglesia de San Francisco — two of the most beautiful colonial churches in South America.

➤ Plaza de la Independencia — a lovely square in the Old City, and the burial place of General Sucre, the "George Washington" of Ecuador. If you are here at sunset you can enjoy a beautiful view of Pichincha, the dormant volcano that forms the backdrop for Quito.

➤ Calle Roca (Roca Street) — a wealthy street in the New City with homes that resemble a green mosque, a stone fortress, and a pink castle.

## Attractions Outside of Quito

### Mitad del Mundo (Middle of the Earth)

The country of Ecuador takes its name from the fact that the equator runs through it. The monument to this imaginary line is only 30 minutes north of Quito. Did you know that, right on the equatorial line and only on the "line", water drains straight down rather than clockwise or counterclockwise? Did you also know that if you stand here on the 21$^{st}$ of March or September, your body casts no shadow? Grab a local bus for a few cents and check it out. You can also negotiate for a cab ride but check the going rate first. There are tours to Mitad del Mundo, but you will pay a premium price and the attraction really does not require a guide.

### The Market of Otavalo

Famous the world over for their beautiful weavings, the Otavalo Indians hold a Saturday market, which is a huge tourist attraction. Smaller markets are also held during weekdays. The main market begins at dawn and ends at noon. There is also an animal market, just outside of town, which is held from 6 a.m. to 8 a.m. Tours to Otavalo are pricey and the buses all arrive around mid morning. A better alternative would be to negotiate a price for a cab for the morning. Do it the day before and arrange to get an early start so as to be there before the tourist crowds arrive, preferably early enough to spend some time at the animal market. Otavalo is about an hour and a half drive north of Quito. Once there, you can change your money at casas de cambios (change houses) or the local bank. Mornings are cool, so dress warmly, watch out for pickpockets, and bargain for everything you buy.

### The Market at Saquisilí

This native Indian market, held on Thursday mornings, is mainly for the inhabitants of remote Indian villages who flood into town to buy or sell everything from bananas to herbal remedies to strings of piglets. Otavalo weavings are also available here. There are eight different plazas selling specific goods, one of which is the animal market, a cacophonous affair with dozens and dozens of squealing pigs. There is no bank in town, so bring plenty of cash (Ecuadorian sucres only!). To our surprise we discovered that no one would accept our dollars or traveler's checks (credit cards were completely out of the question). After a one hour frantic search we found a vendor who would take travelers checks. Fortunately he offered a vast array of wares. The market area is extremely photogenic, but keep in mind many indigenous people do not like to have their photograph taken, so ask permission first. Once again, negotiate a cab for a half-day, dress warmly, watch out for pickpockets, and bargain for everything.

## Avenue of the Volcanoes

This is a portion of the Pan American Highway, which, at one time, was the major route of the Inca Empire from its northern capital of Quito to its southern capital of Cusco. The scenic road is ringed with volcanoes and therefore was dubbed "Avenue of the Volcanoes" by the great explorer Humbolt.

## Cotopaxi National Park

This ecological sanctuary, located along the Avenue of the Volcanoes, is famous for Mt. Cotopaxi. At 19,700 feet (6,000 m), it is the highest active volcano in the world. When not shrouded in clouds, which is most of the time, its snow-capped peak offers a stunning photographic backdrop. Admission to the park is about US$20. There is a small museum, a llama herd, picnic areas, and hiking trails. Hiking at this high altitude can be dangerous unless you are acclimated to the altitude. Bring plenty of water, as there are no concessionary facilities in the park. Sasquisili and the Avenue of the Volcanoes are both located south of Quito, so if you have a full day to spare and like to hike or picnic in a scenic spot, you could consider doing both attractions in one day.

There are so many more exciting attractions in Ecuador, not the least of which is the remote and beautiful Amazonian area. It pains me to stop here, but this chapter is intended to give you only a taste. No matter what you choose to do in Ecuador, I am sure you and your child (or children) will find your vacation to be, as we did — enchanting, extraordinary and totally "Ecuadorable!"

## GROUP #4 – SPECIAL MENTION DESTINATIONS

### EUROPE

For many people a trip to Europe is a trip of a lifetime and rightfully so. You may be wondering why I chose not to include Europe in my list of single parent family recommended destinations. What could be more fun for any family than riding on one of London's double-decker buses or enjoying the exciting view from Paris's Eiffel Tower or picnicking in an alpine meadow in the middle of the glorious Alps? There are so many wonderful ways to travel through Europe as a single parent family — by car, by train, by bus, independently, or with a group. You can go for a week, two weeks, or for U.S. East Coasters, a long mid-winter weekend getaway to London or Amsterdam can be a fantastic bargain.

All of Europe is single parent family-friendly. Europeans are not so "hung up" on the "couples concept" like Americans are. It is quite common to see people of all ages traveling alone, going to the theater alone or dining by oneself. As a single parent traveling independently with one or more children, you will not stick out like a sore thumb. More than likely, you may be mistaken for a resident of Europe rather than a tourist, and this is a positive thing as it will open doors to new and interesting friendships.

So why didn't I include Europe? Mainly because the topic is so vast. To cover the highlights of the major tourist countries of Europe would substantially increase the size of this book. Secondly, I am considering writing a future book dedicated entirely to destinations that are single parent family-friendly. Readers of my Web site, www.SingleParentTravel.net, constantly e-mail me for destination information, indicating the need for this type of book. I welcome reader feedback on this second book idea, especially any suggestions you have for destinations that you would like to see included in this and future books. You may reach me via e-mail at Brenda@SingleParentTravel.net or through my Web site, or you may mail your suggestions to:

Brenda Elwell
GlobalBrenda Publishing
755 9th Street, 2nd Floor
Secaucus, NJ 07094

If you are planning a trip to Europe and want specific destination information on what to see and do when traveling with kids, I suggest picking up a copy of *Take Your Kids to Europe* by Cynthia W. Harriman. The book is written about the travels of a traditional family (two parents, two kids), who spent six months touring Europe, often staying in villas along the way. Although much of the text and modes of travel do not apply to single parent families with two weeks of vacation, the section on what to see and do in Europe for families is excellent and comprehensive. You can pick up a copy at your local bookstore or order it online at one of the many book sites.

## OUR NATIONAL PARKS

Families, traditional as well as single parent, often ask me, "Where should I take my kids on vacation? What's your recommendation?" When I answer, "Take them to a national park," I often get a blank stare in return. Most Americans have little or no idea of what our national parks have to offer. Many believe it is like a big park with animals, which you drive through for a day. Or else they think it is a vacation only for people that like to go camping or "RVing."

As Americans, we are so fortunate to have within our own borders some of the most beautiful, pristine, and remote areas in the world. Our Canadian neighbors share this blessing. I spoke about a few of the American national parks in this book — Grand Canyon National Park, Denali, and the spectacular national parks of southern Utah. There are many, many others — the most popular ones like Yosemite, Yellowstone, the Grand Tetons, the Great Smokies — and those less traveled to, like Big Bend, Death Valley, and glorious Glacier National Park tucked away in a remote corner of Montana. Within Canada's borders — to name only a few — are the incredible, often photographed vistas of Banff and Jasper National Parks, as well as Waterton National Park, the Canadian counterpart to Glacier National Park.

Many of our national parks require some effort, time, and expense to get there, but once there, you are transported to an environment where the air is clear and sweet-smelling, where the rhythms of life are natural, not man-made, and the attractions are free, unlimited, and ever-changing, with no waiting lines! Once you pay your park admission (it ranges from park to park, usually US$10-20 per car, good for a one week stay), you have access to all the scenery, animal watching, hiking, and forest ranger lectures and guided walks that you can squeeze in during your vacation. Your tax dollars pay for maintenance of the parks and forest ranger salaries. Did you notice the title of this section? It said "our" national parks. That's because they *belong* to us.

Lodging accommodations inside the parks range from Spartan to moderate to rustic-deluxe, all of it reasonably priced. To visit a national park is to be transported to another world that washes away the cares and frustrations of our busy hectic lives. The kids will love it and so will you. There is nothing more energizing, and at the same time, relaxing, than to spend a day hiking in the middle of spectacular scenery, having your heart skip a beat when you catch a glimpse of a big moose feeding in a nearby lake, or eating a picnic lunch in a meadow full of wildflowers and spending your evening in a cozy chair by a warm fireplace as you review the day's events with your child or newfound friends. Years ago the Europeans discovered the treasures of America's national parks, which is why our national parks, especially out West, resound with the babble of German, Dutch, Spanish, Czech and many other European languages.

Still have objections about going to a national park? Let me guess what they are...

*"I'm not into camping. I like a hot shower and a comfortable bed at night."*

Fine. Stay in one of the lodges within the park or one of the lodges or motels right outside the park.

*"I/We/My kids will get bored."*

No way. There is so much to do and see that you will be sad to leave and eager to return when your vacation is over. If you are hesitant to spend your entire vacation in a national park, then split your vacation time between the park and a nearby city or other attraction.

*"What happens if it rains?"*

You get wet. Just joking, but not really. You will need to bring raingear unless you are traveling to one of the national parks that has a desert climate. Ranger guided hikes are often held in the rain, unless you are in an area threatened by lightning. The animals are out; they need to eat and forage for food no matter what the weather, and in fact, animals are out more often when it rains. Did you ever book a vacation at the beach or the lake and have it rain? Of course.

If you prefer not to walk in the rain, you can visit the museums, read a book on the park history, play some games and enjoy a hot chocolate in the hotel lobby while you make new friends from around the world. National parks are filled with families and single people of all ages.

*I/We/My kids might get eaten by a bear or attacked or bitten by a wild animal.*

Wild animals do not attack unless they are provoked or threatened. They just want to go about their business of feeding, resting, and taking care of their young, just like you. If the animals see, smell, or hear you coming they will get out of your way. If you approach them or attempt to feed them, you are asking for trouble and may just get what you deserve. Do not feed or leave food for any animals, even the little cute cuddly ones. People food is unhealthy for them and it trains them to beg, which is unhealthy behavior for animals and humans alike. In addition, it is illegal, and you may get a ticket from a forest ranger. The animals know to avoid the well-marked human hiking trails. If you plan to hike in remote bear country, then you should do it in groups and make noise to give warning, such as singing, clapping, or loud chatter. The forest rangers can brief you on animal behavior.

Did I convince you yet? I hope so. If so, here are five helpful guidelines for people who have never been to a national park.

### Plan to stay at a lodge or cabin inside the park

It is a much nicer experience, particularly at the larger parks. If you book early enough you will be able to find accommodations within your budget (Of course there are exceptions. Zion and Bryce National Parks each have only one lodge inside the park and they can be pricey during the busy summer season so you may prefer to stay outside the park. Some smaller parks only offer lodging in nearby towns.).

### Make your lodging reservations way in advance

If you plan to visit one or more of the most popular parks, such as Yosemite, Yellowstone, or the Grand Canyon, I highly recommend booking your hotel reservations at least nine months or a year in advance so as to have a full choice of accommodations inside the park. All deposits are fully refundable and cancellation policies are liberal.

### Pack weather appropriate clothing for your park visit

Depending on the park's climate, you may need sun protective clothing, sweaters or sweatshirts for cool evenings, or raingear. You need not spend a lot of money on gearing up. For years I could not afford to buy hiking boots for my children and myself, so we hiked in sneakers. It was fine. But we did bring a change of shoes. Do bring some type of raingear if appropriate. A cheap plastic poncho tucked away in your backpack will do the job adequately if your budget does not permit classy raingear. National parks are in remote areas. The gift shops are not always well stocked with a variety of styles and sizes, and are often expensive, so it is best to come with the clothes you will need.

**When you arrive at the park, after you check into your hotel or motel, go directly to the hotel that is the center of activities and sign up for every single free ranger guided activity that appeals to you**

The sign up sheet is usually posted at the front desk of the park's major hotel(s). Some activities have limited participants, hence the immediate sign-up. Ranger-guided activities will enhance your park experience, and if you find you don't like the activity, leave. No guilt.

**Soon after you arrive, go to the Park Visitors Center**

There you will find informational exhibits on the park, a gift center with postcards, posters worthy of framing, great history and informational books on the park and surrounding area, and of course those friendly rangers, who will answer your every question with a smile. Ask them to recommend hiking trails and if there are junior ranger activities taking place that your kids would enjoy. If the center offers a short film on the park, watch it with your kid(s). If you are visiting a large national park that has more than one visitor center, drop by them all. Each is slightly different.

National parks are extremely easy to book. Each park has its own Web site where you can learn about the park and book reservations for hotels and other activities such as cowboy cookouts, white water rafting, and mule rides. There are also toll free numbers to call if you have further questions or prefer to book over the phone. At the time you make your reservations I highly recommend that you order one or more guidebooks on the park(s) you will be visiting. Each park offers a standard guidebook — a large glossy paperback with gorgeous photographs and good hiking and activity information. The book will enable you to plan your itinerary in advance.

I hope to see you at one of our national parks. I never let a year go by without visiting at least one, if only for a weekend. It renews my spirit.

# VII

## *Where Do We Go from Here?*

I was recently in my local theater enjoying my Friday night movie fix when a special movie short came on the screen. It was a Coca Cola®-sponsored film short created by an aspiring filmmaker. It featured a smartly dressed businesswoman grocery shopping with her young son. The son knocked over a cereal display and the mother spotted a cereal coupon in the debris, which entitled them to a free trip. In the next scene the mother and son were wearing their cool dude shades, chilling on a tropical beach.

When I saw that film I nearly jumped out of my seat. What was remarkable was the fact that it featured a single parent family in a travel setting. I had never seen that before, ever. The traveling single parent family is, has been, and continues to be, completely ignored by the media, as well as 99.5% of the U.S. based travel suppliers. Single parent travelers fare better in the UK, but even in that part of the world, there is vast room for improvement.

*More than 60% of traveling families in the U.S. are non-traditional families* — single parents, single grandparents, uncles and aunts traveling with nieces and nephews, a gay or lesbian parent or couple traveling with a child, or a married spouse who has chosen to travel alone with a child because his or her spouse cannot come on the trip. Given these statistics, it is nothing short of astounding that travel suppliers continue to show only the traditional family in their ads — Mommy, Daddy, and two children, usually a son and a daughter. A few suppliers, in an attempt to woo the older generation, will show grandparents with a grandchild, but once again it is *always* two grandparents accompanying the child.

The idea of Single Parent Travel first germinated in 1983 during our first single parent family vacation to Europe. The kids and I spent a lovely day touring the Château de Chillon in Switzerland and strolling through the nearby lakeside town. As a special treat, I selected a white tablecloth café for dinner, which adjoined a park. I knew my young children would not be able to sit through a leisurely meal, so having a park nearby was perfect.

They could play where I could see them, and I could enjoy my dinner, a glass of wine, and a relaxing cup of coffee. As I sat watching them play, I realized at that moment I was missing adult companionship. Recently divorced, I was still nursing the wounds of separation and had not yet begun to think about dating. I thought to myself, "Wouldn't it be nice if single parent families had a place to go where they could spend the day with their kids and still enjoy the company of other adults during the trip? Wouldn't it have been nice to share this meal with someone who delighted in ordering something other than French fries? It was at that moment that the idea of Single Parent Travel was born.

Four years later, after completing two years of study toward my CTC (Certified Travel Consultant) degree, I prepared my mini thesis on the topic, "Marketing Travel to the Single Parent." As part of the research for my paper, I interviewed and surveyed single parents throughout the eastern USA to determine their travel needs and desires. Much of the survey results were expected: Single parents did not think of themselves as a niche group nor did they expect to find travel suppliers catering to their needs. Cost was a big factor. Single parents had a travel budget and tried to stay within its limits. Modes of travel varied. And yes, even back then, single parent dads traveled with their kids. The biggest surprise for me was the fact that a large percentage (about 30%) of single parent families were looking for adventure when they traveled. If it fit into their budget, they would consider a trip to the Amazon, or activities such as white water rafting.

After completion of my CTC degree, the idea of Single Parent Travel went dormant. I was busy raising two children, working at a demanding career, and playing soccer mom in my spare time. Not until 2001, when my younger child was attending college, was I able to step away from child-rearing responsibilities and create my Web site, www.SingleParentTravel.net and start writing this book. With the assistance of my daughter, who currently acts as my Webmaster and Publicist, we created another Single Parent Travel Survey. This time, thanks to the Internet and the gracious assistance of Frommers.com and Parents Without Partners, who advertised the survey on their Web sites, we received more than 300 responses from all over the US, as well as overseas from single and married adults who travel alone with children.

*The purpose of the 2001 survey was to accomplish two things:*

1.  To secure meaningful, statistical data on the travel needs and desires of single parents today.

2. To present that data to travel suppliers, thus educating them to the needs and desires of this largely ignored and ever-growing niche market.

It has become my mission in life to educate the travel industry about the needs and desires of the single parent travel market in the hope that they will begin to offer pricing and activities suitable for that market. The results of the 2001 survey are included at the end of this chapter. Several results are notable.

1. Single parent earning power has increased appreciably since my 1987 single parent travel survey and, on average, travel spending is roughly similar to that of traditional families.

2. Single parent families now take more weekends and short trips as opposed to a standard two-week family vacation.

3. A desire for an active, fun-filled and adventurous vacation is a major wish.

4. The non-traditional family has become more vociferous in wanting their travel needs to be recognized.

The three major complaints, which rank far and above any others, are:

1. The single supplement.

2. The lack of activities geared toward single parent families.

3. The lack of companionship with other single parent families.

My thanks go out to all those people who took the time to answer our 2001 survey. We will sponsor other Single Parent Travel Surveys in the future and we urge you to participate. *Your voice is heard.*


## So... where do we go from here?

*Armed with the recent survey information, single parents have helped me to begin to educate U.S. travel suppliers.*

➤ I have been invited to lecture at a number of venues. I recently was a featured speaker on Traditional and Non-Traditional Family Travel at the February ETC (Educational Travel Conference) Conference in Los Angeles, California. This was an opportunity to spread the word to travel suppliers around the world.

- ➤ I have appeared as a guest on several radio stations including KLAC in Los Angeles, FM 107 in Minneapolis, and the "Travel Smart" Program hosted by Jackie Wolfer, which is part of the nationally syndicated "Talk America" show.

- ➤ Travel Suppliers are hearing about us and bringing Single Parent Travel specials to my Web site, www.SingleParentTravel.net, *unsolicited.*

- ➤ My Web site has been featured in major newspapers, magazines, radio shows and Web sites throughout the U.S., including the *New York Times, Time* magazine, the *National Geographic Traveler,* Rudy Maxa's *Savvy Traveler* and Frommers.com.

*I ask you, the reader, to continue to give us your feedback and to promote the idea of Single Parent Travel to the travel suppliers.*

Be a spokesperson for Single Parent Travel. Speak out and let suppliers know your needs. Refer travel suppliers to my Web site and book. Inform me of travel suppliers who cater to Single Parent families. I will be happy to promote them in my monthly newsletter and on my Web site. My schedule permitting, I will be happy to lecture on the topic. E-mail your suggestions and comments to Brenda@SingleParentTravel.net.

*As part of our ongoing desire to service the needs of traveling single parent families, we are pleased to announce the creation of* **SINGLE PARENT TOURS.**

Commencing summer of 2003 my single parent travel company will offer a series of weekend packages and one-week tours to exciting destinations. I will host these tours and design them for single parent and other non-traditional families. Look for further announcements on my Web site and in my monthly newsletters. At the end of this book is a discount coupon for the inaugural season of Single Parent Tours.

We hope to see you on one of our tours!

### Conclusion

It has been a long time since that first Single Parent trip to Europe in 1983, when I conceived the idea of Single Parent Travel. Bringing to fruition a Web site (www.SingleParentTravel.net) and a book, and creating an interactive community of single adults who like to travel with kids (their own or borrowed) has been a labor of love for me. I feel that this is the beginning, the first steps of what will emerge into a growing force in the travel industry.

I hope you enjoyed the stories in my book and found the information useful in planning future family vacations. I welcome your comments and suggestions. What did you like most about the book and why?

What topics would you like to read about in a future book or newsletter? Readers may email me at Brenda@SingleParentTravel.net. If you prefer to write, the address is:

GlobalBrenda Publishing
755 9th Street, 2nd Floor
Secaucus, NJ 07094

Please share your ideas and your experiences. We are part of a community. Until then, from my family to yours – Happy Trails!

*Appendices*

## SINGLE PARENT SURVEY INFORMATION

During the fall of 2001, we hosted a survey for single parent travel. Our hope was to obtain enough "fodder" to take to the travel suppliers and convince them of the needs and wants of the traveling single parent. We are happy to report that more than 340 people responded and provided us with a wealth of information! Thank you all so much. Your feedback will help our mission of making the world a better place for the traveling single parent. This Appendix contains the result of that survey. (A special thanks to my daughter/Web Master/Publicist who spent hours upon hours manually compiling this data!)

### Who are you?

The survey focused on single adults who travel with children. The majority of the respondents are single parents, representing 86%. So who are the rest? Two notable groups of respondents are single grandparents traveling with their grandkids (8%) and married adults who travel frequently without their spouses (7%).

Of the single parents, 61% are the custodial parents and 16% are non-custodial parents. (The remaining respondents were sharing custody or provided no answer.) I am glad to see that both dads and moms travel with their children. The majority of respondents were female (88%), but the men who did respond are highly involved with their children. While this doesn't surprise me, I hope in the future that more single parent dads' voices will be heard. Most (43%) dads are sharing custody or are custodial parents (25%). (The remainder were either not single parents or did not respond to the question.)

Forty-seven percent of our respondents ranged in age from 40 to 49 years. Close behind are the thirty-somethings at 31%.

### Kids, kids and more kids!

The average number of children of respondents was 1.7, just about two kids per household. The majority of you have children aged six through 17. See the chart below.

| | |
|---|---|
| Children under 3 | 9% |
| Children aged 3 to 5 | 14% |
| Children aged 6 to 9 | 35% |

| | |
|---|---|
| Children aged 10 to 12 | 37% |
| Children aged 13- 17 | 31% |
| Children 18 and over | 15% |

## Income and Trip Spending

The biggest surprise was the fact that the majority (21%) of survey respondents had incomes exceeding US$75K. The three remaining categories, — under US$30K, US$30-39K, US$40-49K, were evenly distributed at approximately 17%. Overall, there wasn't much difference between income categories.

Regardless of salary, the majority (45%) spend less than US$2,500 on annual vacations. The next largest segment (31%) spends US$2,501 to US$3,999. From the comments, it was obvious to see that while incomes of the single parent are higher than one would stereotypically expect, as a group, single parents are receptive to bargains, particularly if the bargain targets the single parent family directly.

## How do you travel?

More than half of the respondents take quick trips of seven days or less. From the comments, I surmised that weekend trips are the easiest or most affordable time or money-wise. The next largest trip size, 8 to 10 days, was 31%. Most of you fly (67%) or drive (30%) to get to the annual vacation destination. From the comments, I could see many respondents take multiple methods of transportation, flying, driving, etc., depending on the trip type. The comments were filled with respondents interested in cruising, but very few responded to taking a cruise for their annual vacation. I suspect that might be due to the single supplements in the cruise industry that penalize single parents.

I was surprised to see how many single parents like to travel independently (75%). Those who take a prepackaged tour represented 23%. Again, I think one reason may be that single supplements make prepackaged tours unaffordable.

The question about what type of trip you prefer is always a difficult one to quantify. Roughly speaking, the majority of our survey respondents like a mixture of activities and relaxation or like very active trips. The "other" category was filled with all sorts of comments including visiting family, skiing, hiking, Disney World, camping, ecotours, just to name a few. I laughed when we read the mixed feelings about Disney! From "safe," to "too expensive," to "over-hyped." The comments ran the gamut. My hope is to provide alternative affordable suggestions for Disney, but I have to admit I have a blast whenever I go there, although it is rare due to the price.

My favorite part of the survey was the destination section. Since the majority of the respondents are residents of the U.S., it is only natural that the majority of you travel within the U.S:

21% traveled to a place in the U.S. that was less than one day's drive.
35% traveled to a U.S. destination that was more than one day's drive.
10% of you have been to Europe.
10% to Canada.
7% to Mexico.
8% have taken a cruise.

A few have been to Central or South America, Asia and Africa. We had at least one Aussie who has traveled within her own country!

## Where are you?

The easy answer is: All Over! Literally! I had a few international responses: the UK, Canada, Australia, Belgium and Bermuda. Now that I am in the early stage of my mission of making travel easier for single parents, I am focusing on the U.S. Later, I will see if there is anything we can do for those residing abroad.

The five most represented states in order are:

California
Texas
New York
New Jersey
Pennsylvania

I didn't hear at all from Arizona, Alaska, Delaware, Hawaii, Mississippi, Montana, North Dakota, South Carolina, South Dakota, Utah and Wyoming. If you have friends in any of these states, please tell them to sign up for the newsletter so when I conduct my next survey, their voices will be heard!

The most represented cities/towns were New York, NY and Houston, TX. Other cities/towns that had good representation were Los Angeles, CA; Atlanta, GA; Chicago, IL; Greenville, NC; San Antonio, TX; and Arlington, VA. Our nation's small towns were represented as well with some of our respondents hailing from: Oxford, AL; Jonesboro, GA; Davenport, IA; Mundelein, IL; Chesterton, IN; Leawood, KS; McGregor, MN; Fredericktown, MO; Janesville, WI; and Huntington, WV, just to name a few.

## Comments

The dreaded single supplement was cited as the number one scourge of the single parent family. Two other comments that came up frequently were a desire to meet and get to know other single parent families, and a request for a better balance of activities on trips.

### *Companionship*

"It would be nice to join another single parent/adult with children on an outing or even by the pool at the end of the day."

"[We] would love to go to a resort or destination that [has] other single parents with their kids."

### *Activity Balance*

"Sometimes it's hard to get a good mixture of activities aimed at two different age groups in one package."

"I have found that many resorts, and cruises especially, have various programs for single parents/children but they tend to focus more on children's activities and not on the activities for the single parent."

"Cruises (some) offer child care in the off chance I'd like to enjoy evening entertainment, etc. But ultimately, I like to relax and [my daughter] likes to do typical kids' stuff like swim and play and different kid oriented stuff. However, on past vacations, I have not felt like it was a vacation for me as much as a constant field trip for her. We've done Disneyland and I was dying of lack of adult interaction. I am the kind of person who has no trouble meeting and talking to new people, so that's not the issue. But in order to keep my daughter happy and for her to get the most of the trip, I feel like the entertainment committee. That's not my idea of enjoying a vacation."

"I prefer to stay at fairly luxurious properties, but still vacation WITH my son, rather than sending him to the "'kids club' Very few places seem to have activities that you can do WITH your child... let alone have a truly good restaurant where children are welcome!"

### Tips and Advice

Many of you had excellent advice and tips, which we have included here. Please note that we have not researched these tips ourselves. Further, what has worked for one family, may not work for another. Anyway, on to the tips...

"The most important thing that I have found out is how important research is. When we are planning a vacation, I am on the Web and making phone calls until I have planned out all but one or two of our days. That way, we aren't trying to figure out things to do and making mistakes because we don't have access to the right info, but still have left enough time open to have some flexibility."

"Club Med vacations are great for single parents." I also heard, "Club Med does some for single parents but could do a lot more — especially as baby boomers are getting older but still want to vacation with older kids."

"Cruises are the best for us. We went to Bermuda several years ago and had the time of our lives. With assigned seating we met people and enjoyed that very much. The kids were 15,12, and 8. The Norwegian cruise line charged me for two adults (myself and the oldest child) and the other two went for half price. We had one small cabin, but the two older girls loved the fact that they could go to the movies, or a show. The food was great. Because I am a divorced mom, I cannot handle things like getting the luggage to the room, but the cruise ship had the bags at our door. There was a cruise bus that picked us up and dropped us off not far from home so I did not have the hassle of getting to airport parking or getting a limo home. The service was excellent and I was glad to tip because I had such good service (something not always available to a woman traveling with three children)."

"I've gotten good lodging deals for the added time cost of sitting through time-share sales pitches. This is not a bad way to go."

"Traveling with teen-agers is especially challenging considering the boredom factor. I try to incorporate some fun teenage activities besides the ones I think might enlighten them, such as making sure the hotel has a pool, video games (for occasional use), and other teens for them to meet."

"I have just purchased a used motor home so we can travel as cheaply as others. I am tired of paying a premium for rooms as a single adult."

"Our trips have usually been to visit the children's grandparents in New Orleans for five to six days at a time. The area has many museums, historical sites, and fine shopping that we don't have in rural Missouri. This summer we spent four days at Pensacola beach enroute to our visit in New Orleans."

"I usually take a tour to Europe and let the agency handle everything. I go with Trafalgar because they allow kids to go who are five years old. However, there have never been any other kids on the tours that we have taken."

"I always have [my daughter] sit in her car seat next to me. Regulations require her to get the window seat, so that keeps her entertained. I bring her no-spill cup filled with her favorite juice to pacify her on long trips. It also helps her deal with the pressure build up in her ears as we fly on airplanes."

"The most fun and rejuvenating vacations have been those that I have shared with others with kids around the same age. One or two other small families seems to work best, otherwise the 'kid energy' can climb to dangerously high levels. What I get is:

- adult conversation with people I feel I can understand and feel understood by

- alone time — they let me creep off for 1-2 hours here and there!

- shared tasks — meals, laundry, etc.

- companionship for both me and my son (as much as he loves me, he gets tired of the same old Mom-face all the time!). I'm not the prime source of entertainment that way."

"As a retired Naval Officer, who came up the ranks, I have access to many places that offer low cost accommodations. We use these as a 'base of operation'. I am sure there are other members who qualify for this perk. Take advantage."

"We travel to the Caribbean every summer, usually we go to Mexico and the Iberostar Resort Chain is our favorite"

"I found one resort (all-inclusive) in Jamaica that offers a kids stay, play and eat free program with one adult (most require double occupancy) and that is Starfish Trelawny Beach Resort in Falmouth. It is between Montego Bay and Ocho Rios."

**You Are Not Alone**

Sometimes we single parents just need to know that others have been there.

"If we vacation it is around tax time so that we can use my tax refund to get away."

"Biggest challenge: one income, two weeks vacation, one-week sick leave a year. This means any field trips, any time one or both kids get sick has to fit into this available time. This means one week per year. Under US$1,000. How can single parents make their European dreams come true?"

"Being on vacation (i.e. away from home) as a single parent can actually be more stressful and/or exhausting at times than staying at home, since all the little daily processes that you've automated at home (naps, laundry, snacks, car travel, etc.) have to be consciously and explicitly thought out. On top of the travel-related activities the result is an enormous outpouring of mental and physical energy. Usually it's worth the effort — otherwise why go anywhere — but I have found that I have to be extra careful to build in support and down time for Mom."

"I think it can be great fun to travel with a kid but as a single parent, you have to be very organized and very serious about security, especially when travelling abroad. Some people were very helpful, but most people won't do much to help. In most areas, I didn't declare myself as a single parent, for security reasons. Because that makes you twice as vulnerable."

## Comforting Thoughts

Little reminders of why we continue to travel after all those runny noses, cranky kids and unruly teens:

"My son realizes that a great family vacation does not have to consist of having both parents present and that we don't have to stay at top resorts to have a good time. We have had some memorable times staying in modest accommodations and enjoying the adventures that ensued. I hope he never gets too old for a little getaway with his Mom, because it has been through these trips that I have come to appreciate the specialness of my single parent status."

"The children's fondest memories are our vacations."

"I have traveled to almost every state in the U.S. Now we are on our way to Europe. I believe my kids are doing so well because we travel. With as busy as we are, vacations are very important. It is like our nightly dinner table, with no TV. No one is going anywhere, so we talk and have fun as a family. I would not want to share with a 4th person."

# TRAVEL AGENTS WHO SPECIALIZE IN SINGLE PARENT TRAVEL

**BELIZE**

**Maya Travel Services**
Katie Valk
PO BOX 532
Belize City
**Phone** 011 501 223 1623
**Fax** 011 501 223 0585
**E-mail** mayatravel@btl.net
**Web site** www.mayatravelservices.com
**Specialties/information of interest:** Family travel, scuba/snorkeling, adventure, cultural, Mayan ruins, wedding/honeymoon planner, birding, we are both an IATA travel agency and tour operator

**CANADA—ALBERTA**

**MyTravel**
190 317 7th Avenue
Calgary AB T2P 2Y9
**Phone** 403-266-8095
**Fax:** 403-233-9152
**E-mail** lschuring@algonquintravel.com
**Specialties/information of interest:** All part of the Seven Seas Travel & Cruise Chain.

**Travel & Cruise Quarters**
Andrea Miller
254 - 6100 Macleod Trail S.W.
Calgary AB T2H 0K5
**Phone** 403-251-9065
**Fax:** 403-640-7780
**E-mail** andrea@cruisequarters.com
**Web site** www.cruisequarters.com
**Specialties/information of interest:** Cruise, All inclusive, Hawaii, Las Vegas.

**Travel Time (1998) Inc.**
Terri Jo Lennox, CTC
#209 150 Crowfoot Cres NW
Calgary AB T3G 3T2
**Phone** 403-547-8297/888-544-9333
**Fax:** 403-547-8497
**E-mail** terrijo@traveltime.ca
**Web site** www.traveltime.ca
**Specialties/information of interest:** We handle several clients that are single parents

and have special needs and requests when travelling with their children not the least of which is looking for pricing that recognizes their situation.

**The Travel Lady on Global TV**
**UNIGLOBE South Travel Inc.**
Lesley Keyter
303 Shawville Blvd
Shawnessy AB T2Y 3W6
**Phone** 403-277-6884
**E-mail** lesley@uniglobesouth.com
**Web site** www.uniglobesouthtravel.com

**CANADA—BRITISH COLUMBIA**

**Seven Seas Travel & Cruise**
190 Seymour St.
Kamloops BC V2C 2E1
**Phone** 250-374-7000
**Fax:** 250-374-7033
**E-mail** mary@sevenseas.ca
**Web site** www.sevenseas.ca
**Specialties/information of interest:** All part of the Seven Seas Travel & Cruise Chain.

**Seven Seas Travel & Cruise**
1649 Pandosy St.
Kelowna BC V1Y 1P6
**Phone** 250-861-8000
**Fax:** 250-861-8018
**E-mail** heike@sevenseas.ca
**Web site** www.sevenseas.ca
**Specialties/information of interest:** All part of the Seven Seas Travel & Cruise Chain.

**Seven Seas Travel & Cruise**
156 3055 Massey Drive
Prince George BC V2N 2S9
**Phone** 250 614 7000
**Fax:** 250-561-0054
**E-mail** kbone@sevenseas.ca
**Web site** www.sevenseas.ca
**Specialties/information of interest:** All part of the Seven Seas Travel & Cruise Chain.

**Seven Seas Travel & Cruise**
1553 Third Avenue
Prince George BC V2L 3G3
**Phone** 250-614-7000
**Fax:** 250-561-0070
**E-mail** pat@sevenseas.ca
**Web site** www.sevenseas.ca
**Specialties/information of interest:** All part of the Seven Seas Travel & Cruise Chain.

**Uniglobe Pacific Travel**
Lise Ruest
Saanichton BC
**E-mail** lruest@uniglobepacific.com
**Specialties/information of interest:** I have been a travel agent for just over 13 years. I have been a single mother for 7 years.

**Seven Seas Travel & Cruise**
107 15551 Fraser Hwy
Surrey BC V3S 2V8
**Phone** 604-953-7000
**Fax:** 604-953-7001
**E-mail** diana@sevenseas.ca
**Web site** www.sevenseas.ca
**Specialties/information of interest:** Our agency chain is located in Western Canada and all our offices specialize in Single Parent Travel.

**Carlson Wagonlit Travel**
Nimet Hassam
2496 West 41st Ave.
Vancouver BC V6M2A7
**Phone** 604-264-0552
**Fax:** 604-264-0633
**E-mail** cwtravel@telus.net
**Specialties/information of interest:** We specialize in Single Parent Travel. I am the manager of Carlson Wagonlit Travel, as well as a single parent. I have traveled extensively with my two children, one of whom is disabled.

**Travel by Design**
Michelle, Maureen or Debbie
225-2211 West 4th Ave
Vancouver BC V6K 4S2
**Phone** 604-734-5494/800-519-1819
**Fax:** 604-734-0884

**E-mail** mtaylor@travelbydesign.ca
**Web site** www.travelbydesign.ca
**Specialties/information of interest:** We are the #1 Club Med agent in W. Canada (2nd in Canada) and Club Med is great for single parents as there is no single supplement. We also sell Signature Vacations which also offer a single rate.

**Travelworld**
5 1175 Douglas St.
Victoria BC V8W 2E2
**Phone** 250-382-3121
**Fax:** 250-382-3848
**E-mail** sharvey@travelworld.bc.ca
**Web site** www.travelworld.bc.ca
**Specialties/information of interest:** All part of the Seven Seas Travel & Cruise Chain.

**Camosun Travel**
Mark/Eloise/John
3111 Cedar Hill Rd.
Victoria BC V8T 3J4
**Phone** 250-595-5455
**Fax:** 250-595-5707
**E-mail** info@ctravel.ca
**Web site** www.ctravel.ca

CANADA—ONTARIO

**World Connectors Travel & Tours**
Marlena
13135 Hwy # 27
Nobleton ON L0G 1N0
**Phone** 905-859-6913/866-85-RELAX
**Fax:** 905-859-6915
**E-mail** world@bellnet.ca
**Specialties/information of interest:** Our agency has experience in single parent travel.

**Northumberland Travel American Express**
Sandra, Lisa or Christine
127 Peter St.
Port Hope ON L1A 1C5
**Phone** 905-885-7999/800-465-4810
**Fax:** 905-885-0370
**E-mail** sandra@northumberlandtravel.net
**Web site** www.northumberlandtravel.net

**Savvy Travel**
Savi
219 Sheppard Ave. West
Toronto ON M2n 1N2
**Phone** 416-222-4025/222-3286
**E-mail** savvytravel@on.aibn.com
**Web site** www.travelwithsavvy.com

CANADA—SASKATCHEWA

**CAA Saskatchewan**
Doug Muskaluk
3806 Albert St.
Regina SK S4S 3R2
**Phone** 306-791-4400/800-564-6222
**E-mail** www.caasask.sk.ca
**Web site** doug.muskaluk@caasask.sk.ca
**Specialties/information of interest:** For
the single traveller we offer some unique
services that other agencies do not offer,
including an in-house Notary Service. We
help provide proper documents (letters of
consent) for Single parents travelling trans-
border or internationally (free of charge to
our clients)

**Carlson Wagonlit/All World Travel**
Susan Larsen, CTC/Joy MacIntyre
#2-305 Idylwyld Dr. N. (CP Rail Station)
Saskatoon SK S7L 0Z1
**Phone** 306-934-4664
**E-mail** susan.travel@shaw.ca
**Web site** www.carlsonwagolnlit.ca
**Specialties/information of interest:** Susan
is a single parent with 2 children ages 12
and 13 and has traveled with them to many
destinations. She and Joy specialize in orga-
nizing family travel for single parents as
well as married parents.

INDONESIA

**ABL Tours & Travel**
I Gede Sanat Kumara
Puri Taman Umadui B/21Jl. Gunung Sepu-
tan
Denpasar Bali 80117
**Phone** 62-361-731520
Fax 62-361-735145
**E-mail** abldirector@baliwww.com

**Web site** http://baliwww.com.index.php
http://villas-bali.com    http://baliback
packer.com

SOUTH AFRICA

**The Travel Company Tours and Safaris**
Lynne
106 Katherine St.
Sandown
**Phone** 27118847980
**Fax:** 27117837529
**E-mail** lynne.backos@harveyworld.co.za
**Web site** http://www.travelcompany.co.za
**Specialties/information of interest:** South-
ern African and African travel

U.S.A.—ARKANSAS

**Tripp's Total Travel Management, Inc.**
Suzanne B. Tripp
225 N. Greenwood
Fort Smith AR 72901
**Phone** 479-782-8747
Fax 479-782-9244
**E-mail** suz.tttm@wspan.com
**Web site** www.TrippsTravel.com
**Specialties/information of interest:** We
have several agents who not only have
expertise but do so from a personal basis.
One has a young child, another travels with
her teens. Furthermore, as a sub-specialty
we assist parents who travel alone with their
children on a specific trip.

U.S.A.—CALIFORNIA

**Strong on Travel**
Dale E Strong, CTC
233 Kingsbury Dr.
Aptos CA 95003
**Phone** 831-662-2467
**Fax:** 831-687-0238
**E-mail** dstravel@cruzio.com
**Web site** www.strongontravel.com
**Specialties/information of interest:** Ad-
venture and luxury travel

**The Happy Traveler**
Carol Georges
5703 Oberlin Drive, Suite 100
San Diego CA 92121
**Phone** 858-457-4800
**E-mail** hpytrav@aol.com
**Web site** www.TheHappyTraveler.com
**Specialties/information of interest:** Adventure travel, honeymoon, groups Destinations: Tahiti, Hawaii, Mexico, Caribbean, Europe and Asia.

**U.S.A.—COLORADO**

**Hoffman travel**
Diane Hoffman
1316 E Broadmoor Dr
Loveland CO 80537
**Phone** 970-669-8300
**Fax:** 970-667-4189
**E-mail** hoffmandiane@hotmail.com
**Specialties/information of interest:** I am a destination specialist to Hawaii and Caribbean and I know Western Europe and New York City quite well.

**U.S.A.—CONNECTICUT**

**D&D Travel Services, LLC**
Dennis Hubbs, CTC/MCC
16 Brooke St.
Bloomfield CT 06002
**Phone** 800-613-0282/860-243-9458
**Fax:** 860-243-0494
**E-mail** ddtvl@attbi.com
**Web site** www.ddtvl.com
**Specialties/information of interest:** Family travel, Cruising (Master Cruise Counselors); Caribbean travel

**TourScan, Inc.**
Arthur Mehmel
1051 Boston Post Road
Darien CT 06820
**Phone** 203-655-8091/800-962-2080
**Fax:** 203-655-6689
**E-mail** arthur.tourscan@ix.netcom.com
**Web site** http://www.tourscan.com
**Specialties/information of interest:** Our travel agency has specialized in the Caribbean, Bahamas and Bermuda since 1987. We book many single parent vacations, and we know of many resorts that cater to children of all ages, some all-inclusive and some not.

**U.S.A.—FLORIDA**

**Reservation Station Travel**
Olga Carr
140 Island Way #225
Clearwater FL 33767
**Phone** 800-695-7169
**Fax:** 727-536-6542
**E-mail** olga@reservation-station.com
**Web site** www.reservation-station.com
**Specialties/information of interest:** Cruises, luxury vacations, Disney

**Let's Travel**
Harriot Roberts, CTC
734 W. Colonial Dr.
Orlando FL 32804
**Phone** 407-425-5387
**Fax:** 407-425-1499
**E-mail** harriot@travelagentonline.com
**Web site** www.travelagentonline.com
**Specialties/information of interest:** Upscale and Luxury Travel, FIT (Foreign Independent Travel); Cruises; Rail Journeys; Unique, historical, shopping tours, and group travel

**Coast to Coast Travel Services, Inc.**
Holly A. Biltz
5422 Carrier Dr. Ste. 305
Orlando FL 32819
**Phone** 407-352-7009
**Fax:** 407-363-0588
**E-mail** HBiltz@Vacation.com
**Web site** WWW.CoasttoCoast.Vacation.com
**Specialties/information of interest:** Caribbean, cruises, Las Vegas, Vacation Packages, Hawaii, Central America.

**First In Service Travel**
Phyllis A. Meinsen, CTC
32 Foxhall Lane
Palm Coast FL 32137
**Phone** 386-446-9353
**E-mail** phylndon@bellsouth.net

**Specialties/information of interest:** At one time Phyllis was a single parent.

## U.S.A.—GEORGIA

**Soul & Spice Travel, L.L.C.**
Ms. Ira Lee Mercado
2995 Rosebrook Drive
Decatur GA 30033
**Phone** 404-254-3190
**Fax:** 678-547-3005
**E-mail** soulandspicetravel@yahoo.com
**Specialties/information of interest:** We specialize in themed group departures.

## U.S.A.—ILLINOIS

**Egypt Tours & Travel**
Ashraf
6030 N. Sheridan Rd #104
Chicago IL 60660
**Phone** 773-506-9999/800 TO EGYPT/800 523-4978
**Fax:** 773-506-9996
**E-mail** info@egypttours.com
**Web site** www.egypttours.com, www.egyptiantravel.com, www.visitegypt.net
**Specialties/information of interest:** Single travel, family travel, children with their grand parents travel.

**Bright Side Travel & Cruises**
Joan Wisinski
11745 Southwest Hwy
Palos Heights IL 60463
**Phone** 708-448-6936
**Fax:** 708-448-8613
**E-mail** travel@brightside.agencymail.com
**Web site** www.BrightSideTravel.com
**Specialties/information of interest:** Honeymoons, cruises, Tours U.S.A. & Europe, Family Travel, etc.

## U.S.A.—LOUISIANA

**Island Travel Time**
Madeline Tramarin, CTA, CSS
211 Sherwood Lane
Haughton LA 71037
**Phone** 866-732-7314

**Fax:** 318-390-7650
**E-mail** info@islandtraveltime.com
**Web site** www.islandtraveltime.com
**Specialties/information of interest:** Honeymoons, family reunions, singles (without children). I am a member of ASTA and ICTA

## U.S.A.—MASSACHUSETTS

**PMT Travel**
Dave or Paula Thrower, ACC
84 Wason St.
Medford MA 02155
**Phone** 877-768-8785
**Fax:** 781-723-0571
**E-mail** dthrower@attbi.com
**Web site** www.pmttravel.com
**Specialties/information of interest:** We are specialists with all of Disney travel products including Disney Cruise Lines. We also specialize in cruises and package tours all over the world.

**BARYIA TRAVEL**
Kash Patel
238 Lincoln St.
Newton Highlands MA 02461
**Phone** 617-527-4799
**Fax:** 617-527-4899
**E-mail** kash@baryiatravel.com
**Web site** www.baryiatravel.com
**Specialties/information of interest:** Areas: South Pacific (Australia, New Zealand, and the Pacific Islands Tahiti, Cook Islands, Hawaii, etc.) and Africa. Adventure travel, group travel, sports — golf, etc.

## U.S.A.—MARYLAND

**Travel Time**
Carol Schulman CTC
751 Rockville Pike, Suite 30B
Rockville MD 20850
**Phone** 301-738-8747/800-821-8747
**Fax:** 301-738-9738
**E-mail** trip@calltraveltime.com
**Web site** www.calltraveltime.com
**Specialties/information of interest:** Besides family, we do honeymoons/weddings in the Caribbean/Mexico/Europe and cruises.

## U.S.A.—MAINE

**Bonne Amie Travel**
Aimee J. Ricca
PO Box 442
Rockport ME 04856
**Phone** 866-302-0036
**Fax:** 207-273-3162
**E-mail** aimee@bonneamietravel.com
**Web site** www.bonneamietravel.com
**Specialties/information of interest:** Hawaii, Caribbean, Bermuda, Mexico, New England, Canada, cruises, groups, culinary travel, Disney, Gay & Lesbian travel

## U.S.A.—MINNESOTA

**Carlson Wagonlit Travel**
Richard Newman
6407 West Parkway
Eden Prairie MN 55344
**Phone** 952-941-8900
**Fax** 952-933-7302
**E-mail** rnewman@carlsontravelep.com
**Web site** www.carlsontravel.com/prestige
**Specialties/information of interest:** Family travel and honeymoons

**MLB Travel, LLC**
Mary Behsman
22136 Warner Lane
Elysian MN 56028
**Phone** 507-267-4030; 888-387-7480
**Fax:** 507-267-4214
**E-mail** mlbtravel@myclearwave.net
**Web site** www.mlbtravel.com
**Specialties/information of interest:** Family, cruises, Mexico, Jamaica. Las Vegas and Alaska

## U.S.A.—NEW JERSEY

**Summit International Travel, Inc.**
Peter Or Cherifa
789 Springfield Ave.
Summit NJ 07901
**Phone** 800-527-8664
**E-mail** Summitintltravel@Worldnet.Att.Net
**Web site** www.Summittours.com

**Specialties/information of interest:** Hiking Tours, Biking Tours, Customized Packages/FIT's

## U.S.A.—NEW YORK

**Advantage Travel, Inc.**
Michael McCabe
18 Green St
Albany NY 12207
**Phone** 518-426-0052/888-444-4240
**Fax:** 518-426-0484
**E-mail** mike@advantagetravelinc.com
**Web site** www.advantagetravelinc.com
**Specialties/information of interest:** We also specialize in group travel, same sex partner travel. We are experts for Disney and the Caribbean.

**Carlson Wagonlit Travel**
Keith Stephens/Rick Abraham
315 West 49th St. Worldwide Plaza Arcade
New York NY 10019
**Phone** 212-262-6100
**Fax** 212-262-7407
**E-mail**     admin@carlsontrvl.com     or keith@carlsontrvl.com
**Web site** www.carlsontravel.com
**Specialties/information of interest:** cruises, all-inclusive vacations, honeymoons, gay travel destinations, travel to: Australia, New Zealand, Tahiti, Fiji, Italy, Spain, Great Britain, Amsterdam, corporate & business travel, discount business class & first class tickets

**First In Service Travel**
Erika Reategui
130 West 42 St. Suite 401
New York NY 10036
**Phone** 212-398-6555
**Fax:** 212-398-5352

## U.S.A.—OHIO

**Treasured Vacations**
Ann Marie Schneider
6181 Mayfield Rd. #101
Mayfield Hts. OH 44124
**Phone** 440-646-0640

**Fax:** 440-646-9068
**E-mail** TreasuredVactns@aol.com
**Web site** www.treasuredvacations.com
**Specialties/information of interest:** Cruises, Tours, Packages, Caribbean and customized travel planning.

**Carlson Wagonlit Travel**
Rose B. Arden
750 E. Washington St.
Medina OH 44256
**Phone** 330-723-1200 / 800-321-6750
**Fax:** 330-722-2839
**E-mail** medinatravel@carlsontravel.com
**Web site** www.carlsontravel.com/medina
**Specialties/information of interest:** Disney, Europe, Hawaii, Ireland, Louisiana, N. America, African Safari, Australia, Puerto Rico, Spain, Cruises, golf packages.

**A Better Choice Travel**
Beverly Hajek
7507 Pearl Road
Middleburg Hts. OH 44130
**Phone** 440-234-6300
**Fax:** 440-234-2444
**E-mail** agent@betterchoicetravel.com
**Web site** www.betterchoicetravel.com
**Specialties/information of interest:** We specialize in cruises, all inclusive vacations, & Europe travel

**U.S.A.—PENNSYLVANIA**

**Liberty Travel**
Susan White
569 N Main St
Doylestown PA 18901
**Phone** 215-489-0994
**Fax:** 215-489-0976
**E-mail** WhiteS@libertytravel.com
**Web site** www.libertytravel.com
**Specialties/information of interest:** Alaska, Galapagos, expedition cruising, featured in Conde Nast Traveler 2000, 2001, 2002 in list of "Best Travel Consultants"

**Vacationkids.com, Inc.**
Sally Black
Rr1 Box 1044
Kunkletown PA 18058

**Phone** 610-681-7360
**Fax:** 253-550-4700
**E-mail** Mom@Vacationkids.com
**Web site** www.Vacationkids.com
**Specialties/information of interest:** Complete travel agencies dedicated to family travel. Arranging trips for parents with infants, kids, tweens and teens to all family friendly destinations

**Mia Anderson Travel**
Donna McGee
537 Sarah Street
Stroudsburg PA 18360
**Phone** 570-476-2861
**Fax:** 877-886-2424
**E-mail** dmmcgee@surfbest.net

**U.S.A.—RHODE ISLAND**

**Carlson Wagonlit/Donovan Travel**
Gil Clappin Jr.
508 Main St.
East Greenwich RI 02818
**Phone** 401-885-3500
**Fax:** 401-885-5870
**E-mail** info@donovantravel.com
**Web site** www.donovantravel.com
**Specialties/information of interest:** Disney World, Cruises and European Individual & Group Vacations

**Your Travel Agent**
Christal Shola
766 Hope St
Providence RI 02906
**Phone** 401-272-6200
**Fax:** 401-751-4940
**E-mail** cs@yourtraveldeals.com
**Web site** www.yourtraveldeals.comwebsite
**Specialties/information of interest:** Specials on packages and cruises

**U.S.A.—TENNESEE**

**Outland Travel Inc.**
Donna Davis
6501 Waterlevel Hwy Se
Cleveland TN 37323
**Phone** 800-468-8526

**Fax:** 423-476-2489
**E-mail** donna@outlandtravel.com
**Web site** www.outlandtravel.com
**Specialties/information of interest:** We specialize in single parent, mission trips, soft adventure and specialty groups, such as dance groups, chamber of commerce, etc.

**Travel Management**
Cara Fairchild, CTC
25 West Broad St.
Cookeville TN 38501
**Phone** 800-243-1524/931-528-6491
**Fax:** 931-372-2942
**E-mail** cara@readytotravel.com
**Web site** www.readytotravel.com
**Specialties/information of interest:** Family travel, groups, leisure, foreign independent travel, domestic independent travel, Disney. As a single parent until a year ago with two children, I tend to be the person in our area that people contact...one because of my businesses reputation and two because I have "been there...done that!"

**U.S.A.—VIRGINIA**

**Rose Travel & Tours**
Hemal Desai
4414 Walton Farms Drive,
Richmond VA 23294-6036
**Phone** 804-273-1740
**Fax:** 208-977-1061
**E-mail** Rtnt@Rose-Travels.com
**Web site** www.Rose-Travels.com
**Specialties/information of interest:** Specializing In Indian Sub Continent

**U.S.A.—WISCONSIN**

**Darling Travel**
Claudia Darling
16695 Brehon Lane
Brookfield WI 53005

**Phone** 262-783-6847
**Fax:** 262-790-1083
**E-mail** info@darlingtravel.com
**Web site** www.darlingtravel.com
**Specialties/information of interest:** weddings, honeymoons, adventure, Europe, Asia, Caribbean

**Brookfield Travel & Cruise Corner**
Paula Slesar
19045 W Capitol Drive
Brookfield WI 53045
**Phone** 262-373-1000/800-486-0860
**Fax:** 262-781-2510
**E-mail** inquiries@brookfieldtravel.com
**Web site** www.brookfieldtravel.com
**Specialties/information of interest:** Leisure, Cruises, All Inclusives, Corporate, Incentives & Meetings, Groups

**Brookfield Travel American Express**
Diane Fleming
19045 West Capitol Drive Ste 100
Brookfield WI 53045
**Phone** 262-373-1000
**Fax:** 262-781-2510
**E-mail** dfleming@brookfieldtravel.com
**Web site** brookfieldtravel.com
**Specialties/information of interest:** Cruises, Corporate, Groups/Incentive programs

**Omega Traveler's World & Cruise World**
Susan Norton
2215 S. Oneida St.
Green Bay WI 54304
**Phone** 920-436-6351
**Fax:** 920-497-0503
**E-mail** susan@travelersworld.net
**Web site** www.travelersworld.net.
**Specialties/information of interest:** I am the family travel specialist, as well as a Disney and Hawaii Specialist.

# Index

aa.com 2, 59
Acidophilus 92
ActivitiesForKids.com 72
airlines
    American 2
    Continental 61, 64
    Southwest 62
    Syria 96
    United 61
Alaska 8, 9, 10, 11, 12, 13, 15, 16, 21, 56, 88, 101, **235-47**, 244, 245
    Anchorage 235, 236, **237**
    Coldfoot 244
    Denali 9, 12, 16, 240
    Ester 88, 243
    Fairbanks 242
    Homer 238
    Homer's Spit 12
    Kenai 238
    Kenai Peninsula 12
    Nenana 242
    North Pole 243
    sample itinerary 8
    Seldovia 239
    Seward 239
    Tok 245
    Valdez 246
altitude sickness 90
American Association of Retired Persons (AARP) 37, 46, 63
American Automobile Association (AAA) 3, 5, 37, 46, 48, 63, 250
American Express 48, 141
Apple Vacations 210
Arizona 2, 3, 14, 16, 20, 44, 45, 54, 74, 87, 89, 106, **167-77**, 182
    Flagstaff 172
    Jerome 172
    Monument Valley Tribal Park 182
    Nogales 168
    Phoenix 169
    Scottsdale 169
    Sedona 171
    Show Low 87, 176
    Tucson 167
Arthur Frommer Series 4

B&Bs 12, 63, 152, 191, 199, 200, 205, 236, 239, 242
    requirements 63

Baham, Don 128
Belgium
    Brussels 74
Belize 22, 102
    Belize City 95
Bennett, Colin 134
Best Western 46, 63, 179, 186, 191, 229
Big Mac 115
*Birnbaum's Guide to Walt Disney World* 8
Boersma, Gregg 140
Bolivia 51, 91, 102, 105, 106, 112, 265
    Lake Titicaca 51, 91, 102, 105
Bond, James 220
BritainOnTrack.com 76
British Columbia
    Victoria 130

cab *See taxicab*
California 136, **203-7**
    Bodega Bay 205
    Eureka 204
    Garberville 204
    Mendocino 205
    Sacramento 136
    San Francisco 74, 128, 195, 199, 203, **205**
Canada 3, 41, 42, 73, 86, 155, 157, 270
Canadian Automobile Association (CAA) 5
car rental **95**
    free membership programs 74
    frequent flier points 65
    frequent renter programs 74
    insurance 74
    international 75
car rental agencies
    Alamo 75
car seats 74
car travel *See travel, car*
Center for Disease Control (CDC) 43
Cheerios 103
children
    age 10 and older 52
    airplane manners 69
    behavior 69
    borrowing 85
    buy-in 5
    exchange 149
    flying 67
    freedom 86
    letting go 86

pictures and drawings 18
pre-boarding 69
Club Med 120, 153
Colorado 143, 148, 175
    Colorado Springs 178
ContainerStore.com 35
Continental.com 2, 59
Costa Rica 95, 121, **213-26**, 218, 221, 224, 226
    Guanacaste 220
    Jacó Beach 222
    Monteverde 224
    San Jose 95, **214**
    Tortuguero 218
credit card 64, 74, 94
Culturelle 92

Days Inn 179, 186
Denmark 114
Discovery Channel 81, 120, 220, 254
Disney 2, 8, 35, 56, 131, 132, 133, 153, 260, 282
District of Columbia *See Washington D.C.*
documents 34, 37
    entry *See permission*
Dramamine 11, 90

ear infections 90
Ecuador 11, 27, 28, 90, 219, 260, **264-67**
    Amazon 23, 27, 28, 29, 35, 92, 112, 276
    Galápagos 27, **260-67**
    Guayaquil 260
    Quito 27, 90, 260, 262, **265**, 267
Egypt 47, 49, 92, 96, **248-59**
    Cairo 252
    Giza 85, 252
    Luxor 256
    Nile Cruise 92
    Pyramids 85, 252
Elwell, Marden 123
e-tickets 62
Eurail Passes 76
Europe 6, 18, 30, 35, 42, 54, 76, 78, 79, 80, 82, **268**
EuropeOnRail.com 76
Expedia.com 2, 59, 63, 186, 191

FamilyOnBoard.com 35
Finland 6, 55, 114
first aid kit 29
Flinkman, Lewis 120
Florida 62, 75, 100, 131, 149, 150
    Key Largo 100
    Orlando 56, 75, 131
France
    Paris 116
frequent flyer 61, 64
Frommer's *Budget Travel* Magazine 3
Frommers.com 58, 276, 278

Game Boy® 131
games 68
Google.com 2, 63
Grand Canyon National Park 173
Guatemala 22, 23, 24, 93, 120, 121
    Antigua 93
    Flores 122
    Tikal 22, 23, 24, 120, 121
guidebooks 3, 4

Harriman, Cynthia 268
Hawaii 6, 103, **227-34**
    Haleakala 104
    Hana Road 103
    Honolulu 70
    Kauai 231
    Maui 103, 104, 227, 229, 230
    Oahu 227
    The Big Island 231
Heathrow Airport 77
Hepatitis A and Hepatitis B 42
Heyerdahl, Thor 112
Holiday Inn 46, 63, 121, 183, 229
Holland *See Netherlands*
Honduras 120
    Copan 120, 121
Hong Kong **93-4**, 99
hotel
    bargains 63
    chain 63
    frequent flier points 65
    overseas 63
    reservations 63
    small 63
    Web sites 63
HotelDiscounts.com 193
HotelsOnLine.com 63

Illinois
    Chicago 141
Imodium 92
Inlingua School 99
insurance 34, 86
    car 74
    travel 44
itinerary
    confirmation information 16
    creation 7
    daily activities 14
    example 8
    master copy 21
    personalization 20
    rainy day alternatives 15
    reasons to have 7
    things to include 14
    unexpected 12

Japan 98, 99, 108, 109, 242

Jordan
  Amman 80

Katz, Victor 131
kayaking 12
Kenai Peninsula 12
Kenya 105
Koza, Peter 136

Lamachi, José 112
Landsend.com 35
LastMinuteTravel.com 58
Leningrad *See Russia, St. Petersberg*
LLBean.com 35
Lonely Planet 4
LoveAndLearn.com 72

Malaria 43
Manhattan S*ee New York, New York*
maps 5, 34, 71, 126
  reading 52
Marriott 65
Maryland 73, 165
  Annapolis 165
  Baltimore 165
Massachusetts
  Boston 165
  Cape Cod 152
Master Card 48
Maxa, Rudy 278
Maya Riviera *See Riviera Maya*
McDonalds 114
medical information 86
Mexico 86, 120, 122, 169, 208
  Cancun 208
  Cozumel 212
  Nogales 168
  Palenque 120
  Playa del Carmen **208**
Michelin green guides 4
Montezuma's Revenge 92
Moon Handbook 4
mosquito bites 103
motion sickness 90
Moudarres, Karim 96, 116

*National Geographic* 3, 81, 97, 278
National Parks **178, 270-73**
Netherlands 80
  Amsterdam 268
Nevada
  Las Vegas 178, 190, 192
New Hampshire 73
New Jersey 44, 76, 102, 103, 149, 150, 161, 163
  Camden 163
  Ocean City 163
New Mexico 54, 175
New Orleans 56, 58, 151, 152

New York 13, 22, 87, 123, 125, 126, 150, 155, 156, 157
  Adirondacks 123
  Buffalo 155
  Cooperstown 87, 88, 156, 157
  New York **159-62**
  Niagara Falls 87, **155-58**
  Old Forge 126
  Rome 63, 157
*New York Times* 278
Nickelodeon 120
Nintendo® 131
Norway 114, 115
notarized letter See permission

OfficialTravelInfo.com 3
Ontario
  Niagara Falls 155-58
  Toronto 89, 155, 158
Orbitz.com 2, 59, 194
Oregon 128, 195-203
  Bandon 128, 202
  Brookings 128
  Cannon Beach 197
  Coos Bay 202
  Depoe Bay 199
  Florence 201
  Gold Beach 203
  Lincoln City 198
  Newport 129, 199
  Portland 196
  Tillamook 198
*Outside* magazine 140

packing 29
  car 71
  list 30
snacks 36, 68
Parents Without Partners 25, 96, 150, 276
passport 37, 94
Passport
  for minors under age 14 37
patience 72
Peninsula Hotel **93**
Pennsylvania
  Oxford 163
  Philadelphia 159, **162-64**
Pepto Bismol 92
permission to take children out of the country **39**, 86
Peru 81, 83, 90
  Cusco 81, 82, 83, 90, 267
  Sacsayhuaman 81, 82
  Tambo Machay 81
PlacesToStay.com 63
Powell, Major John Wesley 143
Priceline.com 58

RailEurope.com 76
Rent-a-car *See car rental*
rental car *See car rental*
reservations 55
    activities and excursions 64
    air 61
    hotel 63
    last minute specials 57
    train 78
    types 59
    when to book 55
Riviera Maya **208-12**
Rotary Club 25, 63
Russia
    St. Petersburg 80, 114

Sedona 16, 44, 46, 89
Sheraton 121
Single Parent Tours v, vi, **278**, 301
Single Parent Travel Network *See SingleParent-Travel.net*
Single Parent Travel Specials 3
SingleParentTravel.net vi, ix, 3, 30, 39, 40, 47, 119, 127, 151, 153, 195, 268, 276, 278
Snapfish.com 113
Sweden 114
Switzerland 6, 79, 115, 116, 275
Syria
    Aleppo 80, 96, 97, 98, 105, 106, 116, 249
    Damascus 96, 97, 98, 249
    Palmyra 96, 97, 106

taxicab 83
teen-agers 84
Tell, William 80
Temple University Tokyo 99
Tetanus 42
Texas 76
    Dallas 70
The Economist 115
*Time* magazine 278
Tokyo
    Kyoto 108
ToughTraveler.com 35
tourist boards 2
tours
    fully escorted 6
    packaged 6
    types of 6
towd.com 3
train travel 35. *See travel, train*
travel
    bus 79, 101
    car 71

fly/drive 74
    other modes 82
    planning 2
    subway 101
    train 75, 77
travel agents 3, 62, 154, 186, 193
    ethnic 62
    finding a good one 60
    when to use 60
traveler's checks 48, 94, 266
Travelocity.com 2, 57, 59, 61, 192, 196
Travelodge 179
Typhoid Fever 42

United Kingdom 134
    London 56, 57, 63, 77, 80, 83, 97, 151, 268
    Pembrokeshire 134
    Tenby 134
Universal Studios 131
UNO 68
Utah 140, 141, 144, 148, 174, 175, **178-94**
    Bluff 182
    Mexican Hat 183
    Moab 178
    National Parks **178-94**
    Park City 142
    Salt Lake City 140, 141, 142, 178, 190, 193, 194
    Vernal 140, 142

vacation
    adult traveling alone 151
    alternate ideas 149
    blending families 150
vaccinations 37, 42, 43
Visa 48
visas 40
Visitor's Card 83

Walt Disney World *See Disney*
Washington 128
    Seattle 136, **199**
Washington D.C. 131, 151, 159, **164-65**
Wayne, John 182
Whitehorse, Gilbert 184
Wild Thornbury 120
Women Welcome Women 25
Wright, Wilber 136

Yellow Pages® 2
Young Eagles program 136

Ziploc 126

# ORDER "THE SINGLE PARENT TRAVEL HANDBOOK"

## Check your Local Bookstore or Order by Mail

YES, I want ___ copies of *The Single Parent Travel Handbook* for $17.99 each.

Include $4.43 shipping and handling per book. New Jersey residents, please include 6% sales tax. For orders outside the U.S., please contact Monique Elwell at Monique@SingleParentTravel.net or 1-917-423-1896 for postage costs. (Contact Monique for bulk discount orders.)

| | |
|---|---|
| Number of Copies | _____ |
| Price per book | $17.95 |
| (number of copies times price) Subtotal | _____ |
| NJ sales tax 6% | _____ |
| Shipping & Handling at $4.43 per book | _____ |

**I have enclosed a check or money order for $ _____**

NAME _____
ORGANIZATION _____
ADDRESS _____
CITY _____
ST/Province, ZIP/PC _____
COUNTRY _____
PHONE _____
E-MAIL _____

Send this form with your check to:

GlobalBrenda Publishing, LLC
755 9th St. 2nd fl.
Secaucus NJ 07094-3321

**www.GlobalBrenda.com**

Or Fax to 413-208-6105

## PARENTS WITHOUT PARTNERS

Parents Without Partners is an international, non-profit, educational organization devoted to the interests of single parents and their children. I wanted to mention this excellent organization in my book because of their enormous commitment to single parents, both custodial and non-custodial, male or female, at all stages. For over a year, I have had the pleasure of being both a visiting author on their Web site, www.ParentsWithoutPartners.org, and a contributor to their member's magazine, *The Single Parent*.
Parents Without Partners is a great source to find support from fellow single parents. To join or simply find out more information, visit their Web site, www.ParentsWithoutPartners.org, or contact their international headquarters listed below.

Parents Without Partners, Inc.
1650 South Dixie Highway, Suite 510
Boca Raton, FL 33432
561-391-8833
www.ParentsWithoutPartners.org

*Save $50 on your First Trip with*

# SINGLE PARENT TOURS

In the summer of 2003 Single Parent Tours will offer a series of weekend packages and one-week tours to exciting destinations. I would like to offer a discount of $50 per family to readers of my book. This discount is valid for the summer of 2003. When you book, please give the booking agent the coupon code below.

COUPON CODE: HND02

We hope you join us during our inaugural season!

*Would you like to be informed when the tours are available to book? Then send an email to Brenda@SingleParentTravel.net, or send your name, phone number, fax (if you have it) and address to*

**Single Parent Tours**
755 9th St. 2nd fl.
Secaucus NJ 07094-3321

Fax it to 413-208-6105

**www.SingleParentTours.com**

## HARRY PARISER'S GUIDE BOOKS TO GREAT DESTINATIONS

Harry Pariser is an award-winning travel writer who has written ten different travel guides on the Caribbean and Central America, areas that make great single parent travel destinations. Currently, he has guides to Costa Rica, Puerto Rico, the Virgin Islands, and Barbados available. Harry's books are published by Manatee Press and are available for purchase online at http://www.savethemanatee.com, http://www.amazon.com and http://www.bn.com, as well as at Borders, Barnes and Noble and bookstores in the U.S., Canada and Europe. Alternatively, you can order books through SCB Distributors at 800-729-6423. More information is available online at http://www.savethemanatee.com. Enjoy! The books are informative, easy to read, and have my stamp of approval.